The Three U.S.-Mexico Border Wars

The Three U.S.-Mexico Border Wars

Drugs, Immigration, and Homeland Security

Second Edition

TONY PAYAN

Foreword by Kathleen Staudt

Praeger Security International

 PRAEGER™

An Imprint of ABC-CLIO, LLC
Santa Barbara, California • Denver, Colorado

Library of Congress Cataloging-in-Publication Data

Names: Payan, Tony, 1967- author.
Title: The three U.S.-Mexico border wars : drugs, immigration, and homeland
  security / Tony Payan.
Other titles: Three United States-Mexico border wars
Description: Second edition. | Santa Barbara, California : Praeger Security International,
  2016. | Includes bibliographical references and index.
Identifiers: LCCN 2016025170 (print) | LCCN 2016037828 (ebook) | ISBN 9781440835414
  (hardcopy : alk. paper) | ISBN 9781440835421 (ebook)
Subjects: LCSH: Smuggling—Mexican-American Border Region. | Drug traffic—
  Government policy—United States. | Illegal aliens—Government policy—United
  States. | United States—Relations—Mexico. | Mexico—Relations—United States.
  | Mexican-American Border Region—Economic conditions. | Mexican-American Bor-
  der Region—Politics and government. | Mexican-American Border Region—Social con-
  ditions. | Mexican-American Border Region—Ethnic relations.
Classification: LCC HV5831.M46 T49 2016 (print) | LCC HV5831.M46 (ebook)
  | DDC 363.0972/1—dc23
LC record available at https://lccn.loc.gov/2016025170

ISBN: 978–1–4408–3541–4
EISBN: 978–1–4408–3542–1

20 19 18 17 16   1 2 3 4 5

This book is also available as an eBook.

Praeger
An Imprint of ABC-CLIO, LLC

ABC-CLIO, LLC
130 Cremona Drive, P.O. Box 1911
Santa Barbara, California 93116-1911
www.abc-clio.com

This book is printed on acid-free paper ∞

Manufactured in the United States of America

Contents

Foreword

In this magnificent second edition, scholar and *fronterizo* Tony Payan provides North American border watchers and mainstream audiences an updated and revised edition of his fine book on the three border wars: wars on drugs, wars on immigrants, and wars against terrorists, the latter term broadly imagined in officialdom. The book ought to be required reading for many, including political and policy decision makers, civic activists and youth (the current and next generation of taxpayers concerned about fiscal responsibility), and multiple peoples in the borderlands. Readers will gain insight from this realistic, no-nonsense but eloquent narrative of the border compared with political and media narratives based on the politics of fear during elections and budget-making times in Washington, DC, and state capitals.

For over 150 years, the political construction of a territorial borderline between Mexico and the United States became rigidly fixed, save for the exchange of one square mile with the Chamizal Agreement of the early 1960s. Payan historicizes the border, outlining four stages: the frontier era from 1848 to 1920, the customs era, from 1920 to the 1970s, and the law enforcement era thereafter, which merges into the transformative moment and long, long consequences of September 11, 2001, along with the burdens placed on border people in the Mexico-U.S. borderlands.

The book provides a deft combination of personal conversations, travel observations from all along the border, and carefully documented sources, scholarly and official. Payan begins each chapter with stories and vignettes from his interviews with border people, from the good to the bad and the ugly. Mostly, though, he humanizes border people as generally good, hardworking people who blend a mix of cultures and languages, but who live in the midst of what he calls the new normal: low-intensity conflicts of bureaucratic agencies, organized crime, and corrupt officials—all with damaging consequences for everyday life in the borderlands and the former cross-border interaction that once occurred on a grander scale.

Payan argues that the political singular fusion of three policy wars should be separated, then developed, analyzed, and enforced as independent policy issues with different policy tools. Payan's prose is readable, accessible, and filled with evocative images, an editorial skill that I sometimes worry has long been lost among many in the political science discipline. He makes readers see and feel from the text narrative, despite the absence of pictures. Having read and adopted his first edition in a graduate seminar, I appreciate the seamless way Payan updates and incorporates new material on the base of the 2006 core text.

The book is neatly organized and coherently packaged into five chapters, three of which cover the "wars." After Chapter 1's historical perspectives, Payan dives into the war on drugs, a seemingly futile more-than-40-year struggle. His in-depth analysis of organized crime is among the best analytic treatments. One finds the fuller analysis in Payan, with "pervasive and systemic" corruption in Mexico's epidemic compared with the "concentrated" corruption among U.S. officials that goes a longer way. Payan spares no "side," ideological or territorial, from critical analysis.

If I were to thematically organize his critiques, the themes would focus on economic logics, political logics, and bureaucratic logics. All too often, the political ambitions in bureaucratic politics drive the vision, policy, and future of "border security."

Dr. Payan, with his PhD from Georgetown University, once served as associate professor of political science at the University of Texas at El Paso (UTEP), where I have taught since the late 1970s. I have known him as an inspiring colleague, speaker, coauthor, and coeditor. We coedited the volumes *A War That Can't Be Won: Binational Perspectives on the War on Drugs* and *Human Rights along the U.S.-Mexico Border* (both published by the University of Arizona Press in 2013 and 2009 respectively). These volumes drew on scholarly experts in different disciplines from Mexico and the United States in order to obtain binational and balanced perspectives rather than the nationalist agendas that pervade not only writers in the policy arena but also those academics who analyze in, as John Agnew famously said, the "territorial traps" of state-centric perspectives. At UTEP, students lined up outside Payan's door and filled up his classes, for he always took the noble profession of teaching quite seriously. Border scholars and students miss his presence in the central borderlands and his always acute and insightful commentary on Mexico and the region.

Payan now directs the Mexico Center at the Baker Institute for Public Policy of Rice University in Houston. There, he organizes conferences, research projects, and travels to policy-relevant arenas in North and Central America, plus conferences elsewhere in the world when he is invited as a keynote speaker. Although he no longer crosses the U.S.-Mexico land border on a near-daily basis, his vantage point in Houston is not too far from one of the epicenters of half-trillion-dollar annual binational trade and the legal crossings of millions of pedestrians, trucks, automobiles, and railways (along with the passengers in those legally crossing vehicles). Payan continues to be grounded with border lenses.

The most chilling chapter of the book comes at the end: "The Panopticon Border." Readers of Jeremy Bentham, Michel Foucault, and even George Orwell's *Nineteen Eighty-Four* will recognize the growing high-tech atmosphere of a surveillance-driven near-police state staffed in a monstrously large bureaucracy, the U.S. Department of Homeland Security and its $60 billion annual budget. As he states, "Whoever thinks the border is chaotic and is out of control has clearly not been to the border." Payan's book is a warning call not only for border people about the tension between freedom and bureaucratically-driven security, but also for mainstream peoples in North America.

By the close of the book, Dr. Tony Payan shares with readers some tough talk for what he calls a "tough new normal" at the border and some innovative policy proposals. He jolts us, I hope, into action and organization to protect borderlanders from an all-intrusive state and to preserve this "reluctant partnership," as he calls it, between Mexico and the United States that creates countless U.S. jobs. Payan is the preeminent scholar of the U.S.-Mexico borderlands, but he is also our strongest border voice— a voice to whom all should listen and take heed.

Kathleen Staudt

Preface

This book was originally published in 2006. It was the result of a long trip along the U.S.-Mexico border. I drove up and down the borderline, from San Diego/Tijuana to Brownsville/Matamoros. I stopped at every port of entry, talked to U.S. Customs and Border Protection and Border Patrol agents, took thousands of pictures, spoke with many borderlanders, observed all kinds of border processes (pedestrians, trucks, cars, trains, and even cattle) for hours anywhere I could, and reviewed many numbers on immigration, security, trade, and other statistics. When I took that trip, it had already been almost five years since the terrorist attacks of September 11, 2001. By that time, the dust of the attacks had settled, but the wars that those attacks spun were raging, from Afghanistan and Pakistan to Iraq. The world was still turned on its head. The George W. Bush administration, however, was beginning to be criticized for both the attacks on Iraq and the pervasive and even detrimental effects of new and expanded government powers on the civil liberties of Americans. The country that united behind the strategy to face the terrorists was becoming divided once again.

The U.S.-Mexico border too was in convulsion. As I mentioned in the preface to the first edition, the border paid a very high price for the attacks of September 11. Even though it had nothing to do with the attacks, it became the focus of a permanent war on terror. In addition, all sorts of issues were conflated with the war on terror, including immigration, drugs, and national security. But the border was a complicated place in its own right, something that perhaps made it easier to zoom in on it as an implied "cause" of the 9/11 security crisis. The years 2005 and 2006, for example, were years of maximum apprehensions of undocumented border crossers—almost 1.2 million per year. This helped galvanize all the talk about building a wall between Mexico and the United States—something that would eventually get funded in 2007 through the Secure Fence Act. Moreover, the war on drugs was heating up in Mexico and would eventually become a brutal massacre that would last for years—from 2006 to 2012—and result in the estimated deaths of 120,000 Mexicans. Many of those deaths took place in border cities and towns, from Tijuana to Ciudad Juárez to Reynosa and Matamoros. Moreover, the U.S. government was on full alert on the homeland security front. Terrorist attacks in Europe and the Middle East had Americans wondering when terrorism would hit the border or when the border would be the obligatory entry point for terrorists who would want to "do America harm." Moreover, the Homeland Security Department—that enormous bureaucracy focused on threats of all kinds—was slowly consolidating its power. Federal bureaucracies were in full expansion, asking for more funding, more personnel, and more equipment; claiming jurisdiction over more and more territory; and establishing a de facto state of exception within 100 miles of the border. The militarization of law enforcement was proceeding apace, and the border was a prime example of that.

It was understandable 10 years ago that security should trump prosperity, civil rights, local autonomy, democracy, and so on. Security was primordial after the apocalyptic attacks that we all witnessed on television. After all, without security, there is no economy, no justice, no peace. But 15 years after the terrorist attacks of September 11 and 10 after this book was first written, it is worth asking where we are, what we have accomplished, what we have gained, what we have given up, and whether it might not be time to review what we have done to ourselves and to the border, the borderlands, and borderlanders. It is worth asking whether there is a better way to manage the border than the way we do it today.

First, we can assert with nearly absolute confidence that nothing in the many reports, articles, and books written after September 11 show that the border itself—however lawless it may have been—had anything to do with the terrorist attacks. Moreover, there is no evidence whatsoever that any terrorist activity has taken place at the U.S.-Mexico border. We know that the terrorists did not come through the U.S.-Mexico border and they did not come from Mexico. They had a clear political purpose—as terrorism nearly always does—that had very little to do with the border. To attempt to argue the opposite is at best naïve and at worst malicious.

So, we must now turn to the idea that security, though important, has become the end, the means, and the values that rule our daily lives, our morals, our social solidarity, our humanity, our vision of our rights and privileges, and so on. Security has indeed become an absolutizing concept—as if risk could be reduced to zero percent. That is of course illusory. For when security is made the only absolute and everything is brought under it, we will end up with a social environment that is more akin to tyranny than to democracy; we will end up with an obnoxious bureaucracy underpinned by fear and arbitrariness. Nowhere is this more evident than at the border, where the security apparatus has become nearly unbearable. Border security agents are the cops, the investigators, the adjudicators, the judges, the jury, the executioners, and there is hardly any ability for anyone to protest or to appeal. There are no grounds to challenge, even minimally, any of those agents. They have all the power. Border users have no rights. Security has become an ideology—there is no challenging it or its scaffolding.

In addition, the billions and billions of dollars spent every year on border security both have been thinly justified by a threat—terrorism—that has not materialized or even come close to it, and have not produced, at the end of the day, any more security. Let me explain. All the added budgets, high-tech gadgets, and personnel have not revealed any terrorist plot against the United States at or from the U.S.-Mexico border. Thus, in terms of "homeland" security, the border does not appear to be a major source of threats to the nation. Second, undocumented immigration has actually gone down. And while some of this may have to do with the added difficulties to cross the border illegally, precisely due to the overgrown security apparatus, the reality is that we do not yet know what exactly the cause of this dramatic drop in undocumented migration is. It can just as easily be argued that after 2008 the economic conditions in the United States were such that there were simply no jobs to be had; it can also be argued that it is becoming a nightmare to live in the United States without documents—employers no longer want to hire undocumented migrants for fear of fines or jail; migrants cannot access housing; they cannot make use of any public benefits whatsoever, in spite of what many may say; they have no health care, welfare benefits, unemployment compensation, or public assistance; and there is always the fear that they can be detected easily and deported anyway. This has made many Mexicans who had been living in the United States simply leave the country or concentrate in *colonias*, those destitute, marginalized, and poor areas found dotting the border in South and West Texas and in Arizona and New Mexico. The result is that Mexican migration is in fact negative—more Mexicans are leaving and being deported than are coming to the United States today. They are not coming for many reasons; and more and more are leaving as the United States is becoming simply unlivable for most undocumented migrants, in spite of what many anti-immigrant activists may say.

Third, the war on drugs is the most egregious failure of the border security agencies. Drugs have their own logic—well beyond the border.

They originate far from it; they go deep into the heart of America. And they do not seem to have any correlation with increased surveillance on the border. Drugs, by the government's own measures, are today more readily available, more varied in the kinds of substances available to consumers, and cheaper. There is hardly any relationship between investment in the drug war and the access to illegal drugs in the United States or the ability of the security bureaucracies to stop them. Moreover, drugs have now moved home: Marijuana is now legal in most states in one form or another and California—the biggest market—will likely legalize it this year 2016. And the border security machine has not stopped the latest surge on heroin use in the United States. Illegal drugs, somehow, are making it through and they seem to be able to do hardly anything about it.

In addition, the new security environment has created the largest security-oriented bureaucracy the United States has ever seen, with ever more expansive powers and seemingly unending resources. The U.S. Department of Homeland Security has become unwieldy and unaccountable for what it does. It has created a state of exception for itself and its activities—all in the name of security. So, by almost any measure, the border has paid a high price for the war on terrorism. The state of exception that the Department of Homeland Security and the Border Patrol have created for themselves along the border deserves further scrutiny, precisely because it has implications for our rights and our ability to move unimpeded by those who pretend to keep us safe but may only be building their own organizational interests at our expense.

In that sense, it is important to examine the behavior of these agencies. Due process and human rights—of migrants and residents and even citizens—have come to matter less when handled by border agencies. And there is plenty of evidence that border bureaucratic discretion is expanding and abuses of all kinds of rights are growing. These agencies feel justified based on fear and paranoia. Anybody that questions their motives is immediately suspect and treated as such. They are slowly chipping away at the ability of citizens to protest, to hold the agencies accountable for what they do, and to impose limits on their power. To grow their organization into an unquestionable security machine and their agents into quasi-apparatchiks, they continue to conflate all kinds of issues. The war on terrorism is indistinguishable, in their view, with the war on drugs, with the war on crime, with the war on undocumented immigration. Everything is deemed the same kind of threat at the same level and any violator is therefore a national security threat.

Security, of which these agencies are in charge, trumps prosperity, and they feel like they can put a hold on all economic activity for any reason, without explanation, no matter what the cost. No appeals have been successful. Even the business community has had to adjust to their rules and regulations, and they never give an inch or engage in any kind of dialogue that may in any way require that they explain what they do and why they do it. The result is that they cost billions of dollars—not only what we tax-payers invest in them but also in millions of human and vehicle hours held at will all along the border. No one has truly estimated how much the security apparatus really costs, but billions in wealth is laid waste on the border every day.

Beyond the economic cost, respect for individual rights and trust and tradition is being obliterated. At the border, no one has any rights whatso-ever. The security agencies can stop anyone at any time for any reason under whatever circumstances they decide, without any explanation. The border is becoming unlivable, not only on the Mexican side but along the borderline and within 100 miles of the borderline inside the United States. And it is unlivable to this day. Border bureaucrats are overbearing and even outright abusive—and someone I spoke to about it said they have a "customer service" problem! The reality is that they enjoy com-plete discretion and can even kill without any accountability. No one can question their charge: security at all costs. They accept no challenges, and if any border user dares challenge them, they will bring every re-source they have to bear in order to punish them. They make no conces-sions. They hold the lines for hours. There is a sense of intimidation and fear. Border users know it and move as stealthily as they can. The worst thing that can happen is to fall in the hands of one of those border bureau-crats. You could end up spending hours and hours in detention and the outcome is completely unpredictable.

Indeed, there could have been nothing better for these imperialistic bureaucracies at the U.S.-Mexico border than September 11. They made themselves the sole guardians of all security at the border, and security is their ideology. They took advantage of this horrific event to legitimate and assert themselves, to grow their empire—to make themselves indispensable guardians of the new paternalistic security state and to expand their discretion and limit anyone's ability to hold them account-able. They have, in effect, gone rogue, without anyone noticing, except those that have to deal with them at the border. But no one can challenge them. They have, after all, the key to our security—or so they claim.

The result is that the border is truly dysfunctional. It is poorly managed. It costs billions of dollars in security and more billions in deterred eco-nomic activity. The border has become an expensive transactional cost. Our rights hardly matter. Accountability is nil. And frustration grows by the day among border users of all kinds.

This book, in its second edition, attempts to question some of this new border order and those in charge of it. It shows that security has become an ideology and that those in charge of security have gone roguish, with-out much justification for it—even by their own standards. But it also shows that unless we question the very ideology of securitization, they will continue to prevail and create more chaos than they resolve, and in the process these bureaucrats will prosper from this chaos. It is time, I argue, to find a new way to manage the border, a North American way to bring a new order to the border—one that will work for all citizens from both sides of the border, one that will bring about security but also prosperity to all, one that will respect the rights of all, and one that will hold border security bureaucracies to limits on their power and account- ability for their actions. I can only hope that you enjoy the reading and that it causes you to think about what we are doing and why we need a new way to view our border.

ACKNOWLEDGMENTS

I would like to thank the many people who listen to me talk about these issues time and time again: Kenn Kern, Irasema Coronado, Kathy Staudt, Tony Kruszewsky, Nivien Saleh, Erika de la Garza, Pamela Cruz, and many others. And I continue to dedicate my ponderings on the U.S.-Mexico border to Ralph L. Scott, a proud El Pasoan and life-long bor- der resident and my mentor, counselor, and life coach who passed away on January 5, 2006.

CHAPTER 1

The Three Border Wars

A TALE WITH TWO SIDES

Héctor Rodríguez gets up in the morning before the crack of dawn. He showers, shaves, and gets dressed quickly. By the time he gets out of his bedroom, his wife, a Mexican citizen, has already packed a brown-bag lunch for him and their two children. Héctor is a U.S. citizen who works for a construction company in El Paso, Texas, but lives in Ciudad Juárez, across from El Paso. His wife works at a local radio station in Ciudad Juárez. The children attend elementary school in the United States. Hector and the children cross the international bridge to El Paso every morning as early as they can to avoid the long waiting lines at the port of entry (POE). Once on the U.S. side, he drops the children at school before heading to his workplace. He picks up the children in the late afternoon and makes his way back home. His wife comes in later in the day. They have supper together and prepare to go to sleep.

Martín Sánchez has always been considered the "black sheep" of the family. Unable to pay for school beyond grade six, he started doing drugs early on. He hung around with some local gang members suspected of robbing several local banks in Nuevo Laredo. From there he was recruited by the powerful drug-smuggling organization known as the Juárez Cartel. He now works for them. Martín has a criminal mind in every way. He has even participated in several kidnappings and killings.

The stories of Héctor and Martín are a powerful image of the border. The two men and their lives are representative illustrations of life at the southern edge of the American empire. These men embody the good and the bad; the beautiful and the ugly; the ordinary and the anomalous of life where Mexico, a developing nation, and the United States, the world's only superpower, meet.

Indeed, the United States is recognized as the most powerful nation in the world. Its economy is the largest; its technological advances are phenomenal; the accumulated wealth of the country is enormous; its military is unparalleled in the history of the humankind; its achievements are admirable. You would think, like almost any impoverished Central American or Mexican peasant working hard on his small patch of land does, that the United States is a paradise on earth. But according to many, all is not well in paradise. Well, at least, not all is well on the borders of paradise. According to many American politicians, very conservative groups, and even some U.S. media commentators, the border is nothing but "turmoil, chaos and lawlessness." To hear politicians like the governor of Texas, Greg Abbott, or presidential candidates in 2016 tell it, the border is "broken" and it urgently needs a wall. Their rhetoric is supported by stories of drug traffickers running life on the border;[1] there also are stories of illegal alien invasions coming from the south[2]—some of them Central American unaccompanied minors that pose a major threat to the welfare of the country; and occasionally there are stories of Middle East terrorists trying to enter the United States from Mexico by sneaking across through Arizona or New Mexico—none of which are actually true. Former secretary of homeland security Janet Napolitano even said that from time to time terrorists enter the United States from Mexico. She suggested that terrorism was spilling across the border.[3] The U.S. Congress periodically enters the fray, calling the border a "frightening place" and a place where "business centers are closing down, tourism is declining, and the general population is demoralized by the level of lawlessness."[4] This is the world where Martín Sánchez lives. If you live in the United States away from the border and listen to the stories of the media and the speeches of members of Congress, you would think that the U.S.-Mexico borderlands are a wild, wild West, where living conditions are unbearable and life is "solitary, poor, nasty, brutish and short."[5] And there is some truth to this view of the border. Anyone familiar with Martín Sánchez's life as a gang member or a drug trafficker or who has read the stories of the hundreds of women assassinated on the border can have a look at the kind of border that Representative Myrick described, when she stated that Hezbollah car bombs were going off on the border.[6] But the world of Héctor Rodríguez is seldom paid attention to or covered by the media, even if it really is much more common on the border than the life of Martín Sánchez. The overwhelming majority of borderlanders are decent, hardworking, law-abiding citizens, with the same dreams and aspirations of any middle-class family in the United States or Mexico.

Today more than ever, the U.S.-Mexico border is experiencing one of the most difficult and defining periods of its 150-plus-year history, particularly since September 11. As the next chapters will make clear, the problems of the border are serious. The Martín Sánchezes of the border

are also many, and they make life on the border a frightening thing sometimes. But there is also plenty of evidence to tell another story that can
debunk some of the dizzying rhetoric regarding the border. There are also
the millions of Héctor Rodríguezes. In other words, there are two sides to
the border tale.

For those of us, 15 million people as of 2015,[7] like Héctor Rodríguez,
who live on and move across the border on a regular basis, the portrayal
of our strip of land—running nearly 2,000 miles along the southwest
and about 100 miles wide on both sides of the international boundary—
as a violent, chaotic, lawless war front is largely inaccurate, although
sometimes it may have seemed to be so, especially during the height of
violence on the Mexican side between 2008 and 2012. Most border residents are law-abiding, hardworking citizens of either Mexico or the
United States. Most people who live on the border get up every day, with
the same preoccupations of any other family in the United States: work,
school, family life, and in general carving out a good life for their community. The overwhelming majority of border crossers does so to shop, work,
study, visit family, and seek good entertainment. They are men and
women who view themselves as bridging two worlds. Just as there are
terrible stories of crime and violence, there are also stories of heroism
and courage on the border. And the story of Héctor Rodríguez is not
unique. Frank is a maquiladora manager from Michigan who goes to
Ciudad Juárez to work every day. Frank recently married a Mexican
woman and now lives the life of a borderlander—and to hear him say it,
he loves it. Robin is a housewife in Chula Vista who likes to go shopping
in Tijuana. Maria takes her two children to school from Nuevo Laredo to
Laredo every morning and picks them up at three in the afternoon.
Raúl is a dedicated husband who takes his family shopping from Monterrey to McAllen every year. Mariana and Mabel are two students at the
University of Texas at El Paso (UTEP) who commute every day from
Ciudad Juárez to El Paso. Like Héctor, Frank, Robin, Maria, Raúl,
Mariana, and Mabel, there are millions of stories of border residents
who live cherished lives on the U.S.-Mexican border. Unfortunately, it is
not the millions of good lives on the border that give it its reputation.
It is the thousands of bad lives that determine what the border is for the
rest of the world. The bad seems to outweigh the good. And judging by
the 2016 presidential campaign, that is still the case.

But before I delve into the border today, it is important to take a closer
look at the history of the border over time with a view to how this strategy
of escalation has worked through nearly a century of U.S. efforts to
control the border. This exercise can help enlighten our view of what is
happening at the border at present, and perhaps even give us an opportunity to glance at where the border is going in the future.

THE MEANING OF THE BORDER

When one thinks about the U.S.-Mexico border, images of chaos, disorder, poverty, pollution, crime, and insecurity are often evoked. An American tourist who arrives at the border and crosses to Tijuana from San Diego or to Ciudad Juárez from El Paso frequently testifies to this. In 1999, Scott Rogerson, a *Weekly Alibi* journalist traveling on I-10 at 70 mph, wrote his impressions regarding the border:

Driving south to El Paso you come over a rise and the first thing you see is a vast sprawling city choking the Rio Grande valley. If you were on vacation and had never been there before, you would think El Paso is a much larger city than what your map indicates. But as you descend further and draw nearer you notice the rat maze of shacks covering the hillside along the valley and realize it looks like no other American city you have ever seen before. Then you grasp the reality. The hillside is Mexico. The rat maze of shacks is a cardboard colonia.[8]

His rather unflattering portrayal of "the border" constitutes a common impression by visitors to almost any town along the nearly 2,000-mile stretch that separates the United States and Mexico. But those who dismiss the area as a dusty, poor, and wretched land miss the long and magnificent history of the U.S.-Mexico border and the varied tapestry of wealth and poverty, hope and despair, backwardness and progress that is manifest, for example, in the lives of its residents, who number nearly 15 million and live in 14 pairs of cities that dot the border. Regardless of the impressions the occasional visitor may have, few can capture the flavor of the border who do not live and move and have their being there.

Rogerson's description of the border reflects a temptation to lump three distinct concepts together: the boundary, the border, and the borderlands. The boundary is the physical line between the two countries. It was set in 1853 in the Gadsden Purchase Treaty, which reads:

Article I: The Mexican Republic agrees to designate the following as her true limits with the United States for the future: retaining the same dividing line between the two Californias as already defined and established . . . the limits between the two republics shall be as follows: Beginning in the Gulf of Mexico, three leagues from land, opposite the mouth of the Rio Grande . . . thence . . . up the middle of that river to the point where the parallel of 31°47′ north latitude crosses the same; thence due west one hundred miles; then south to the parallel of 31°20′ north latitude; thence along the said parallel of 31°20′ to the 111th meridian of longitude west of Greenwich; then in a straight line to a point on the Colorado River twenty English miles below the junction of the Gila and Colorado rivers; thence up the middle of the said river Colorado until it intersects the present line between the United States and Mexico.[9]

And except for a renegotiation of the Chamizal tract dispute, finally settled in the 1960s,[10] the boundary has been the same since then. If the
boundary refers to the physical line drawn between the two countries,
defining the border is much more difficult because it is the geographical
area where the national and cultural characteristics of the two nations
meet and mix and where their respective governments implement
policies concerning much more than the international boundary. This geographical area varies depending on where one is along the nearly
2,000-mile boundary line. Moreover, the 1983 La Paz agreement between
the United States and Mexico defines the borderlands as the band of land
that stretches about 62.5 miles north and south of the boundary line.
This region includes communities not on the border itself, but in relative
proximity to it. The U.S.-Mexico borderlands therefore contain nearly
15 million residents in both countries. Their number is projected to reach
between 20 and 25 million people by 2030,[11] although their growth has
slowed down considerably in the last few years and may not reach the
predicted numbers.

These residents of the U.S.-Mexico border straddle two languages, two
cultures, two legal systems, two economic systems, two currencies, and
two political systems, and most of them do so with great ease. Borderlanders are neither fully American nor fully Mexican. They have made
their own hybrid culture.[12] Anyone visiting the Segundo Barrio in El Paso
or the Logan Neighborhood in San Diego will immediately notice that.
This fact may surprise many a Midwesterner who finds himself or herself
in a place that does not resemble either Mexico or the United States.

What the border looks like today and what its 15 million residents experience day to day is the product of its historical legacies and its political,
social, and economic context. To understand—to truly understand—the
border one has to look to the past as much as to the present. In effect,
the border has not always been the way it is today. There is a natural tendency to freeze the border in time as a bedlam, as if it had always been a
place of great turmoil and disarray. In reality it is an extremely dynamic
place whose meaning and physical appearance, whose practices and activities have shifted continuously for a period of 150 years, even as the physical
line has remained unmoved. A look at the U.S.-Mexico border across time
will quickly reveal that it has suffered a substantial transformation over
the last century and a half, and current perceptions of the border as an
immoral, dirty space are relatively new and come and go. To understand
the evolution of the area and to appreciate what is happening there today,
we need to take a look at its major transformations since 1853.

The history of the U.S.-Mexico border begins in the mid-nineteenth century. Although the physical boundary between the two countries took its

final shape in 1848 with the Treaty of Guadalupe-Hidalgo and in 1853 with the Gadsden Purchase, the way in which we view the border has changed over time. Its meaning to people living on it has undergone dramatic changes, which can be categorized as different stages of meaning, according to the emphasis given to the border, principally by the U.S. government. In effect, the U.S. government is the primary agent determining the meaning of the border, by dictating how open or closed it should be and what the rules governing transboundary activity should be. Residents on both sides of the physical boundary are generally left to adjust, adapt, and react to decisions made in Washington, DC. They do so by accommodating their lives and routines as best they can to the newest policy whims that come from Capitol Hill.

Shaped largely by the U.S. federal government, the meaning of the border to its residents has gone through four historical stages, which I will label as follows: the frontier border, the customs border, the law enforcement border, and the security border. Each of these stages can be measured by specific changes on the ground along the border, changes that have taken us to the current situation on the ground: the three border wars analyzed in this volume.

THE FRONTIER ERA

Between 1848 and roughly 1910, the prevalent meaning of the border was that of a "frontier." The Southwest of the United States was a place of open spaces and expressions of freedom. The boundary line that separated the United States from Mexico defined citizenship and civic duty, but it did not constrain mobility or access. And neither government had the ability to stop or regulate economic activity. People and cattle were free to roam back and forth without impediments. The spirit of the U.S.-Mexico border at this time is best captured in the romantic narratives of the cowboy and the cattleman. The region was marked by weak ties to centralized authority and removed from the large-scale economic activity of the eastern United States.[13] It was a place left to its own devices, and border crossers traveled freely, uncontested by governmental institutions. During these decades, there were no border bureaucracies to speak of, with the exception of a handful of U.S. Customs agents who worked only a few hours a day at certain checkpoints.

On matters of immigration, there were few laws regulating immigration on the U.S.-Mexico border in the second half of the nineteenth century. Congress was preoccupied with immigration from Europe and overlooked migration movements from the southwestern border. The Chinese Exclusion Act of 1882 targeted Chinese immigrants who came to work on the railroad lines of the Southwest. It did not refer to

Mexican immigration at all and it barely mentioned land borders. Four intervening congressional immigration acts[14] also said nothing about immigration laws governing the U.S.-Mexico border. All of the acts of Congress of that time related closely to labor laws, indicating that immigration was viewed more as an economic or a labor issue rather than a law enforcement issue. The Immigration Act of 1891 instructed the Treasury secretary "to prescribe rules for inspection along the borders of Canada, British Columbia, and Mexico so as not to obstruct or unnecessarily delay, impede, or annoy passengers in ordinary travel between these countries and the United States."[15] The Immigration Service it created focused on immigration arriving "by water" but not by land, and it is likely that there were no Immigration Service officers along the border, perhaps with the exception of Leonidas B. Giles, who was stationed at El Paso, Texas, in 1893. In that year, 119 of the 180 Immigration Service officers were stationed in Ellis Island alone compared to 1 along the U.S.-Mexico border. In 1899, there were only about four Immigration Service inspectors along the entire 2,000-mile border. It is worth noting that the Immigration Service at that time was under the Treasury Department, and on February 14, 1903, it moved to the Department of Commerce and Labor, a fact that reflected a preoccupation with the relationship between immigrants and economic issues, particularly labor, rather than with immigrants and law enforcement or immigrants and national security. The government considered immigrants as workers, not as potential criminals who posed problems of law enforcement or national security. Even if the immigration acts well into the 1900s were increasingly restrictive, there was almost no preoccupation with land immigration from either Canada or Mexico. Both the economic and labor orientation of most immigration controls and the absence of concern with the U.S.-Mexico border lead us to conclude that the mood along the U.S.-Mexico border at the time was that of the frontier. People, goods, services, and then vehicles moved freely across the border subject to hardly any inspection. Into the first decade of the 1900s, Mexicans were still allowed to move in and out of the United States unencumbered by any bureaucracies. Typically, Mexicans arrived in the United States, they were questioned, their entry was recorded, and they were free to enter the United States and even settle there. In the first decade of the 1900s, the mood began to shift along the border, but the focus was not on immigrants of Mexican origin. Marcus Braun, an Immigration Service inspector, investigated the U.S.-Mexico border in 1907 and found that Syrians, Japanese, Greeks, Chinese, and other third-country unskilled labor were using the U.S.-Mexico border as a passageway to the United States. This led the Immigration Service to classify immigrants entering through the Mexican border into "legitimate immigration" and "illegitimate immigration." Chinese, Japanese, Middle Easterners, and others coming in through Mexico were considered "illegitimate immigrants." Mexicans continued to be considered "legitimate immigrants." It was at this time, in 1908, that the government began to keep complete records of arrivals across the U.S.-Mexico border.[16]

The national mood that demanded immigration controls at the turn of the century originated in the industrial areas of the East Coast and slowly expanded to the South and Northwest. The Southwest, however, was largely indifferent to the national mood to control immigration. It did not embrace the notion that border crossers had to be controlled until later. Other than the occasional political rhetoric concerning the Chinese or the Japanese in California, the Mexican border was largely exempt from the anti-immigrant movement that marked other parts of the United States. Mexican border crossers were made liable for a head tax upon crossing. Those who could not afford to pay the head tax did not enter through an official POE. Instead, they crossed at some other unguarded point between ports of entry. Importantly, there are no records of anyone arrested, detained, or deported because of such "illegal" entries. In the words of Theodore Roosevelt, the U.S.-Mexican border was to be "closed to all but citizens and bona fide residents of Mexico." Such was the frontier border.

Soon after the final settlement of the boundary line in 1848 and 1853, border towns sprang up, many of them, such as Laredo and El Paso, Texas, heavily identified with Mexico. Mexicans also crossed into the United States and founded entirely new towns such as Brownsville, Texas. In fact, the lower valley of Texas saw the greatest creation of towns, although the western border in New Mexico, Arizona, and California remained largely empty. For decades, only U.S. cattle barons and agricultural interests profited from abundant empty land by monopolizing trade routes across the border. An examination of photographs of the time shows that on most of the nearly 2,000-mile-long boundary, there were no fences or significant obstacles to the movement of people. The pairs of towns along the border were divided by a short wire fence just a few feet high, when there was a fence at all!

Like immigration, trade across the U.S.-Mexico border went unregulated for a long time. It was the railroad that connected the border with zones of major economic significance in the United States, and thereby cities like Nuevo Laredo, Piedras Negras, Paso del Norte (Ciudad Juárez), and Nogales on the Mexican side and Laredo, El Paso, Nogales, and others began to prosper on the U.S. side. Products, like people, could easily cross from one side to the other. Contrabandists were an important part of the border economy. They smuggled anything into Mexico, from coffee to textiles. Smuggling has been part of the border since its inception because "one side of the river always had something that was lacking on the other side." By 1850, the Mexican government saw contrabandists as criminals. With their activities, contrabandists deprived Mexican producers of their Mexican market share and the Mexican government of its revenue. Meanwhile, border residents considered trading across boundaries an acceptable and even respectable activity.

Smuggling, as a border reality, thus has always been present.[17] What has changed over time is the nature of the goods smuggled. During the second half of the nineteenth century the government of Mexico, in order to remedy revenue losses, imposed tariffs on the importation of numerous agrarian and manufactured goods. To enforce these laws it created a special customs police (*contraresguardos*), which was far too small to prevent smuggling. Mexicans and Americans, therefore, continued their nearly free-trade practices across the border without much difficulty. Smuggling was facilitated by the general lack of governmental bureaucracies on the border. At that time, drugs were not a concern to central authorities on either side. For one thing, drugs had not yet been made illegal. In addition, drug use among border residents—or in the country as a whole—was minimal, if it existed at all.

The U.S.-Mexico border was an open border where individuals could cross at will. Even though, strictly speaking, it was illegal to cross between official ports of entry, the U.S. government had neither the wherewithal nor the desire to guard the border; bureaucrats on the border were limited to a few at official ports of entry; and no one patrolled the line between them. In the 1880s, Jeff Milton was the first border patrolman to ride along the Texas border on horseback with a revolver on his belt. Still much of the efforts of the early pioneers of border patrolling were directed against "illegitimate" immigrants, that is Chinese and other "undesirables," but not against Mexicans. When Congress began to require Mexicans and Canadians to pass literacy tests and pay a head tax of US$8, many avoided the official ports of entry and crossed between them. The real struggle with illegal immigration begins here, with these requirements now imposed on Mexicans and with the increasing abuse of the openness of the border by some Asian and European immigrants, who preferred to skip the cumbersome process at New York and other ports and decided to enter the United States from Mexico.

Although many have complained that cowboy and frontier narratives often romanticize the nineteenth-century border, this century was, in a way, an era of bliss characterized by a lack of attention to the border, unimpeded mobility, free trade, and practically no inspection of border crossers—without denying that some illegal activities were taking place. This era of relative bliss for border crossers came to an end with the turn of the century. The pressures of twentieth-century modernization were gathering on the border like dark clouds in the sky.

THE CUSTOMS ERA

Three major events changed the face of the border forever. These events had little to do with the border itself—as it is often the case, but they changed it profoundly. They ended the frontier era and rang in the customs era.

The first great nail in the coffin of the frontier border was the advent of the Mexican Revolution, which began on November 20, 1910. To prevent the turmoil from spilling into U.S. territory, the government established a series of forts along the border. During this time, the number of illegal crossers decreased considerably, only to rise again after 1920, when the Mexican Revolution ended. The $8 head tax of 1917 and the literacy tests were making it very hard for many Mexicans to migrate or even just to travel to the United States as easily as they had done for decades before. Many, however, had become eligible to move to the United States because of persecution during the Mexican Revolution. The Mexican upper class, for example, immigrated en masse to the United States, with all their capital, much of which began to feed business financing in the Southwest. Others were simply refugees of the violence of the revolution. Many of the members of my own family, for example, came from Mexico during that period, fleeing from the Mexican Revolution. The Hispanic character of many border cities was reinforced at that time by mass migration into cities like Nogales, El Paso, Laredo, and Brownsville.

The second major circumstance that was to transform the character of the border was the growing anti-immigration wave in the United States that reached the Southwest via the Chinese Exclusion Act of 1882, intended to exclude all Chinese from migrating into the United States. Amendments to this act extended the provision for another 10 years in 1892. By 1902, the Chinese Exclusion Act was further extended, this time indefinitely. Although Mexicans had been able to move back and forth freely for decades, suddenly they were no longer part of the daily life on the American side of the border. Instead, they were considered "foreigners" who did not possess the right to mobility across the boundary. This was a fundamental shift in attitude brought about by the growth of the state and the consolidation of nationhood in the empty lands of the Southwest. This attitude of the American public, translated into harder legislation, began a century of gradual closing of the border. The U.S. government began to bureaucratize the border and systematize inspections. In 1924, the U.S. Congress created the Border Patrol as part of the Immigration Service. Their duty was to guard the border to prevent illegal crossings of both people and merchandise, and to apprehend those who would aid a migrant who had not gone through the normal immigration clearing process. The Border Patrol began with just a few hundred agents, but they continued to increase over time, reaching more than 11,000 agents by 2005 and 20,000 by 2013—most of them on the U.S.-Mexico border. In fact, it was not until World War II that the Border Patrol reached 1,500 agents responsible for guarding the entire U.S. border, not just in the Southwest. By the 1930s, the Border Patrol was reorganizing, introducing new technology, and professionalizing its training. The stricter immigration laws had translated on the border ground to a much larger, professional border patrol force integrating the latest in surveillance technology. The Border Patrol numbers would only grow and their use of technology would only get more sophisticated. There was no turning back.

A second factor that changed the meaning of the border was the Prohibition era. On January 16, 1920, Americans woke up under the Eighteenth Amendment of the Constitution forbidding the manufacture, sale, or importation of alcoholic beverages. As a result, customs inspections became more prominent to enforce Prohibitionist laws. The new amendment created a new black market that demanded most of the attention of customs inspectors and even the Border Patrol. The U.S.-Mexican border began to see the smuggling of alcohol hidden in other cargo or crossed by mule between ports of entry. An increasing number of customs agents had to focus on enforcing customs laws derived from the Prohibition era. Because the new quotas on immigration imposed by Congress in 1921 and 1924 only fueled the market for illegal labor, bureaucrats along the border came under growing pressure to enforce not only immigration laws but also customs laws, and the latter occupied more and more of their time. Even after the Prohibition laws were repealed, customs inspections continued to focus on numerous other goods crossing the border. Customs exemplifies what some call "the natural law of bureaucracy": it is easier to create and grow a bureaucracy than it is to dismantle and control it. Customs, like the Border Patrol, would only expand in size over the next few decades. By 1929, a new act of Congress began to require that Mexicans have a visa to enter the United States and stiffened the penalties for entering the country between official ports of entry. This was indeed the end of a privilege enjoyed by Mexicans for decades and further divided local communities.

The third element that changed the border was World War I. Although its effect was not felt directly on the border, World War I made clear that the United States was becoming a mature power, a prosperous economy, even as Mexico turned on the wheels of a revolution that would barely place it on the path to modernity. This drove a wedge between the two countries, driving home the economic disparities that have marked the border to this day. Mexicans would begin to view the United States as a place of both political and economic refuge. Eventually, this disparity in wealth and income grew and determined the current geopolitical relationship of the two nations in its modern iteration. If immigration works somewhat like osmosis, the wealthier side will inevitably attract people from the poorer side. And this was certainly the case after 1920. Asymmetry works to create incentives and disincentives to move, often illegally to the more prosperous side of the border. Much of what occurred in the twentieth century and is likely to occur in the first part of this century will be largely determined by this unequal relationship, including another potential bracero (guest worker) program, which was proposed in various immigration reform bills in 2005, 2007, and 2014.

These three chains of events conspired to close the border in two important ways: to restrict the movement of people and to regulate the traffic of all commercial goods between the two countries. During this "customs era," the border was characterized by a fixed, harder line that revoked the frontier milieu permanently. The United States increased its surveillance and stiffened its customs protections. Bureaucrats began to keep records of all cross-border transactions, which increased their paperwork, and which in turn increased the number of agents working on the border. The momentum was toward greater vigilance at the border, creating a deeper sense of separation between the two nations. Still, much of the inspection activity was focused on goods being transported across the border. Surveillance between ports of entry remained very light and sporadic, and cross-border interaction, even undocumented interaction, was relatively easy. People still went back and forth between ports of entry. In fact, up to the 1970s, it was quite easy to cross the border, even illegally. I myself recall crossing the border in the 1980s with great ease.

The Law Enforcement Era

There is no single dramatic event that inaugurated the "law enforcement border." Instead, the transition to this era on the border occurred slowly over time. Beginning with the Nixon administration, ideologically conservative forces in the United States rose to prominence, which began an emphasis on law and order that dominated the American political landscape by the 1980s. This new conservative revolution left no stone unturned. Ronald Reagan's administration was sent to Washington, DC, in 1980 to do just that: bring "law and order" to its fullest expression. In this scheme of things, the border could not be the exception, and so it underwent a quiet revolution, further restricting mobility between the two countries.

The focus of the law enforcement era was on two major issues. One was the massive undocumented migration that had been rising with Mexico's rapid demographic growth and urbanization from the 1940s to the 1970s and culminated with several million Mexican citizens living without authorization inside the United States. In the view of many, the flood of undocumented border crossers who took advantage of the relative openness of the border between official ports of entry to settle in the United States was now unacceptably high. Indeed, the number of illegal entries at the South Texas border even in the 1950s had risen so rapidly that the Border Patrol began to transfer agents from the Canadian border to the Mexican border. With the number of undocumented workers, the Border Patrol saw a considerable increase in its own budgets and personnel. There was a sustained sense of urgency regarding the problem of undocumented migration, and the U.S. government began to step up its efforts to "guard" the border against this "alien invasion."

Moreover, in 1982 the U.S. government began to put pressure on the Colombian drug cartels that smuggled cocaine via the Caribbean. Because of the squeeze on the Caribbean, the Colombian drug lords sought an alliance with the Mexican drug-smuggling organization of Miguel Ángel Félix Gallardo, which operated on the U.S.-Mexico border. This new alliance brought the cocaine trade to the border, in addition to the existing heroin and marijuana trade that had already flourished on the largely unguarded border in the 1970s. By the mid-1980s, the Colombian-Mexican drug cartel alliances were smuggling tons of drugs across the border.[18] This raised some serious concerns, and the U.S. government began to beef up its efforts to combat drugs on the U.S.-Mexico border. This, added to the problem of immigration, which had already been redefined as a law enforcement problem and concentrated in the U.S. Justice Department, made the border a place where law and order had to be imposed from above. Evidence suggests that the overall funding to combat drug trafficking focused on the U.S.-Mexico border, mostly devoted to law enforcement measures. Policing became the new way of dealing with any issues along the border.[19]

The law enforcement era was reinforced in the 1990s. By 1993 and 1994, three law enforcement operations to guard the border were set up. One was *Operation Hold the Line* in El Paso, Texas; a second was *Operation Safeguard* in Arizona; and the third was *Operation Gatekeeper* in California. These three operations were military-style operations with new high-tech gadgets and added patrol officers and vehicles. They were supposed to be posted every quarter of a mile (within sight of each other) in order to stop the flow of undocumented workers and illegal drugs. Although this was unsustainable as a general strategy, it reinforced the view that the border was a lawless place where more law and order was required. It also inaugurated an era of border militarization that would continue to this day. Moreover, it would create a border security-industrial triangle that built enormous vested interests in perpetuating the image of the border as a dangerous place.

It was at this time that some local communities on both sides of the border began to lose the historical connections that had bound them together and cross-border social and family relations started to weaken.

Fences began to go up and there were already some proposals to build a steel wall along the border, principally in urban areas. Some walls were in fact built. This was the end of the old "cross-border intimacy" that borderlanders were accustomed to.[20]

THE NATIONAL SECURITY ERA

Unlike the "law enforcement era," which descended on the border with the transformation of the United States into a more conservative society, the national security era of the border was inaugurated with a single event: the attack of September 11, 2001, on New York and Washington, DC. With the post–September 11 lash out, perhaps no other area of the country was as affected as the U.S.-Mexico border. But the response of the U.S. government *on the border* was to some extent a curious response. Those who diagnosed the failure to deter the terrorist attacks of that day focused on immigration procedures, on cross-border commercial practices, on the openness of the border, etc. Thus the diagnosis of the failure of the government fell heavily on the U.S.-Mexico border, even though the border had very little to do with the terrorists of September 11. Few focused originally on the real failure: a lack of intelligence coordination to detect and apprehend potential terrorists in the United States entering anywhere, whether at sea ports, airports, or land ports of entry.[21]

With this border-centered diagnosis of the terrorist attacks came the many short- and long-term reactions of the U.S. government and their costs, many of which also focused on the border. In the short term, the border was temporarily shut down. Families were separated; students could not get to school; cross-border commuters could not get to their jobs; and retail business experienced a slowdown. In El Paso alone, there were 50,000 fewer business transactions in the month following September 11. The waiting time to cross the border increased to up to four to five hours due to the careful inspection of every vehicle crossing the border. The import/export sector, too, experienced additional costs because of the delays in trucking their merchandise across the ports of inspection. The added fuel, hours spent on waiting, and human-hours lost represented a considerable expense in the days following September 11.

The long-term effects were also important. The first and most important effect was the redefinition of the issues along the border. Whereas border issues were previously a matter of law enforcement, everything was redefined as a matter of national security. There was a "securitization" of all border issues that was made permanent by the creation of the U.S. Department of Homeland Security, where many of the agencies that deal with border issues are now located. Besides the redefinition of border politics as national security issues, the focus of the Department of Home-land Security reorganization was to a large extent the border and its activ-ities, not so much the interior of the country, except perhaps for the international airports. After September 11, the budgets for border security and surveillance increased even more than they had in the 1980s and 1990s, reaching $7 billion in 2006. Some budget proposals called for much more. In 2005, for instance, Congressman Bennie Thompson demanded an increase in the number of Border Patrol agents, from 11,000 to 21,000. President Bush, however, vetoed that increase at that time. Eventually, however, the numbers did rise to 21,000 and the border security budget reached many more billions of dollars.

With the "securitization" of all matters pertaining to the border and the increases in budget and personnel came also a change in the general atti-tude toward border crossers. Before September 11, officers on the border tended to treat border crossers poorly. But now, every vehicle and every person entering the United States is considered a suspect, a potential harm to America. Today, border agents have gone beyond simple lack of courtesy in treating border crossers. They are now, unaccountably, free to violate all kinds of due process rights and even human rights, and abu-sive treatment of border crossers has become the norm.[22]

It is interesting to observe that five years after September 11, not much has changed on the border. Two important factors make this evident. First, illegal drugs continue to stream in at the same levels as before, despite increased budgets, personnel, and a new Department of Home-land Security. And the drop in undocumented crossers, while partially attributable to increased law enforcement, may also be due to the economic conditions within the United States after the 2008 financial crisis and the abysmal job market for everyone as well as to Mexico's own changing dem-ographic statistics. Thus all that these changes and reforms seem to have accomplished is a redefinition of the concept of security to include all border issues, a new and more hostile attitude toward border crossers, and a new layer of bureaucratic paperwork for all. But none of these reforms seem to have fixed the more fundamental problems of the border. To do so, what is required is a long-term plan, with a much wider vision and stronger politi-cal leadership than the current political leaders of either country are willing to provide. For now, the security era is here to stay.

One can only hope that the fifth era of the border will be one where the border will be dismantled, rather than reinforced, by conceptions of law enforcement and national security and viewed as a resource for both countries.[23] "Debordering" will likely become a historical necessity for both countries in due time and we might as well begin to imagine what an open border will look like. The question is when will it happen and of course whether things will get worse before we get there.

THE CLOSING OF THE BORDER

An examination of the history of the border over its 150 years or so reveals that the border has been closing. With every era, the border has become even more guarded and more tightly controlled. The result of every escalation along the border has been massive bureaucratic reorganization and the addition of more resources and personnel to control the border. However, the approach throughout the twentieth century was quite the same: more law enforcement with greater punishment for border lawbreakers. And yet, the approach is the equivalent of an escalation that has not paid off.

OUR LIVES IN THE HANDS OF OTHERS

Unfortunately, border residents have little control over the image and reputation of their homeland. They do not even control their cross-border life. They certainly do not make or even influence the policies and rules that structure their cross-border interaction. Those policies and rules are made in the capitals, Mexico City and, more specifically, Washington, DC, thousands of miles away from the border itself. Through border policy, the lives of millions of people who reside in the borderlands are strongly contoured by policies from far away. This is why the perceptions of politicians and policy makers regarding the border matter. It is their perceptions that give rise to policies presumably designed to determine how the border and its "intractable" problems are to be dealt with. Border residents simply live with the consequences of the decisions made in the halls of Congress or the corridors of bureaucracy. For this reason, an alert border resident shudders when politicians grandstand to talk about illegal drugs, undocumented immigration, and homeland security on the border. This is not to say that there are no mechanisms to consult "stakeholders" at the border; but often by stakeholders, policy makers mean large transportation companies, manufacturers, and other large corporations that are legitimate border users, but they exclude the residents of the border itself.

Yet these are the three issues that are most talked about today when it comes to the border—drugs, immigration, and homeland security. There are thousands of media stories, congressional hearings, statements by various groups of civil society, press releases, and declarations by governments and leaders on the wretched condition of the U.S.-Mexico border.[24] Illegal drugs, undocumented immigration, and the potential for a terrorist attack filtering through the border are the most often cited reasons for a governmental impetus for a new border security policy coming down from Washington, DC.[25] This is particularly true since September 11, although the terrorist attacks of that day have only accelerated a trend already in progress. How the lives of the vast majority of those living along the border are affected or what their needs may be is largely irrelevant. Washington, DC, has decided that the border is a chaotic, lawless, unwieldy place that must be brought "under control."[26] To that effect, the U.S. government speaks of the drug war, the efforts to combat undocumented migration, and the war on terror. Drug traffickers, undocumented workers, and terrorists must be stopped at the border. The rhetoric is couched in militarized language. These three "border wars" consume most of the time of any politician or policy maker even willing to take a hard look at this troubled part of Paradise.

The perception of the border as a bedlam has clearly not been good for the border or the people who live on it. But it has not been good for decades. For more than 40 years, the U.S. government has waged its two longest wars on the border: the war on drugs and the war on undocumented migration. Besides these two wars, the last 15 years have seen the development of yet a third border war: the war on terror, as it manifests itself on the border. To the three fundamentally distinct problems of the border—illegal drugs, undocumented migration, and homeland security (guarding against terrorists)—the U.S. government has come up with three similar solutions: a border war. And these wars are largely fought on the U.S.-Mexico border.

A DEMOCRATIC DEFICIT

The talk of "border wars" is particularly disturbing to border residents when it comes from Washington, DC. If politicians and policy makers perceive the U.S.-Mexico border as a dangerous place that poses a threat to the national security of the United States, they will be inclined to create and implement policies to "close the border" or to "bring it under control."[27] Many of them are fond of declaring a war on this or that problem, with an even stronger centralizing effect in dealing with border issues. Thus, when it comes to the border, decisions on how to deal with its issues come from above, not from below. Over the history of the twentieth century and into the twenty-first century, most laws and policies relating to border control were created in Washington. Yet their deepest effects have been felt by the people who live, work, do business, and study on the borderlands—those who live on the front line, so to speak. Moreover, whenever politicians change the laws and establish new rules that govern cross-border interaction and create new bureaucracies, residents of the borderlands are never consulted. They are denied the fundamental right to a level of self-government in their cross-border interactions because boundaries are a "federal jurisdiction."[28] The fact that borderland residents do not have an input into how the government deals with the area's issues indicates a democratic deficit. Border residents do not govern themselves; they are governed from above.

CONFLATING THE ISSUES

In Ciudad Juárez, I interviewed a former drug trafficker, who wanted to remain anonymous for obvious reasons. My interviewee told me a joke when I asked him about the interrelation between drug trafficking, human smuggling, and the war on terror. He said that he saw some connections between the first two—and he showed me some of these connections as he saw them—but he did not see a connection with the third. He joked and said that no decent drug trafficker would want to be seen with a terror suspect because then the U.S. government would really come after him. This joke made me think about how these three wars are different on the border, and how they are interrelated. In the eyes of the U.S. government today, they are one and the same thing.

President George W. Bush declared a global war on terror in September 2001.[29] It soon became obvious that this global war would necessarily have consequences for border management. That was a logical follow-up. What was not logical was the fact that this new global war on terror would conflate the issues into a single image of a dangerous border that posed a national security threat to the very survival of the United States and then proceed to declare an all-out war to "control the border." Robert Bonner, former director of U.S. Customs and Border Protection (CBP), best illustrated this conflation of the issues. He said that "the existence of CBP makes us vastly better able to protect our nation from all external threats, whether illegal migrants and illegal drugs, terrorists, terrorist weapons, including weapons of mass destruction."[30] Bonner's words clearly show that the U.S. government was not interested in disaggregating the border into various regions or component problems, even for the purposes of analysis. His words also show that the government was not interested in dealing with each of these issues one at a time. Instead, the government was going to view a lack of control of the border as a single national security threat and it was going to deal with it with a single strategy: by declaring war on the presumed threats coming through the southern border.

To the observant border resident and the trained academic eye, illegal drug trafficking, undocumented migration, and homeland security at the border are very different problems. Yet the United States has lumped them together by creating a single Homeland Security Department and dumping most border issues into it.[31] Moreover, every one of these issues was given a similar treatment. It would be very hard to make the case that the Border Patrol, with the same training, personnel, equipment, and manuals, could fight drug traffickers, deter undocumented workers, and prevent terrorists from crossing the border. Yet they are commissioned to do all three. But it is absurd to think that these border phenomena are the same. And it is even more absurd to imagine that the solution to all three is the same, waging a generalized war that has made the border more insufferable than it already was. It is incongruous to think that drugs are smuggled the same way as human beings or that either of these is a national security threat as opposed to being a serious crime or that drug traffickers would necessarily associate with Middle Eastern terrorists when they do not share the same motive for their activities, etc. In sum, neither the problem nor the United States' blanket solution to these distinct problems is a long-term, wise strategy for the border. Conflating the issues can only prevent the U.S. government from dealing more effectively with each of them. Creating what looks like a single strategy with a unilateral, short-term focus seems counterproductive as well, given that the problems of the border are better solved in partnership with one's neighbor, with a long-term focus to tackle the very origins of each concern.

PLANNING TO SECURE THE BORDER: SAME OLD, SAME OLD

The National Intelligence Reform Act of 2005 included a request for 10,000 more Border Patrol agents, to take the total to about 21,000 agents. Eighty percent of the new agents would patrol the U.S.-Mexico border. That would bring the total number of agents guarding the southern border to nearly 18,000, a veritable army. President Bush cut that number and his FY2006 Budget authorized only 210 more agents. A January 24, 2005, letter signed by many Republicans asked President Bush to reinstate the request "in order to secure our borders against terrorists." The numbers would eventually reach 21,000 under the Obama administration. The request for an increase of 10,000 more Border Patrol agents, however, is the type of request that has been repeated in Washington for decades when it comes to the border. Timothy Dunn has argued that the U.S. government has one single approach to deal with the border: to move steadily to a militarized strategy with increased personnel and resources and a low-intensity conflict strategy.[32]

Nowhere is this logic of escalation more evident than on the ground along the nearly 2,000-mile southern boundary. Throughout the twentieth century, when a problem surfaces or spirals out of control along the border, the U.S. government has defined it and then responded with an escalation strategy.[33] The rhetoric too escalates. Instead of law and order, over time the discourse has turned to one of invasions, wars, national security threats, lack of control, and now, terror. September 11 only sped up this logic of escalation. Even as late as 2005, the White House proposed a

Secure Border Initiative that would represent more of the same: a unilateral, law enforcement approach. The Secure Border Initiative focuses on:

More agents to patrol our borders, secure our ports of entry, and enforce immigration laws

Expanded detention and removal capabilities to eliminate "catch and release" once and for all

A comprehensive and systemic upgrading of the technology used in controlling the border, including increased manned aerial assets, expanded use of UAVs, and next-generation detection technology

Increased investment in infrastructure improvements at the border—providing additional physical security to sharply reduce illegal border crossings

Greatly increased interior enforcement of our immigration laws—including more robust worksite enforcement[34]

Thus, over the heads of the nearly 15 million residents along the border, the U.S. government bureaucracies operating on the U.S.-Mexico boundary engage drug traffickers, undocumented workers, and presumed border-jumping terrorists with little regard to local solutions or the creation of a larger frame within which to solve these issues—ideally together with Mexico—in order to secure the border once and for all. Instead, the focus is a unilateral, short-term approach centered largely on law enforcement. No attention is paid to the larger social and economic forces that motivate people either to smuggle drugs, or to cross the border to work without documents, or now, say many in the U.S. government, to jump the border as terrorists with the intention to "harm America."[35] There is indeed little thought given to the construction of a long-term, bilateral solution to the troubles that plague the border. The European way of dealing with its internal border issues is nowhere to be found in North America.[36]

In sum, border control programs have come and gone, and what they have in common is that they have largely relied on more agents, more facilities for detention, more technology, and generally more enforcement. Every proposal and bill includes more of the same. Thus the border today constitutes the front line of three ongoing wars that need to be analyzed as such, as the continuation of the same old strategies and tactics. This book will argue, however, that so far the three border wars have been utter failures, given the poor results the U.S. government has had over time. Drugs are just as abundant; undocumented workers continue to cross over; and no credible reports of terrorists crossing the border to blow themselves up in the United States have been recorded publicly.

ARE THE THREE BORDER WARS JUSTIFIED?

The issue of a logical law enforcement escalation along the border is important. The problem of unilateral action by the United States is also crucial. The economic sustainability of the approach is fundamental. But there is an even more critical question that must be asked about the three border wars that we are about to examine in this book. Even if it were fully justified to view these three great issues on the border as the same problem and to wage a massive law enforcement, quasi-military war against them, using the same strategies, the same tactics, the same bureaucracies, the same training, the same equipment, etc., at an increasing cost, we would have to look at whether the wars of the border are both limited and successful. In other words, the question of whether there is in the future a successful end to the problems of the border is key. Unfortunately, there is no end in sight to the battles of the border. They seem to be unlimited and, worse yet, unsuccessful. Nearly all historical evidence over decades shows that the border has never been under control and is not likely to be under control in the near future. More of the same guarantees only a less democratic borderland with a more repressive police state operating along the border.

A close look at the history of the border can help us put the U.S. approach in perspective. The war on drugs has been going on for more than 40 years.[37] The war on undocumented migration has been going on for more than 40 years as well.[38] These two wars are in fact America's longest wars. And now we have the war on terror on the border. The war on terror, away from or at the border, has no end in sight, and while its successes in the Middle East or in terms of deterring terror attacks in the United States may be acceptable, it has not produced a single successful "terror bust" on the border. The government's inability to declare victory in these wars is particularly serious if we consider that the current approach is not only monetarily unsustainable in the long run—it is an expensive approach—but also has not solved and is not likely to solve the problems of the border.

Moreover, the approach also often alienates Mexico diplomatically and there is little reason for that country to cooperate with U.S. border issues, although some sense of cooperation has begun to grow again in the last luster. The United States, however, insists on going it alone when it comes to the border, with an expensive bureaucratic apparatus of many agents, budgets, and gadgets, and a strict law enforcement approach that has not paid off because there may not be anything there to pay off in the first place. This is the path of empire, attempting to secure its outer perimeters at an increasingly higher cost. History has shown that this path is doomed. Consequently, in the process of analyzing what it is like to live and work and study and move about on the front lines of these border wars, I also want to expose the absurdity of dealing with the border unilaterally. That is, the United States treats the boundary as if beyond the borderline there were simply an abyss, and the "national security threats" on it come from that dark chasm that Mexico is assumed to be.

THE SCOPE OF THE BOOK

It is against this background—a mixed picture of the border, a democratic deficit, three distinct border wars, and a single government response to all of them—that this book is written. These pages argue that illegal drugs, undocumented migration, and homeland security at the border are three problems interrelated mostly by the fact that they happen on the border. They need to be analyzed independently, taking into account their unique characteristics as well as those of the border itself. Each problem has its own dynamics, its own actors, its own motives, and its own scenarios—even when there are points of interception among them. Bluntly put, they are not the same issue and they should not be treated as such. To examine each of them and to demonstrate why a single U.S. strategy against three distinct problems is not a workable solution in the long term, I rely on real-life border stories to draw attention to these issues, their origin, their nature, and their day-to-day development. I try to bring the reader to the daily activities of a drug trafficker, or the ordeals of an undocumented worker, or the way the border is changing by the new homeland security regime. Although all these stories happen along the same geographical location, it is important to separate them because it becomes easier to see the absurdity of dealing with three entirely different issues in the same way, waging an all-out war on the border that is at once transforming and hurting life there and driving a wedge between two neighbors.

At the end of the book, I outline a longer-term solution to the problems of the border. But that longer-term solution requires hard work, much patience, and strategic investments by both the U.S. and the Mexican governments. I also argue, however, that the political will and the leadership vision are not there yet, even if there is now a glimmer of hope, mostly because so many of us are pushing for a new approach. No one yet, in either country, however, has dealt with the border within the larger framework of an integrating North America as a whole. The solution, by default, has been a border strategy that has not paid off and is not likely to pay off in the near future, but whose costs keep mounting. Law enforcement is expensive, alienates neighbors, and has proven to be an inefficient solver of long-term, deep-seated issues such as illegal drug trafficking, undocumented migration, and now terror (if any) at the border. A war of attrition on the border does not seem to be successful today nor is it likely to be so in the future.

Let us now disaggregate the three fundamental border issues to show the logic behind each of these border problems. This separation of the issues will help analyze them separately and understand what is behind each of them. This same examination should expose the futility of the twentieth-century approach ratcheted up further by the Bush administration in the early years of the twenty-first century. It should also expose the fact that under President Obama not much has changed. It could be perhaps because he was too busy with health care reform initially and then gridlocked by an uncooperative Congress, unwilling to make any changes to border policy. But in the end, the current approach is choking the border, diminishing the potential for prosperity in the twenty-first century, and costing billions of dollars that would best be invested in modernizing border infrastructure, managing trade more efficiently, creating more integrated labor markets, and investing in border communities. That, however, is still to be seen as we will soon move into the third decade of the century.

CHAPTER 2

The Drug War on the Border

A BIRD'S-EYE VIEW

In November 2005, a marijuana-laden dump truck got stuck in the Rio Grande in Hudspeth County, Texas, while fleeing back to Mexico from U.S. law enforcement officials.[1] In September 2005, Aldo Manuel Erives, a former Border Patrol agent in El Paso, was sentenced to 10½ years in federal prison for allowing drug couriers through a checkpoint without inspection.[2] In December 2004, Robert Dean Harper and Timothy Gavin Hynd were arrested by the Highway Patrol in Tucson, Arizona, for attempting to smuggle 610 pounds of marijuana inside coffins.[3] In July 2003, Ismael "El Mayo" Zambada, Mexico's number one drug trafficker, evaded the U.S. Drug Enforcement Administration's (DEA) 19-month-old "Operation Trifecta," even while U.S. authorities reported capturing 240 suspected drug smugglers in the United States and Mexico, and seizing six tons of cocaine.[4] A half-mile tunnel is discovered and a massive bust of coke and pot is seized under the Tijuana-San Diego border.[5]

Incidents like these now happen far too frequently on the border and all of them have something in common—they are part of a war on drugs that the U.S. government is waging on the U.S.-Mexican border. Mexican and American newspapers and magazines are full of stories like these. A quick Internet search will yield hundreds of thousands of drug war stories over the last decades of what is now America's longest war—longer than any other military engagement and longer than the war on terror.

When President Richard Nixon declared a war on drugs in 1969, the U.S.-Mexico border became, for all practical purposes, the frontline of a never-ending war between the U.S. government and the drug-smuggling cartels. The border is where the government and the drug-smuggling organizations wage some of their fiercest battles, and where both sides suffer most of their defeats and score most of their victories in a largely futile game because the results of the war on drugs have so far been meager, even by the government's own standards.[6] And no place has paid a higher price for the drug war than the U.S.-Mexico border. Thus it is worth asking: What exactly is the relationship between the border and the drug war? Why keep on waging this unending war? The answer is, simultaneously, simple and complex.

ECONOMICS AND GEOGRAPHY

Two fundamental truisms combine to explain America's longest war. The first of these was pronounced by Charles Caleb Colton (1780–1832) who wrote that "commerce flourishes by circumstances, precarious, transitory, contingent, almost as the winds and waves that bring it to our shores."[7] The other maxim is even simpler: geography is destiny. That is, a standard map can reveal more about the tactics and strategies of the players in a given issue than all other explanations combined. Analyzing the war on drugs on the border requires that we consider these rather deceptively mundane observations because they are the key to uncovering the dynamics and fate of the struggle to eliminate the production, trade, and consumption of mind-altering substances in the United States. The supply route flourishes along the border because of these two forces: economics and geography.

IT'S ECONOMICS, STUPID!

To begin to understand the illegal-drug business, we need to recognize that humans have innate desires, especially for pleasure. Almost all human desires produce economic activity. When one is hungry, there is resort to a supplier of food. When one desires stimulation, one seeks a place for entertainment. In the United States, there are some 25 to 30 million people who regularly desire and gratify the pleasure that mind-altering drugs produce, according to the National Institute on Drug Abuse.[8] Just as grocers provide food and entertainers provide entertainment, so do illegal-drug dealers provide mind-altering drugs. The market for psychotropic drugs is like that for any other commodity. There is a product, there is a supplier, there is a middleman, and there is a consumer. Economics, then, can help explain the entire activity of the drug trade.[9]

Even when a government makes the gratification of an innate desire illegal, the innate desire still remains; and very likely there are still willing suppliers of the desired good. The result is the creation of a black market. In the illegal-drug black market, all the elements of a normal economy are distorted by the combined factors of the illegality of the desired good, the law enforcement apparatus to ensure compliance, the risk premium charged by suppliers, and the furtive decision making of consumers. In such an economy, the rewards and risks are both magnified by public policy. For example, a unit of marijuana of 0.5 grams costs about $1.70 to produce. On the street, when illegal, it may sell for $8.60. A profit margin of $6.90 per 0.5-gram-unit in a free and open market would not last long. To reinforce this point, in Colorado, the first state to implement legal marijuana, prices per unit have fallen between 16 and 30 percent since it was legalized—not considering that it is now heavily taxed as well. In an open market, it is clear that competition eliminates this excessive profit. The $6.90 profit per unit is the risk premium that draws the "criminal" to willingly engage in a highly dangerous activity: producing and trading marijuana. Without the risk, markets stabilize prices and eliminate the huge profit margins. Moreover, a black market creates a class of criminals because government prohibition of the product will drive black-market players underground, creating a clandestine network of producers, traders, and consumers. Participants in such a market are thereby made criminals. Add to that the huge costs of enforcement and incarceration. In an open market, these players are simply buyers and sellers. An added advantage is that the state seems to save taxpayer funds in two ways: by dismantling the law enforcement apparatus dedicated to enforce drug laws and by collecting additional taxes. In 2015, Colorado was slated to collect more than $125 million in taxes, fees, and permits, in addition to indirect collection from the nascent marijuana tourism industry revenue.

Throughout the history of humankind, borders and black markets have been closely related, usually because individuals are willing to engage in smuggling the forbidden goods across the borderline. With this understanding, it is easy to see why smuggling is pervasive. The connection between economic incentives and criminal behavior was intuited by Adam Smith in *The Wealth of Nations* when he said that "nobody will be so mad as to expose himself upon the highway, when he can make better bread in an honest and industrious way."[10] And yet, on the Mexican border—and beyond, there are people mad enough to engage in organized crime on the sheer basis of the profits to be made from the drug trade. These can be exorbitant. Drug trafficking is the most profitable organized crime in the world—although some argue that human trafficking is equal to or right behind it—and America is the most important market for illegal drugs. The estimated annual income from drug trafficking and dealing is virtually impossible to calculate. The UN Office on Drugs and Crime estimated it could be as much as $400 billion worldwide and *The Economist* argues that it could be as high as $150 billion.[11] On the U.S.-Mexico border, the profits are estimated to be $80 billion. I think this is overestimated in any event because no one can accurately calculate how much money there is to be made, but it is easily in the tens of billions of dollars. The sheer profit incentive for anyone to partake in this activity is enormous.

To the estimated annual profits from the drug-trafficking business add the current conditions of high unemployment, underemployment, self-employment, and low incomes in Mexico—there is little evidence of wage convergence between the United States and Mexico, even well after NAFTA.[12] This will yield a tremendously fertile ground of thousands of men who are willing to risk their lives for a share of the drug trade profit. According to the World Bank, Mexico had an unemployment rate of 4.9 percent in 2014.[13] Moreover, considering that in Mexico even part-time and self-employed people (e.g., vendors in the streets) are considered employed, we are left with an exorbitant number of individuals able and willing to pick up a trade that promises quick riches. That means there are several million people in Mexico with no jobs and desperate enough to allow themselves to be recruited by organized crime. Worse yet, salaries in Mexico are abysmally low—about $4 a day—mostly due to the fact that the Mexican government has a general wage policy designed to keep salaries down to attract foreign investment. This leaves many families in extreme poverty and willing to engage in illicit activities to make money.

Moreover, the Mexican labor force adds roughly 1 million workers per year but has steadily produced only about 500,000 jobs per annum. That means that every year 500,000 people are very much on their own. Many choose to enter organized crime networks and even more move on to the United States as undocumented workers. Moving to the United States illegally, however, is increasingly more difficult. The state of the U.S. economy since 2008 has discouraged Mexican migration, which may have reached net zero by 2015. At the same time, the border is now so difficult to breach that many no longer consider it worth spending months or even years in prison for crossing illegally into the United States. Thus many of these individuals—and they are overwhelmingly men—are rationally making their calculations on the basis of utility maximization. They measure both benefits and risks to the best of their knowledge, and many conclude that it is worth risking life and liberty for the kind of profits that can be made in the drug trade.[14] What else can explain the fact that most drug traffickers die young and the rest get old in jail, and there remains a never-ending supply of men willing to take the place of the dead or the jailed?

NI-NIS

To make matters worse, organized crime in Mexico, including drug trafficking, is fueled by what is now known as the Ni-Nis. In Spanish, *Ni-Ni* means "neither-nor" and it is now a term that refers to young adults who *neither* study *nor* work, essentially hanging out in the streets. These Ni-Nis are thought to be the raw labor for much of organized crime in Mexico, including the organizations that operate smuggling drugs across the border. According to the Mexican Statistics Bureau (INEGI), there may be as many as 7 million Ni-Nis in the country.[15] That constitutes a serious problem and one that easily fuels both organized crime and eventually an exodus to the United States as the economy recovers and new jobs that appeal to migrants begin to increase in number.

LOW WAGES AND DRUG TRAFFICKING

Returning to the issue of wages, income levels in Mexico are still well below those of the United States. The minimum wage in Mexico is about $4 a day in 2016. In the United States, the minimum wage is $7.25 an hour and much higher in some jurisdictions. As one climbs up the wage ladder, the disparities between the two countries generally grow even starker. Whatever scale one uses, however, the wage disparity across the U.S.-Mexico border is enormous, even in the context of the greater prosperity of the Mexican border states and the lesser prosperity of the U.S. border counties, particularly in the lower Rio Grande Valley in Texas. These border asymmetries have a strong effect on the incentives for individuals to participate in the drug trade. It is quite common in El Paso, Texas, for example, to see young Mexican and Mexican American men and women being led in handcuffs to jail where they are processed for attempting to smuggle drugs hidden in their vehicles. These young men and women—as young as 18 years—are often convinced by drug traffickers to cross a load of drugs on a one time basis in exchange for hundreds or even thousands of dollars. The amount of money offered to many of these B1/B2 visa holders (crossing card) is several times what they would make in a single month. If they get away with crossing the load of drugs— and many do— they receive a handsome reward with hardly any strings attached.

But temptation is everywhere—not just among the Ni-Nis or low-wage earners. Just five years ago, a student's mother came to see me at the University of Texas at El Paso (UTEP) to talk to me about her son. He was a Mexican student at the university and held an F-1 visa—a foreign-student visa. He had been recruited to smuggle drugs across the border by a group in Ciudad Juárez. He did this for a few months, eventually buying an expensive truck, dressing much better, and spending generously, even as he pursued his engineering studies at UTEP. Eventually, he was caught by CBP, convicted at a federal court in El Paso, and spent nearly five years in a federal prison in Alamogordo, New Mexico. The reason: easy money. But he lost his career and mobility into the

United States, and now has to hide from the owners of the drugs he "lost" when he was caught. He moved to southern Mexico to live as discreet a life as possible. However, the latest I have heard is that he is back cooperating with drug traffickers.

To make matters worse, human development in Mexico is still lacking. Many of these men (and some women) are unskilled or low-skilled labor. As such they cannot obtain well-paying jobs. They are willing to try a trade that requires only the ability to behave like a thug, handle a gun, be a bodyguard, or drive a vehicle loaded with illicit drugs. Some of them become *sicarios*—salaried killers working for the cartels. These are skills that are easy to acquire because they do not require long-term training. When in the 1980s Mexico became a transshipment point for drug cartels from Colombia—which had been squeezed by U.S. counterdrug efforts in the Caribbean—the initial scouts sent by the Colombian drug lords to liaise with their organizations in Mexico found many Mexican men and even women willing to collaborate with them. That labor pool is still there and readily available. The only problem is that organized crime has become much more diversified in its focus within Mexico and many of them are now criminal groups that kidnap for ransom, extort money from businesses, rob and assault, and engage in human trafficking and smuggling.

Wealth is yet another issue to consider. We are dealing with business and money, after all. The attraction to the drug trade is, albeit not absolutely, fed by wealth disparities along the border. Thus much of the drug trade along the border cannot be attributed to the morality or immorality of the border, or the good or ill intentions of those who participate in the production and trafficking of illicit drugs, but to the sheer economic incentives that the business itself offers and the structural forces influencing border asymmetries such as differences in income levels, unemployment, and the low-skill levels of many Mexican workers. Given today's technology, everyone is aware of such disparities and there is a seething social resentment from the have-nots toward the haves. Slowly, this frustration turns into desperation and eventual crime—even if poverty is not the only variable that feeds a life of crime. Such is the "dark force"—economics, really—against which the U.S. government must direct its drug war.

THE EXPLANATORY POWER OF A STANDARD MAP

Real estate agents have long known that their business is about location, location, location. For drugs and the border, the same rule holds. The U.S.-Mexico border is the busiest border in the world. According to the Bureau of Transportation Statistics, 11.3 million trucks with 8.5 million loaded truck containers, 41,000 trains with 2.1 million loaded train cars, 103 million personal vehicles with 190 million people, 298,842 buses with 4.6 million bus passengers, and 41.6 million pedestrians crossed the U.S.-Mexico border in 2015.[16] This is in addition to the 250,000 individuals who attempt to cross illegally every year between POEs— a number that has collapsed by more than 60 percent since its peak in 2005. Mexican migration has in fact slowed to a crawl. That number of crossings, no matter what, is staggering for any agency to keep track of and to inspect thoroughly. Border inspectors must necessarily rely on random checks to detect illegal drugs or contraband coming from Mexico. Many rely on their own senses and even low-tech checks like tapping a vehicle's body or gas tank to detect anomalous sounds, using mirrors to see underneath vehicles, or asking questions that may make the driver nervous—still the best methods, according to many—to determine whether to do a secondary inspection or not. As an agent said, looking for drugs among millions of vehicles is like looking for a needle in a haystack. The windows of opportunity for those who would use the border to smuggle illegal drugs are enormous. According to a former drug trafficker I interviewed in Ciudad Juárez, many of the tons of drugs such as cocaine, heroin, and methamphetamines smuggled into the United States make it across in passenger vehicles through POEs rather than between them—although an increasing number makes it across through underground tunnels and many of them make it across the border hidden in trucks. The DEA's own web page proudly exhibits several narratives and pictures of operations conducted along the U.S.-Mexico border. And to this day they cannot estimate very accurately how much drug smuggling actually goes on.

With all the opportunities for smuggling drugs, the many men willing to work in the drug trade, the economic incentives to do so, the unabated appetite for drugs by the American public, and the nearly 2,000-mile U.S.-Mexico boundary, the border and illegal drugs cannot be separated, nearly half a century into a declared drug war. An estimated 70 to 80 percent of all the drugs consumed in the United States come across its southwestern border, except marijuana, which has become legal and quasi-legal in many states in the United States, cutting into Mexico's market share of that drug. The general routing through Mexico is certainly determined by the map; cocaine is a perfect example of this. Mexican traffickers obtain the cocaine from South American businessmen and transport it into and through Mexico. This is not difficult to accomplish. The Mexican police are completely unable or unwilling to stop this. In fact, some important segments of various Mexican police forces actually cooperate with the drug dealers and protect and escort their drugs. Once the drugs reach warehouses within Mexico, they are moved overland to the border and then into the United States by various methods discussed later in this chapter. Mexican rural areas are peppered with clandestine air strips where drugs arrive or where planes refuel on their way to their final destinations. Even well-established airports serve as the entry for South American drugs into Mexico, including Mexico City's international airport where several important drug busts occur every year.

THE WAR ON DRUGS EXPANDS BEYOND THE BORDER

Starting in 2007, President Felipe Calderón of Mexico, in a coordinated effort with the United States through the Mérida Initiative, began a major assault on organized crime in Mexico. The Mérida Initiative committed US$1.4 billion over several years to help train and equip Mexican police as well as beef up its intelligence services and carry out operations against the drug cartels. Through a series of interviews with officials in his administration, it has become clear that President Calderón truly believed that drug-trafficking cartels as well as other criminal groups were threatening the very viability of the Mexican state. He made fighting criminal cartels, which by his estimation had replaced the Mexican state in several cities and states across the country, the priority of his administration.

President Calderón's actions against drug traffickers and other organized crime in Mexico included deploying the military—both army and navy—to cities and states deemed taken over by criminal organizations. He also replaced several police forces with military personnel or had military personnel accompany local police to eliminate their collaboration with criminal syndicates. He also rehabilitated the federal police and increased the intelligence capabilities of the Mexican government. Under President Calderón, all of Mexico was in a state of permanent war against drugs.

QUESTIONABLE RESULTS

After six years of a sustained onslaught on organized crime in Mexico, what are the results of the expanded war on drugs? By 2012, it had become clear that the drug-smuggling landscape was changing. First, Mexican cartels expanded their staging operations in Central America. Honduras, Guatemala, and even El Salvador became major drug-trafficking areas, replacing certain regions of Mexico that had come under governmental scrutiny. Second, an examination of organized crime in Mexico clearly shows that Calderón's attack on criminal groups created a three-layered war: intercartel wars, intracartel wars, and a government–organized crime war—these are explained further below. The result of this was a weakening and fragmentation of the Juárez Cartel, Tijuana Cartel, and Gulf Cartel, which broke up into criminal franchises with local

presence in many parts of Mexico rather than a single, hierarchical structure with control of a specific smuggling corridor. Los Zetas—a vicious
and murderous group with a diverse criminal agenda more akin to a
mafia cum drug-trafficking organization, and which were the major target
of Calderón's efforts—were nearly obliterated as such, but instead of dis-
appearing they gave way to numerous cells operating in Mexico's kidnapping for ransom, business extortion, and general crime. Third, the number
of groups increased substantially, making it impossible for ineffective
local police forces to fight them but also difficult for the federal police to
track and sweep up all of them.[17]

Fourth, the field battles among cartels and between the government
and the drug-trafficking organizations and other criminal groups
produced around 120,000 violent deaths and around 23,000 people disappeared. To many Mexicans this was simply an unacceptable price to
pay for what many still think is quintessentially an American problem.
They promptly voted President Calderón's party out of office in 2012
and retuned the PRI, which promised to reduce the violence. And finally,
Mexico's efforts simply expanded drug-trafficking cartels' operations into
Central America, where governments are weaker and more vulnerable to
intimidation and corruption. One unintended consequence of this was a
dramatic increase in public safety and security issues in northern Central
America and a massive exodus of citizens from the Northern Triangle
(Guatemala, Honduras, and El Salvador), resulting in an increase in
undocumented migration from those countries through Mexico and into
the United States.

THE BALLOON EFFECT

The balloon effect phenomenon is one of the major criticisms of the U.S.
drug war. It uses an analogy, a balloon, to indicate that when you apply
pressure in a particular region, criminal activity simply moves to another
region, much like when you apply pressure on a latex balloon the air simply moves in another direction rather than disappears.[18] This may have
been confirmed in the drug war once again. As Mexico and the United
States applied pressure to the large cartels within Mexico, many of them
moved their drug-trafficking operations to Central America, as already
indicated.

NO MORE WEAPONS

The close collaboration between Mexico and the United States, however, was not without its disagreements. Many Mexicans viewed
increased American presence in Mexico during the Calderón years as

undue interference in Mexican affairs. According to some interviews I conducted, the Americans took advantage of a chaotic situation and operated freely throughout Mexico. Whenever they faced resistance in a particular government agency, they simply shopped around their operations in another agency, creating fragmentation and even competition within the Mexican government itself.

Another important point of contention was the issue of weapons. At some point, Mexico became convinced that what was fueling the bloody war on drugs in Mexico was, in part, a steady flow of weapons from the United States, most of them smuggled one at a time by border residents, both American and Mexican. And this was not entirely unfounded. Though many in the U.S. tried to deny it, the reality is that most weapons used in crimes in Mexico were indeed American weapons. President Calderón took a stand and gave a major speech about weapons, calling on the United States to regulate its gun market—something clearly politically difficult in the United States. The U.S. government has been losing the battle to regulate and track weapons in the country and could do very little. Still, CBP assigned agents to check cars exiting El Paso. These random checks, however, have resulted in few confiscated weapons and little money—the other intended target. What it has done instead is slowed southbound traffic, adding to the nightmare of border users who must now wait long hours to both enter the United States and exit it. Moreover, CBP acquired a perfect excuse to begin to control exits from the United States, further growing its bureaucratic empire and making living on the border nearly miserable.

A WAR THAT CANNOT BE WON

Ten years after the first edition of this book, it has become increasingly clear that the war on drugs cannot be won. Drug addiction is still widespread. Drugs are today easily available, cheaper than ever, and, what is worse, now come in a wider variety than ever before. Forty-five years later, $1 trillion of U.S. taxpayer monies, and hundreds of thousands of deaths—from overdoses at U.S. hospitals to drug trafficker bodies strewn about from Colombia to Mexico—the war on drugs rages on with few results. Many have begun to conclude that it is a futile war and it is time to address the problem through new approaches, including treating drug addiction as a public health issue—so-called harm reduction strategies.

Evidence from the field of economics makes it clear that illegality actually adds a risk to any activity, but also a risk premium, which in turn becomes a handsome profit, and which down the line incentivizes new entrants into the market for the illegal good. Success is always temporary. Illegal markets, like legal markets, eventually adjust. A frontal attack on a particular group providing an illegalized good may reduce the supply temporarily, but the demand does not go away and the supply is fairly elastic. Thus drug traffickers simply shift strategies to continue supplying drugs.

THE BEGINNING OF THE WAR

The border and illegal drugs as we know them today do not have a long history, even if contraband does. The relationship between illegal drugs and the border begins in the 1960s—although it can be argued that illegalized goods have been part of the border landscape since Prohibition in the 1920s. But America's specific love affair with illegal drugs began in the counterculture of the 1960s. Since then, the country's appetite for psychotropic substances has escalated from marijuana to heroin, cocaine, and the hardcore chemical drugs consumed in nightclubs around the country.[19] Because mind-altering drugs were already illegal, the growing appetite for them increased not only the risks of dealing in drugs but also the profits of doing so. These profits, however, increased more than the risks because the incentives for people to deal in drugs grew considerably, not only in Mexico but also inside the United States.[20] An increasing number of illegal-drug producers and smugglers found it profitable to enter the business of selling illegal drugs.

Because the border was wide open, the cost of smuggling drugs into the United States through the 1960s and 1970s was relatively low, and by the early 1980s, the illegal-drug-smuggling business was booming along the border. There were numerous small gang-like groups in Mexico that operated to smuggle drugs into the United States. The market was large and growing, and the willing suppliers were also many. Mexico was a major supplier of marijuana and heroin, particularly Mexican brown heroin. Cocaine came mostly from Colombia via the Caribbean.

During the early 1980s, the United States implemented a series of operations in the Caribbean to stem the flow of cocaine from Colombia.[21] Colombia also came under pressure from the United States to fight its most important cocaine-smuggling cartels in the 1980s. In response, by the mid- to late 1980s, the Colombians began to look for different routes to smuggle their cocaine, thus expanding the drug war strategic game. They discovered Mexico, whose location and open border with the United States could be remarkable assets. Two thousand miles of largely unguarded border into the largest drug market in the world could not go unnoticed. The Colombians found a willing counterpart in Mexico, Miguel Ángel Félix Gallardo, a well-known Mexican drug smuggler who had consolidated many of the small-time smugglers in the 1970s into a single organization and by then controlled much of the illegal-drug trade along the border. His marijuana- and heroin-based organization was already in place and ready to serve as a conveyor belt for Colombian cocaine. The alliance between the Colombian drug lords and Félix Gallardo's organization produced a formidable drug cartel that would operate through most of the 1980s. Félix Gallardo, a quiet man who preferred to negotiate and avoided violence for the most part, became the drug lord of the border. He consolidated the Colombian-Mexican multidrug corridor into a formidable business, run mostly out of Guadalajara, Mexico.

But again, the drug war is a strategic game. President Ronald Reagan called drug smuggling one of the greater threats to national security. Thus, in response to the development of the Colombian-Mexican connection, the United States redirected massive antidrug efforts to the U.S.-Mexico border.[22] The efforts were largely expended with considerable insensitivity, bringing the U.S.-Mexico relationship to some of its lowest points. In 1985, for example, Enrique "Kiki" Camarena, a U.S. DEA agent, was kidnapped, tortured, and murdered in the state of Jalisco, prompting a diplomatic crisis between the two countries. This incident clearly shows that the war on drugs has produced some of tensest moments between the two countries, whereas President Calderón's antidrug efforts between 2006 and 2012 show that it has produced some of the deepest collaboration between the two as well.

Félix Gallardo was finally arrested in 1989 in Mexico. He continued to run his operations from inside his prison cell, but his collaborators outside were in a constant struggle for control of the organization's operations on the border. With his many lieutenants vying for control of the drug business, Félix Gallardo sent a message to them from his prison cell. To receive his message they met in a posh hotel in Acapulco. Through his messenger, Félix Gallardo told them that given that the U.S. government, "the real enemy," was stepping up its efforts to destroy his organization, intraorganizational disputes had to be settled. In response to U.S. action, he ordered a territorial division of his organization. Each "lieutenant" would control one smuggling corridor. He then exhorted them to live in peace among themselves and to stay within their own territories. Thus it was at this meeting that the modern drug cartels with their respective corridors would emerge: (1) the Tijuana Cartel, (2) the Sinaloa Cartel, (3) the Juárez Cartel, and (4) the Gulf Cartel.[23] Starting in 1989 then, the U.S. government would not have just one criminal organization to fight but four. By the year 2000, these four organizations came to move at least 80 percent of all the drugs that enter the United States. American counterdrug measures did little to undermine the Félix Gallardo cartel but did do enough to inspire the 1989 division of his organization into a group of drug-smuggling oligopolies that became even more difficult to fight—a harbinger of the further organized crime group fragmentation that would come with the "successes" of the 2006–12 period.[24]

Over the last decade or so, Mexico has managed to kill, imprison, or extradite most of the drug kingpins from the 1990s and 2000s—nearly 80 of the 100 most wanted kingpins. Unfortunately, they have only been replaced with more ruthless, bloodier, and crueler drug lords, in addition to those who have branched out to turn on the Mexican population through numerous criminal activities that have made Mexico a generally unsafe country, where many do not dare travel any longer. For Mexico, the drug war has only thrown the country into a spiral of criminality that has been hard to contain altogether. In sum, the security situation in Mexico today is more dangerous because in that it is more widespread geographically, in the variety of its activities, and in its cruelty.

BUSINESS OR WAR?

This brief, historical even if impressionistic view of the birth of the drug cartels and their eventual fragmentation into dozens of groups over time, together with a quick look at the market forces that operate behind the drug trade, shows that the illegal-drug business and the U.S. drug war on the border is a strategic game, lodged strangely between market forces and warlike strategies to fight it. As the United States squeezed the Colombian drug cartels headed by savvy "businessmen" in the Caribbean, the Colombians sought an alliance with the Félix Gallardo organization in Mexico. This led to a formidable business-like alliance and an increase in drug trafficking on the U.S.-Mexico border even as the U.S. and the Mexican governments made inroads into fighting the drug-trafficking activities of the Félix Gallardo organization in the 1980s. After the reorganization, the four cartels proved resilient against nearly all drug war strategies and tactics. To every attempted crackdown by the U.S. government, the cartels responded by becoming highly flexible organizations that adapted and adjusted quickly to nearly any adverse circumstance. Whenever the U.S. government attempted to escalate the drug war, the cartels changed their modus operandi: they invested in more sophisticated methods to smuggle drugs across the border; they recruited new members; they corrupted more officials; and they sought innovative ways to remove obstacles to the business of the organization. The four drug cartels became veritable business corporations that outlived their original founders. In spite of the billions of dollars annually that the U.S. government spent during those years[25] on the drug war, the four cartels continued to thrive and smuggle in 70 to 80 percent of all drugs consumed in the country. And like corporations, they continued well after the entire workforce changed—always refreshed by new, ever more astute and innovative illegal-drug entrepreneurs who are willing to take the risks in exchange for the profits. In effect, in regard to the drug cartels and U.S. tactics to destroy them, what did not kill them made them stronger.

It is ironic that their fragmentation and transformation into an array of smaller cartels, some smuggling drugs and others charging right of way, such as the Tijuana Cartel is reputed to do today with other groups that smuggle drugs through their territory, came only when the United States and Mexico closed ranks in a brutal, all-out war effort beginning in 2007. But drugs did not go away with the weakening of the cartels. Instead, one of them, the Sinaloa Cartel, took advantage of the chaos and became a much larger cartel, with enormous power and a vast empire within Mexico, and branched out to operate not only in all of North America but also in South America, Europe, and even Asia. It is today a truly transnational drug-trafficking organization, capable of responding to changing circumstances in both the war on drugs and the illegal-drug market. Their power to evade the law, to corrupt powerful politicians, and to make unimaginable profits has remained. Other cartels have disintegrated, but not disappeared. They have become a scourge all along the U.S.-Mexico border. They control smaller smuggling corridors and have expanded their criminal activities. At one point or another over the past decade, Tijuana, Ciudad Juárez, Nuevo Laredo, and Matamoros, all border towns, have collapsed under the weight of the violence exercised by these groups vying for power and control, sometimes block by block. In 2010, Ciudad Juárez, for example, was considered the most murderous city in the world, with 217 murders per 100,000 people—greater than in the most violent cities, such as Caracas (Venezuela), Rio de Janeiro (Brazil), and San Pedro Sula (Honduras).

The drug war on the border is a cat-and-mouse game between law enforcement agencies and drug cartels and other criminal groups that would use the border to profit. This game is a constant process of escalation.[26] Law enforcement agencies increase their resources, hire more personnel, and introduce the latest technology to intercept illegal drugs. The drug cartels respond with ever more creative ways to go around the latest law enforcement efforts. In this escalation game, the U.S. government is the general loser, scoring tactical victories (drug busts usually published as tons of this drug and tons of that drug and routine arrests of this low-level trafficker or that kingpin) but losing the overall war against the flow of illegal drugs. A diachronic analysis of illegal-drug quality and availability in the U.S. streets shows that in spite of all the United States' tactical victories, illegal drugs are just as abundant as they have ever been and there is always more evidence that their price is dropping and their quality is increasing, signaling a steady, unabated supply.[27] On top of this, the marijuana movement continues to score against the federal government, further making evident the futility of the drug war.[28]

BUREAUCRATS VERSUS DRUG CARTELS:
UNEQUAL ENEMIES

Researching drug trafficking is in many ways as revealing about the business and the criminals as it is about the bureaucratic logic that lies behind the drug war. Just as in any war, where no two armies use the same manuals containing standard operating procedures or training in the same strategies or tactics or having the same constraints placed on them, the U.S. government's drug war has forced two very different types of "enemies" with two very different sets of rules to confront each other. These important differences have resulted in a distinct disadvantage for the U.S. drug war bureaucracies vis-à-vis drug cartels. This confrontation means not only that U.S. bureaucracies are at a disadvantage and clearly in a losing battle—more akin to a hamster running inside the wheel—but that the results they have produced for nearly half a century are practically nil when it comes to stemming either the illegal drug supply or the demand for them.

First, bureaucracies are very rigid hierarchical structures that do not allow for much flexibility in responding quickly to contingencies. Any substantial changes in the budget or personnel or in the programs and operation procedures take a long time to accomplish and often require legislative action, a notoriously slow process. The decision making is also a process that requires many meetings and much planning and long implementation periods. Bureaucrats cannot by definition hide and are often rather obvious in their work. They also have to self-monitor continuously and are always under the public and congressional eye. Although the large drug cartels are generally pyramidal, they are not rigid structures at all. Changes in the organization are made very quickly, largely because the decision making is centralized in a few capos and their lieutenants. This enables the cartels to be extremely flexible and adaptable. Often changes are implemented as a matter of routine to stay ahead of law enforcement organizations. More recently, the number of criminal groups has grown, and it has become more difficult to track them, particularly because they seem to appear and disappear with great ease—sometimes vanishing as soon as the leader is caught or killed and sometimes merging with another group, splintering into two or more groups, changing leadership, or moving from one place to another. Smaller groups are also more supple and quick to respond to changes in their environment. Specialization has also emerged: some are drug-trafficking groups, others retail-level dealers; others charge for the right of way on the territory they control; and yet others operate in cells dedicated to different criminal activities. There is really only one large cartel that emerged unscathed from the 2006–12 bloody period, the Sinaloa Cartel—perhaps the only traditional cartel left in Mexico. And the U.S. government has not been able to make a dent in its activities. Joaquín "El Chapo" Guzmán, its top leader, who was caught in Culiacán, Sinaloa, on February 22, 2014, and spent some months in prison, managed to escape on July 11, 2015, with hardly any consequences for anyone on either side of the border. This irritated American law enforcement, but there was not much they could do. His recapture on January 8, 2016, has also not been felt in the activities and power of the Sinaloa Cartel, signaling largely that he had become irrelevant to the organization. Worse, many of these new smaller groups are more like independent cells, numbered in the hundreds, and difficult to dismantle because they come and go, and when they go they are always quickly replaced by others. Think of al-Qaeda, which was defeated as a major terrorist organization but ultimately survived in many different groups that continue to wreak havoc here and there.

Second, U.S. drug war bureaucracies are saddled with handbooks full of ethical and legal rules and requirements. In addition, the labor force has certain rights and benefits. They often claim their rights vigorously. They are not available 24 hours a day. Any law enforcement bureaucrat is accountable for human rights and for due process, and is constantly under the scrutiny of the public, the media, and watchdog groups. A sloppy law enforcement officer not only makes his or her agency liable but can also cause the criminal to escape from the U.S. judicial system because of due process violations. In contrast, in a drug cartel there is no handbook and there are no ethical and legal requirements. The only "handbook" is the decisive calculations and will of the bosses or capos, which trickle down to the workforce mostly through word of mouth. Cartel communications are quick, without the long memoranda and paperwork trail that is required of a bureaucracy. Moreover, there is no due process to speak of. Drug cartels or criminal groups are not accountable for due process or human rights, inside the organization or outside it. Deception, lying, and murder are legitimate weapons in the arsenal of operating procedures available to a criminal group. Such instruments are obviously not available to a disciplined, law-abiding bureaucracy, even if every so often an agent breaks the law.

The result is that whereas bureaucracies do not change or adapt easily, criminal groups can change swiftly upon command and adapt quickly to new circumstances and grow and change and come and go. Their workforce is available 24 hours a day and it is generally highly disciplined. Threats, torture, and death await a member who fails to follow orders. That is the difference between the U.S. drug war bureaucracies and the criminal organizations they are up against. These conditions constitute a nearly insurmountable structural difference between U.S. anti-illegal-drug bureaucracies and the organized criminal groups they face, and it likely contributes to the ability of criminal organizations to defeat most U.S. drug war strategies and tactics and maintain their booming business all along the border and in the U.S. illegal-drug market. This is not to say that U.S. bureaucracies do not have successes or are completely powerless, but clearly they have been engaged in a losing battle for nearly five decades now. Speaking with a former DEA official in El Paso, Texas, who spent more than 30 years on the force, he acknowledged, indirectly, that he may have spent his life fighting a war that cannot be won.

A POSTMODERN SPECTACLE: THE SOCIAL MEDIA

One of the most intriguing aspects of the war on drugs is that with the advent of social media and widespread use of cellular telephony, the battle for attention has come to the drug war. Sometime ago, I was driving in Ciudad Juárez and talking to a former drug trafficker. He told me that the traditional cartels tended to use violence in relatively discreet ways. Many undisciplined members of the workforce were executed quickly and buried deep in backyards or even in some rented homes under the concrete of the dining and the living rooms. He pointed out the house where a famous drug trafficker who was executed by order of his boss was buried. For nearly two decades, there might have been public executions and disappearances, but the public was, for the most part, spared the horrors of drug-trafficking violence. Not so today.

Over the course of the drug war in the last 15 years, there were multiple signs that it was becoming a psychological struggle. While public executions and shootouts continued, new tactics of fear and intimidation emerged. There were dozens of bodies left, bloodied for public view in streets and parks and squares. There were heads rolled onto a dance floor in Michoacán in 2006. There were bodies hung from bridges and overpasses. There were beheadings and shootings filmed and posted on YouTube. There were pig heads nailed onto headless bodies abandoned on roads. There were banners threatening authorities and members of other cartels or copycats unfurled for everyone to see in cities across Mexico. There were sadistic dismemberments made public through social media. And there were interrogations followed by executions recorded and posted in social media venues. The spectacle was gruesome and nauseating. And it was intimidating and terrifying.[29]

The war on drugs had taken a macabre turn, one that targeted cops and members of other gangs, one that relied on ghastly displays of violence and destructive bio-power. Mexicans were simply horrified and demanded change. And public opinion turned against the Mexican government because many citizens believed that they were fighting a war by and for the Americans but in Mexican territory.

THE NARCO-JUNIORS

It is noteworthy to point out that there have been at least four generational shifts in the drug war. The first was the very traditional and somewhat pedestrian drug traffickers of the 1960s to 1980s. These were trained to some extent by the old alcohol smugglers of the Prohibition era. They were taught the business of supplying illegal goods. They flourished under the aegis of a Mexican police that was not interested in fighting crime but in administering crime, and a political class that had ties to crime and even profited from it. They grew into well-established organizations, the most prominent of which was the Guadalajara Cartel. It consisted of a relatively hierarchical structure, but one that was loosely put together and operated under a profit-sharing arrangement both within and with Mexican government officials and bureaucrats. Miguel Ángel Arellano Félix was the "capo di tutti capi."

The American attack on Colombian drug cartels drew the cocaine business to Mexico, and the arrest of Arellano Félix in 1989 led to a division of this massive drug-smuggling cartel into four territorially based groups, as already mentioned. These four cartels, Tijuana, Sinaloa, Juárez, and Gulf, lived side by side, largely staying away from each other's territory. The fall of their leaders in the 1990s brought a new generation of more ruthless capos, quicker to use violence, greedier with their money, and more paramilitarized in their tactics. These large organizations began to pose a great threat to the Mexican government and learned quickly how to adapt to American pressure on Mexico to go after them.

The next generation, perhaps with the exception of the Sinaloa Cartel, which remains relatively intact—although there are rumors of internal transformation—is a group of drug traffickers much more sophisticated in their tastes, travel, financial arrangements, and managerial style. This generation tended to stay away from violence, preferring to delegate kidnapping, torturing, and killing to armed branches of the cartel. They also separated the cartels into subsidiaries—cultivation, transformation, transportation, financial assets, and so on. Some of the members of this generation were caught jogging in Mexico City—such as Vicente Carrillo Leyva of the Juárez Cartel, caught in 2009 at the age of 32, and Vicente Zambada Niebla, caught at the age of 40 also in 2009 and also in a posh neighborhood in Mexico City. Slowly, this group is being ravaged by drug war efforts by Mexico and the United States, but new generations always ready to take over emerge almost as quickly as some are caught. Interestingly, unlike their predecessors who preferred to live in border towns and states and build a social base there—hence the names of the cartels—this new group of individuals prefer to live quieter, albeit luxurious lives, in towns like Guadalajara, Querétaro, and Mexico City. Some of them even send their children to schools in the United States.

And that takes us to the narco-juniors. These are young, tech-savvy, well-educated, well-traveled, attention-hungry, millennial-generation men and women, who like to flaunt their wealth in social media, drive expensive cars, live in tony apartments throughout Mexico, spend time in Europe, eat in the best restaurants, and dress in the most expensive brands. These are known in Mexico as narco-juniors. The wealth and knowledge of crime has been passed on by their fathers and their grandfathers. They are equally ruthless, but generally delegate the dirty work to the grunt workforce of ruthless *sicarios* (killers for hire, by job or salaried), who often work for very little. The recent movie *Sicario* (2015) is quite revealing of this new class of killers that do the dirty work for many of the new drug traffickers.

The business of drugs is changing on both sides of the border—new generations of drug traffickers and new generations of sophisticated drug consumers. The actors also change. But the game is the same: the black market for illicit drugs, those who would supply them for a handsome price, those who work to stop them, and those who consume the drugs. And so have elapsed the last 50 years.

"MODUS SMUGGLINDI"

On a midday afternoon, Pedro, a 26-year-old, sits nervously waiting on line at a Nogales POE. He finally makes it to the inspection point. The U.S. border official leans toward the window of the car on the driver's side. He looks at Pedro who flashes his crossing card to the officer. The officer asks Pedro where he is going. Pedro, fashionably dressed, says that he is going shopping. Pedro is very nervous but contains himself quite well. His heart is racing, but he disguises his nervousness well. The official stands back up and waves him through. Pedro has just made it. His car has a bundle of cocaine hidden in a secret compartment behind the dashboard. He drives the car to a house in Nogales where an automatic garage door opens. Once inside the locked garage, the drugs will be recovered from the car and stored; they will be readied to be taken to Phoenix or Denver and beyond from there.

Smuggling drugs in a "fixed" vehicle, known as a "clavo" (nail), like the one Pedro was driving, is one way to smuggle drugs—the most common. But there is no single method for transporting drugs across the border. The drug cartels employ a variety of smuggling methods. Still, it is possible to classify their modus operandi.

The POE versus the Non-POE Axis

Most drugs enter the United States through the POEs at the border. According to a former member of a drug cartel I interviewed in Ciudad Juárez, cocaine, heroin, and methamphetamines are too valuable to risk crossing between POEs, in the wilderness. They can be intercepted by a Border Patrol agent and the loss to the organization would be considerable.[30]

Like in any other business, drug smugglers prefer to minimize risk and reduce uncertainty. The method to accomplish this is by working hard to build "networks" of employees and bureaucrats who are willing to offer protection to the organization's operations through payoffs (corruption). This ensures that the cargo crosses safely into the United States. They are willing to pay not only Mexican but also American officials handsome rewards in order to minimize the risk of losing the merchandise. It is mostly small-time drug smugglers that risk crossing drugs between POEs, and usually only marijuana. Marijuana is not as valuable—and less and less so as it becomes legal in the United States—potential losses are not so high, and the risk of crossing between POEs is often worth it, as the Hudspeth County incident referred to earlier shows.

The People versus the Vehicles Axis

In spite of the occasional media hype regarding the intersection between undocumented migration and drugs, the overwhelming majority of undocumented migrants cross on foot between POEs, while most drugs are hidden in vehicles that cross at POEs. Very few risk crossing the border on foot carrying illegal drugs. These are mostly novices or work for small-time drug dealers. Some may pose as backpackers or attempt to cross drugs hidden on their bodies or in clothing at POEs. They are recruited by small-time smugglers and trained to hike certain routes that may or may not coincide with the preferred routes of undocumented workers. The Tohono O'odham Nation of Arizona has reported the arrest of some drug smugglers who cross on foot with their knapsacks full of cocaine or marijuana. Their reservation in south central Arizona has witnessed this problem.[31]

Smuggling drugs on foot between POEs is rare, however. An Internet search for stories of individuals "busted" crossing drugs by walking either between POEs or even at POEs yields very few cases of this modus operandi. There are, of course, stories of people caught trying to smuggle illegal drugs hidden on their bodies and in clothing or in their bags and luggage through legitimate POEs, but as U.S. officials get better at detecting the nervousness of a border crosser or odd shapes on their bodies or in their bags, crossing drugs on foot is just too risky. Also, the amount of drugs that a pedestrian can cross is small, compared to the amounts that can be crossed hidden in a vehicle. Those who get caught end up in local courts rather than federal courts, because they tend not to exceed the amounts that would force them into federal court with higher penalties. These pedestrian drug-crossers cannot provide much intelligence either, because they tend not to work for the large drug cartels but for smaller entrepreneurs and sometimes are hired on the spot for a few dollars! One individual reported that he was offered $50 to cross drugs on his person. Others reported that they did it because they were coerced or threatened. Yet others reported sheer economic need.[32] What a drug dealer offers is sometimes several times a Mexican resident's monthly salary, which can go a long way to help their families. But overall, pedestrians are nowhere near the favored modus operandi of drug smugglers. They are inefficient and too risky.

A more preferred method for smuggling drugs is vehicles (cars, vans, and pickup trucks). Vehicles are often modified with special compartments built in where drugs can be hidden. As explained earlier, a vehicle prepared in such a way is known as a "clavo" (nail). The secret compartments tend to be in the gas tank, behind the dashboard, in the spare tire, or in some other nonsuspicious compartment in the body of the vehicle. The drugs are wrapped in tin foil, plastic wrap, or other packaging material. The packages are sometimes basted in substances that range from gasoline to oils and perfumes so as to disguise the smell, permitting the load to be undetected by the sniffing dogs. According to my interviewee in Ciudad Juárez, the drug cartels have sniffing dogs to test the "clavos." If their sniffing dogs detect the smell, the appropriate steps are taken until they cannot detect it. Only then is the vehicle sent to the POE.

A "clavo" can make it across the border in two ways. The first is by taking a chance. The vehicle shows up in the hope of not being detected. Sometimes they are; sometimes they are not. Whether they are detected or not depends on a number of factors, including the presence of sniffing dogs, the nervousness of the driver, and the thoroughness of the inspection. "Clavos" are sometimes sent in groups, with one easily detectable so that agents are distracted by that one "bust" and neglect thorough inspection of the other vehicles crossing at that moment. The busted "clavo" is the price to pay for reducing the risk of the other "clavos" being caught. This works partly thanks to the "spies" posted on both sides of the border by the drug cartels. It is not uncommon to see idle men, often posing as vendors, whose job is to "spot" for the cartel, watching the work patterns of U.S. officials and looking for a "lazy" or "distracted" officer who might not bother to double-check a vehicle. This information is relayed to the cartel operatives, who immediately send a pre-prepared "clavo" to that checkpoint at the POE. This is becoming harder to do, as officers are now moved every 15 minutes or so from one booth to the next and they are considerably more alert to what is going on. Still, it does happen.

A better way to reduce uncertainty and risk for a cartel is to smuggle a "clavo" in an operation that has been prearranged with a U.S. official working at a POE. This modus operandi involves the corruption of U.S. officials. Every year produces several dozen cases of corrupt

U.S. officials who are willing to cooperate with a drug cartel. Most U.S. agents who become corrupt are motivated by greed. An agent usually makes an annual salary of between $30,000 and $50,000 depending on rank and longevity in the job. A drug cartel is willing to pay anywhere between $10,000 and $20,000 to that same agent for allowing a "clavo" to come across by waving it through the POE inspection point. This corruption has not ceased, in spite of efforts to stop it.[33]

A two-day documentary on corruption by National Public Radio showed that several factors matter in tempting a U.S. official to become corrupt. One is greed, of course, but blood ties also matter. Many officials are tempted by their own relatives across the border. Corruption by U.S. officials has an enormous impact on facilitating the drug trade and is perhaps more perverse than the corruption of Mexican officials. A corrupt Mexican official may offer protection by overlooking the operations of the drug cartels, but the drugs are still in Mexico. A corrupt U.S. official may allow tons of marijuana and produce millions of dollars in profits by waving dozens of "clavos" through over time. That one official undermines all the efforts of his or her organization and constitutes a considerable loophole through which the drug business can profit enormously.[34]

THE NORTH AMERICAN FREE TRADE
AGREEMENT CONNECTION

The large cartels ride the formal NAFTA economy as well and they have done so for more than 20 years now. There are about 6 million trucks that cross the U.S.-Mexico border every year.[35] They carry 70 percent of all U.S.-Mexico trade, now an estimated total value of US$600 billion. NAFTA in the end turned out to be a heaven-sent blessing to the drug cartels. Trucks not only serve as a massive conveyor belt for drugs. Over time, the four large cartels have come to rely on trucking as the primary conveyor belt of illegal drugs across the border. Tons of marijuana, cocaine, heroin, and methamphetamines ride hidden in the millions of trucks that cross the border. These same millions of trucks also move the drugs on U.S. highways to the major metropolitan areas throughout the country and from there they go on to the retail-level market across the country.

What makes this possible is revealed in a simple mathematical reflection. Of the 6 million trucks that cross the border, only a fraction of them can really be inspected. It would be extremely costly and time-consuming to run a thorough inspection of every truck. It is also commercially unacceptable. Technology is helping to catch more of the hidden drugs: the gamma ray and X-ray scanners similar to a car wash sprayer that trucks now go through are helping considerably, but still only a fraction are detected. Dogs are also helping, but they are simply insufficient. In a recent visit to Otay Mesa in Tijuana/San Diego, I was told that it is now becoming harder for drugs to be smuggled in trucks, but that it still goes on and trucks certainly moved them along American highways to further destination points throughout the country. Cartel technicians, however, are also always looking for ways to beat the newest technology. Their organizations give them the resources to invest in such research. They are also very innovative, as we have already seen, always looking for new ways to smuggle drugs across the border. In that sense, criminals and bureaucrats are just playing a strategic game, where one organization responds to the moves of the other in a never-ending chase.

CUSTOMS AND TRADE PARTNERS AGAINST TERRORISM

U.S. bureaucracies realize the impossibility of inspecting every truck crossing the border and catching every load of drugs hidden in them. To circumvent this problem—and the potential of a terrorist attack on the border—the Department of Homeland Security built a new trusted-traveler system for trucks and cargo called Customs and Trade Partners against Terrorism (C-TPAT).

Begun in 2001, C-TPAT is largely a trust-based system that consists of networks of intimate knowledge and mutual trust among U.S. officials, importers and exporters, and truck drivers. The drivers and the trucking companies are registered and precleared with CBP as is the merchandise. C-TPAT participants are required to apply for preclearance to avoid delays at inspection points—which do not always work, as many truckers complain, because a single truck identified as "loaded with drugs" can get the rest of the line stuck until the issue is cleared out. The C-TPAT system calls for trucks to be loaded at the warehouse or factory in the Mexican border town, then a seal is placed on the cargo container to expose any break-ins or subsequent opening in order to hide illegal drugs in them. CBP agents may or may not break the seal upon inspection at the POE, but when they break it, they do not generally replace it. This sometimes allows a trucker to load illegal drugs kept in stash houses in border towns and move them via the major highways into metropolitan areas throughout the United States. C-TPAT, billed as essentially a supply chain security program for international businesses, is supposed to prevent such cheating and build trust among those participating in cross-border businesses.[36] As CBP has put it,

Begun in November 2001 with just seven major importers as members, as of June 2011, the partnership has grown. Today, more than 10,000 certified partners that span the gamut of the trade community have been accepted into the program.

These include U.S. importers, U.S./Canada highway carriers; U.S./Mexico high-way carriers; rail and sea carriers; licensed U.S. Customs brokers; U.S. marine port authority/terminal operators; U.S. freight consolidators; ocean transportation intermediaries and non-operating common carriers; Mexican and Canadian man-ufacturers; and Mexican long-haul carriers. These 10,000-plus companies account for over 50 percent (by value) of what is imported into the United States.[37]

The C-TPAT system has proven to be fallible at many points, but it has actually slowly resolved many of these issues, including implementing a system of secondary inspections that involves moving trucks to secon-dary and tertiary checks without holding up the line. Even so, many trucks are not preinspected because they do not participate in the system and they can easily hold up the line. At Otay Mesa, however, I recently learned that a few thousand trucks are now responsible for more cross-ings because they come and go continuously. Inserting a new truck into the trusted chain is expensive, so owners use the same trucks over and over again. But the rewards the cartels offer to anyone willing to break the rules are too high. Truckers can be tempted into breaking the trust deposited in them. A truck operator from Laredo in 2005 explained that some trucks, after leaving the warehouse in Mexico and before they arrive at the POE, take a "detour." At an appointed place, the seals are broken, the drugs loaded, and the seals replaced. Sometimes, it is not noticeable that the seals have been violated, although CBP inspectors are gaining experience in detecting whether a seal has been tampered with.[38] More-over, 19 years later, inspectors have in fact gotten very good at detecting tampering. The problem is really that the volume is just overwhelming and always ahead of inspection capacity.

One of the major problems remains Mexican law enforcement. The Mexican police, principally at the state and local level, collaborate with drug-trafficking organizations and offer protection to these trucks, sometimes escorting them on their routes in Mexican border towns. During an interview with a guide in Ciudad Juárez, he took me to Avenida Las Américas where a local policeman was standing directing traffic. The guide and I approached the police officer. The officer, who knew the guide, described the police force's willingness to "escort" a load of drugs in town so that no one would stop the truck on its route to the POE. Such services are regularly offered by the Mexican local police forces. During the violence of 2006 to 2012, they even served as *sicarios* or paid killers for the cartels. Many also engaged in organized criminal activities during their free time. To this day, it is hard to trust that the police are doing their job. At lunch in El Paso during a May 2004 conference on "Border Security: The New Realities," a Mexican business-man bitterly stated that their cargo was sometimes "contaminated" by corrupt drivers and even corrupt cops. Businesses often lose the merchandise and even the truck, which under forfeiture laws is seized by CBP when the truck is found to be carrying illegal drugs. To avoid this, many business owners and managers in Mexican border towns had bought small cars and hired drivers to "escort" the trucks all the way to the POE. But these escorts too can be co-opted or threatened into cooperating.

New technology is being introduced to keep track of the 18-wheelers carrying the majority of trade between the United States and Mexico. GPS devices are being installed in the trucks to ensure that the company knows where a truck is at all times. Even so, there are too many transactions to keep track of. My Laredo interviewee said that often trucks are detected off their appointed route, perhaps even 30 or 40 miles south of the border. At that point, the trucking company must decide what to do. If they decide to report it to law enforcement authorities on the Mexican side, they risk losing the semitruck and having the driver jailed. Generally, they first call a lawyer who can deal with the issue before reporting it to the authorities. The extremely risky legal protocol often leads to informal inquiries with the driver, without involving any government authorities at all. No real follow-up may happen at all.[39] Table 2.1 summarizes the current state of affairs in regard to smuggling methods.

TUNNELS AND MORE TUNNELS

On February 27, 2002, U.S. officials discovered a 1,200-foot tunnel running between a private home in a farm east of San Diego and a home in the town of Tecate, Baja California. This sophisticated tunnel was used to smuggle tons of cocaine, marijuana, and other drugs between Mexico and the United States for perhaps as long as three years. On April 19, 2004, U.S. officials reported that they had discovered more underground tunnels that were being used by drug traffickers. On November 26, 2010, U.S. officials discovered yet another massive tunnel, some 2,600 feet long connecting Tijuana and San Diego. And yet another tunnel, this one 2,400 feet long, was discovered on October 22, 2015. Since September 11, U.S. officials have discovered more than 100 passageways that usually run between buildings on the Mexican side and the U.S. side of the borderline. Over the least 15 years, there has been an explosion in the number of tunnels, perhaps the result of better detection of drug smuggling at ports of entry. Whatever the cause may be, these tunnels have been used to smuggle tons of cocaine, heroin, and confection drugs into the United States. There have also been reports that they are used to smuggle migrants as well, although that does not seem to be the primary use of these tunnels.

What is most surprising about these tunnels is their sophistication. Their construction requires heavy financial investment and sophisticated

Table 2.1

The Changing Modes of Smuggling

	Pedestrians	"Clavos"	Trucks	New Methods
POE	Older method. Not much preferred any longer and now rarely used.	Still a favored method of small-time drug smugglers and still used extensively by cartels. The payoff if smugglers succeed is quite large.	Preferred method of the largest cartels and other smaller drug smugglers.	Sophisticated camouflage of drugs in containers, compartments, etc.
Between POEs	Not preferred and hardly ever used—in spite of all the rhetoric. If used at all, it is mostly small loads of marijuana by "backpackers." It just does not pay off, as the chances of getting caught are too big and the loads too small.	Not preferred and seldom, if ever, practiced. There were rumors and even examples in the news of runs across the borderline by ATVs loaded with drugs, but this does not seem to have been a method used systematically.	Nonexistent —trucks just do not travel across the border line between POEs.	Small planes, submarines, tunnels, drones, and other more sophisticated and relatively new methods. Larger planes are also used between South and Central American and Mexico, but hardly ever to the United States.

engineering in tunnel construction, but also very stealthy methods, as tons of dirt have to be removed from the site without being noticed. Some of the tunnels have lighting, ventilation, water drainage systems, supporting structures to prevent caving, and even rails to move drugs quickly from one end to the other. A testament to the difficulty of building the tunnels is the fact that most of them have been discovered unfinished.

Thus, in addition to surface patrolling, U.S. law enforcement agencies now have to procure equipment such as ground-penetrating radars and large earth-excavating drills in order to discover tunnels running between the two countries. Even so, most tunnels are discovered through human intelligence rather than technological means.

Driving along the border highway in Mexicali, Baja California, and in Calexico, California, it is easy to see how building tunnels in certain areas would be easily accomplished—as opposed to Texas, where digging under the river would require an effort no cartel has yet been willing to invest in. It should therefore come as no surprise that the Tijuana Cartel pioneered these tunnels, although their use has expanded to the Sinaloa Cartel on the Sonora-Arizona border as well. Peering through the fence to the American side, I observed a paved street with a typical U.S. neighborhood row of homes. The distance between one house on my right and on my left could not have been more than a four-lane avenue with the median as the border between the two countries. It is easy to observe neighborhoods in several places in California and Arizona adjacent to each other divided only by the fence itself and streets that run right into it. The distance between one house and another—one in Mexico and one in the United States—is often a few hundred feet. Tunnels are entirely feasible under these conditions, and if successful, they can be the route for many tons of drugs before they are even discovered.

These tunnels are yet another indication that the war on drugs is a strategic game. As the U.S. government makes it difficult to cross drugs over the border, drug cartels respond by appealing to more creative ways of doing business. The narco-tunnels are one more strategic response by the drug capos in the never-ending drug war.

UNMANNED AERIAL VEHICLES

The strategic game between U.S. law enforcement and organized criminals when it comes to drug smuggling is unlikely to end. It only escalates. As unmanned aerial vehicles (UAVs)—also known as drones—have become more readily available, cheaper, and easier to use, both sides of this futile war are now using them. The year 2015 was a turning point in the use of drones for drug smuggling. Several were detected carrying drugs between Baja California and California.

Although U.S. law enforcement officials have said that this is a rather expensive method and they do not expect drones to become a major smuggling method, the reality is that they are more and more sophisticated, GPS programmable, increasingly cost-effective, not easily detected by radars, and there is no danger of anyone being caught if the drone does not make it to its destination. Drones are the "ideal drug mule," as the

DEA has put it. They need very little attention, do not protest, lack any ambition, and can make many trips day in and day out.

Cartels have proven to be incredibly adaptive to new technologies—they went from vehicles, to human mules, to low-flying Cessna planes, to Jet-Skis, to tunnels, to makeshift submarines, and now to drones. Just as law enforcement has been using drones to spy on the cartels, the cartels have now turned the technology on U.S. law enforcement and have used it to smuggle drugs into the country. This is the essence of strategic games—and it should prompt us to ask whether we should not begin to redefine the problem of addiction differently than as a criminal issue and seek to reduce the business of smuggling by dealing with drugs as a public health issue.

THE BUSINESS COMES HOME

The marijuana legalization movement has made enormous strides in redefining the debate surrounding the use, possession, and sale of this psychotropic substance in the last few years. As of this writing, four states had already legalized marijuana altogether. Dozens of others have decriminalized its possession or legalized its use for medical purposes—often broadly defined. And although marijuana remains illegal under federal law, history points in the direction of eventual complete legalization. But what does that mean for the border?

There is already some evidence that Mexican marijuana is "losing business" to the wave of marijuana decriminalization and legalization occurring in the United States. As it stands, Mexican marijuana was already considered low-quality by many American consumers. There is a culture around marijuana whose exploration goes well beyond the scope of this book, but for our purposes, suffice it to say that U.S. growers have been experimenting with THC content and other characteristics of the plant and have now produced "higher-quality" marijuana strands. The result has been that Mexican cartels dealing in marijuana are being displaced by American producers and are likely to lose even more market share in the future.

The consequences are becoming obvious. One of them is that a potential reduction in the marijuana profits for Mexican smuggling cartels will turn them more aggressively to market other drugs. Although there is some controversy as to exactly which drug is more profitable—with most studies arguing that cocaine and heroin are much more profitable than marijuana—the sheer volume of marijuana consumption in the United States implies an enormous financial loss for the Mexican cartels. This means that they will have to rely on other, heavier drugs, which remain illegal in the United States and perhaps only they can supply.

They will now push more cocaine and heroin as well as other confection drugs. On the upside, this means that U.S. law enforcement will likely have additional resources to tackle these so-called more dangerous drugs.

Indeed, since 2011, the amount of marijuana confiscated at POEs has fallen by about one-third, signaling a slowdown in marijuana smuggling across the border. This drop in turn means that American consumers are turning to more easily available and higher-quality strands of American marijuana and abandoning their former suppliers. Mirroring this fall, heroin seizures have tripled and meth seizures have quintupled. Seizures are considered a good gauge of how much is being smuggled, even if we do not know exactly how much makes it through. Clearly, some Mexican farmers are converting their crops from marijuana to opium poppies, and as meth labs in the United States are being aggressively dismantled, new mega labs are surging in Mexico. This issue has become so salient that it was put back on the table at the North American Leaders Summit in Canada in June 2016. Heroin and meth are profitable in smaller quantities as well. Interestingly, cocaine seizures are also down, but cocaine has seen these ups and downs before.

Finally, it is important to note that the last three years have been crucial in this transformation. Not only has marijuana made it to American's mainstream as a tolerable and tolerated drug, but Mexico's president Enrique Peña Nieto, unlike his predecessor, President Felipe Calderón, is not as keen on fighting the drug cartels. He made it clear from the very beginning of his administration in December 2012 that he would not be dragged down to the bloody battles of the Calderón administration (2006–12), which produced an estimated 120,000 drug war–related deaths. Rather, he believes that this is an American problem. This has meant that the remaining smuggling groups have had a relatively easier time expanding their business in Mexico and contending with American law enforcement.

CORRUPTING THE WARRIORS

Nearly everyone who lives along the U.S.-Mexico border knows that Mexican officials are corrupt. The last 10 years have revealed the incredible corruption that pervades Mexican law enforcement. This corruption has in fact forced Mexico to reconsider the structure of its police forces—so as to attempt to extinguish hundreds of municipal police forces and to create only 32 state police forces and a single federal police in the hopes that they can be more easily controlled. This plan has simply not prospered. There is too much resistance at the local and state levels. But corruption is not unique to Mexican cops—although it is nearly systemic on the south side of the border. The corruption is no secret to U.S. officials either. Anthony Placido, the DEA's top intelligence official between 2005 and 2010, testified that "the single largest impediment to seriously impacting the drug-trafficking problem in Mexico" is Mexico's police corruption.[40] The capture of Joaquín "El Chapo" Guzmán for the third time in January 2016 in fact creates a dilemma for Mexico. He may know too much about police and military corruption in Mexico and reveal it to Americans in plea-bargaining processes. I, too, have personally witnessed acts of corruption by Mexican customs officials. Most Americans, however, would like to believe that U.S. border officials are not corrupt. And yet many are. The culture of payoffs flourishes on both sides of the border—even if it does not reach the epidemic levels of the Mexican side.

Walking into the federal courtroom in El Paso, any researcher becomes quickly aware that there are always ongoing corruption cases against U.S. officials. U.S. officials have used personal vehicles to drive into Ciudad Juárez from El Paso and bring back a load of drugs. Others have waved undocumented immigrants through. Because the officer is well known among his peers, they would usually let him through without inspection. In one such case, the officer even drove the same car past the second checkpoint, in Sierra Blanca, Texas, and then turned in the drugs on the other side, safely on their route to Dallas or Houston or elsewhere. He was discovered only because another person driving his vehicle was stopped beyond Sierra Blanca. Upon inquiry, it was discovered that he had crossed the same vehicle not long before and had turned it over to someone else at Sierra Blanca. A sting operation caught him in the act and he is now serving time. Between 2005 and 2012, there have been 177 agency employees charged with smuggling (See Figure 2.1). Corruption is a serious problem in fact. A June 29, 2015, report by a CBP Integrity Advisory Panel shows that corruption at the border remains a problem.[41]

The rewards for corrupting a drug warrior on the border are potentially very high. U.S. officials are powerful and even intimidating figures on the U.S.-Mexico border and at the interior checkpoints, such as Sierra Blanca, Texas, or Deming, New Mexico. They can stop you in your tracks or they can let you move freely inside the United States. And they guard the richest illegal-drug market in the world as well as one of the most profitable job markets. Drug cartels are constantly looking for the lazy or the greedy official, and the incentives may pay an officer's income many times over. A U.S. official makes about $80,000 a year, while a drug lord may offer to pay him tens of thousands of dollars for every single drug load he waves through at the POE.[42] And there are almost 79,000 CBP and Border Patrol agents combined. Surely some of them can be corrupted.

Federal investigators know that corruption among U.S. officials can be a serious problem if not checked and they are constantly investigating

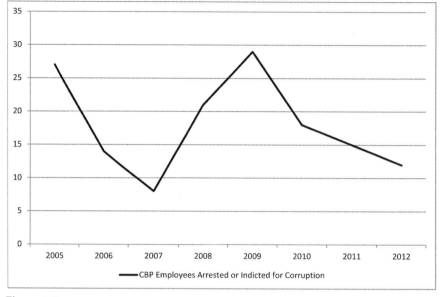

Figure 2.1

Number of CBP employees arrested or indicted for corruption. (GAO Border Security: Additional actions needed to strengthen CBP)

discrepancies in officials' incomes and their lifestyles, in order to follow threads that often lead to entire rings of corruption, such as the sting in Chicago where 18 U.S. officials were caught. While nearly 200 corruption cases have been discovered in the last 10 years because of drug smuggling or alien smuggling, only a fraction of them are being caught, and drug smugglers are constantly recruiting new officers. The cartels have an entire team looking for ways to make connections with U.S. officials and tempt them to join the other side. This group is, according to a member of the Juárez Cartel I interviewed, part of the public relations division of a cartel. Sometimes small measures do help. At POEs today, officers are moved in and out of inspection booths every 15 or 20 minutes and communications during the short shift are prohibited.

Corruption among U.S. officials is particularly damaging because, with a wave of his or her hand, a single official can be responsible for tons of drugs that make it to the streets of U.S. cities and provide millions of dollars in profit for a drug cartel. Again, all the officer has to do is wave a vehicle through in exchange for handsome rewards. Although Mexican corruption is widespread and systemic—and therefore very expensive to the cartels because they have to pay off too many people—American corruption can go a very long way toward producing enormous profits for everyone involved by just paying a single officer. A lone U.S. official can do much harm and essentially undermine the work of all his coworkers by opening a huge hole in the border protection net that they are supposed to constitute. An analysis of the type of crime committed by U.S. officials accused of criminal activities shows that the overwhelming majority of them engage in drug trafficking, bribery, human smuggling, and, finally, lying about their activities.[43]

Corruption is a fundamental component of any illegal industry. Drug trafficking could not be the exception. Corruption greases the wheels of the drug-smuggling business and assures its flow. The motivation is the same: greed. Corruption practices have also contributed to strengthening the hand of the large drug cartels because they are increasingly the only ones that can afford the millions of dollars that it takes to keep the wheels of the drug-smuggling business rolling. The small-timers simply cannot afford to corrupt officials on either side of the border who increasingly demand more and more of the drug smugglers in a perverse game of reverse extortion.[44] And this is what leads us to suspect that the many smaller gangs that have proliferated in Mexico have simply stayed in Mexico and profited from other businesses, such as kidnapping for ransom, extorting money from businesses, and other illegal activities. Thus most of the violence has stayed in Mexico and there is very little spillover into the United States. Border counties have in fact some of the safest cities and towns in America, even in the face of all the violence that occurs just across the borderline.

Mexican illegal-drug-driven corruption is pervasive. It is systemic. It reaches thousands of individuals both horizontally and vertically within the country. A drug cartel may have several thousand direct employees—from buyers to spotters to smugglers to weapons procurers to *sicarios* (or gunmen) to accountants—but indirectly it pays off hundreds, if not thousands, of people, particularly law enforcement officials and politicians. And there is no magic formula for Mexico to extricate itself from this corruption network if it refuses to touch its own political, entrepreneurial, and law enforcement communities. The Peña administration (2012–) has in fact been soundly criticized for adamantly refusing to do anything about corruption. Border law enforcement agencies in Mexico are heavily penetrated by the drug cartels because they are indispensable in ensuring that the operations of the drug cartels can be conducted without interference by government operatives not on the payroll of the drug cartels. And there are reports that at least part of the military is also involved—although the Mexican Navy seems to be exceptionally clean for Mexican standards and thus the U.S. and Mexican governments heavily rely on them for special operations, such as the recapture of "El Chapo" Guzmán in January 2016. Moreover, criminals are now more professionalized, hiring highly educated individuals who serve as public relations officers that recruit the help of other professionals, including accountants, businessmen (to launder money), law enforcement officials, doctors, lawyers, and the like. This is particularly true of the Sinaloa Cartel, as the other three large cartels have been severely weakened by the 2006–12 onslaught by the Calderón administration.

American officials do not offer this kind of protection and access to cartels or their operatives. American corruption is considerably less extensive and it is nowhere near as systemic as Mexican corruption. Still, American corruption has a much larger concentrated impact than Mexican corruption. It goes a much longer way than Mexican corruption. Crossing the international border continues to be the riskiest operation for a drug smuggler. It is the toughest link in the chain. A single corrupt American official is enough to let through tons of illegal drugs, producing hundreds of millions of dollars in profits for a cartel, by as simple an act as waving a "clavo" or a truck through a checkpoint, or by being lazy and not doing his or her job well. Corrupting a U.S. official pays much more handsomely than corrupting nearly any official in Mexico. Most of the time, U.S. officials' corruption is uncovered because their lifestyle appears to surpass their earnings.

Interestingly, the escalation of U.S. antidrug efforts, the many measures implemented by CBP to self-monitor, and the increased effectiveness of U.S. officials at POEs have made it increasingly more difficult and more expensive to bribe them. The higher the risk for the corrupt official implies higher payoffs by the drug cartels. A corrupt official will demand more money to wave a "clavo" through the inspection point. Economically speaking, as the risk increases, the payoff does too. Drug smugglers may now disburse millions of dollars to buy officials on both sides of the border. Both the heightened vigilance and its consequent higher payoffs are squeezing the small-time smugglers out of business. Of course, one consequence of this strategic game that law enforcement and criminal organizations play is that the latter rely on many new alternative methods to smuggle drugs—planes, tunnels, drones, etc. One way or another, they are getting the drugs across.

THE PROTECTIVE SHIELD OF THE BORDER POLICE

Walking along Avenida López Mateos in Nogales, Sonora, I came to a corner where a young woman was selling newspapers. The headline of the local paper, *El Imparcial*, was more than clear: *"Tres Ex-Policías Ejecutados"* (Three Former Policemen Executed).[45] Digging into the newspaper columns, it became clear that these former policemen had actually been drug law enforcement agents in the states of Sonora and Sinaloa in the past. These men are examples of the conditions of law enforcement in

Mexico today. It is very difficult in any one Mexican border town today to disentangle drug trafficking and law enforcement. A good percentage of Mexican law enforcement officials along the border with the United States are bought off by the drug traffickers or criminals or neutralized by explicit or implicit threats. In 2010 in Ciudad Juárez, an estimated 20 percent of a 2,300-person-strong municipal police force was likely completely co-opted by organized crime. And 200 police were killed in the line of duty during the worst years of the violence, 2008–10. Cops in Mexico are part of a vibrant network of corruption. The strategy has long been the same—"plata o plomo" (silver or lead)—and it has extended to politicians who refuse protection or passage within Mexico as well. In other words, you take either the bribe (silver) or a bullet to the head (lead). A significant number of mayors, city council members, and police agents have been gunned down in Mexico for simply refusing to cooperate. At a minimum, police officers who do not want to become corrupt will simply keep silent to protect themselves and cover the corruption of their fellow officers. This is a rough equivalent to the "blue wall" in U.S. police departments.

Whatever the situation of the police officer, the choice that any new police officer in Mexico faces is to keep silent, to actively participate in protecting the drug trade or other organized criminal activities, or to resist and be killed. Such was the case of the new chief of police in Nuevo Laredo in June 2005. For weeks no one would accept the job in that drug cartel–controlled border town in the state of Tamaulipas. Finally, Alejandro Domínguez was convinced to take the job. On that hot day of June 8, 2005, only a few hours after taking the job of city police chief, Mr. Domínguez was gunned down. Even though the Mexican federal government practically occupied the city with federal police agents and army soldiers and placed nearly 700 police officers under house arrest, more deaths continued to occur over the following days. Many argued that the major battle was between Los Zetas, a group of army soldiers who have organized to provide protection to the Gulf Cartel that controls the region, and the Men in Black, a group fighting for control of the territory on behalf of the Juárez and Sinaloa Cartels. Regardless of the unprecedented presence of Mexican federal policy and the military, the choices for any police officer in a Mexican border town remain unchanged. Most cannot remain neutral and sooner or later take sides.

The choices do not end there, however. Often, police officers desert the force to become active members of the drug trade and other criminal activities turning on Mexican citizens. They become bodyguards, operatives, or even *sicarios* who carry out the executions of those "condemned to death" by a drug lord or a criminal boss. Drug lords prefer to recruit former policemen because they are already trained in the use of weapons and in torture techniques, and know everyone else inside the police force, not to mention the weak points of the law enforcement organizations. Police chiefs are also quite afraid all along the border to this day. During the worst violence, 2008–12, many lived in the police headquarters, isolated from most of the force, and sent their families away for fear of retaliation. Such was the case of Julián Leyzaola, the chief of police of Ciudad Juárez, who was eventually shot in 2015 anyway and now sits in a wheelchair. Drug lords never forget and certainly never forgive.

Thus, in many instances, the job of the police forces in border towns becomes serving as a protective shield for drug trafficking and neutralizing any real government action against the drug-smuggling organizations, and they do a very good job of it. Street-level cops provide day-to-day protection to the drug lords. They often give advanced warnings of any government action against a cartel. They moonlight, guarding drug shipments and warehouses. And many of them have been known to serve as *sicarios* for the drug lords when there is the need to eliminate a rival. In fact, the actual operative personnel of any given drug cartel is often composed of former policemen or policemen moonlighting for the drug cartel. The drug trade is so profitable that many policemen are tempted to leave their jobs outright and join the drug organizations. Such was the case of the three former policemen executed in Nogales the day before I arrived there—Pablo Gracía Noriega, Jesús Martínez Luna, and Jesús Heriberto García Valenzuela.[34] One of these three had been in charge of directing the major operations by the state police against the drug lords. These cases are found by the hundreds and dot the entire border to this day. Unfortunately, this practice is spreading to other parts of Mexico in spite of all the efforts to reform the police.

VICTIMIZING THE CRIMINALS WITH BRIBES

The relationship between law enforcement and drug smuggling in Mexico is so complex that it is hard to understand as new twists and turns show up. My interviewee in Ciudad Juárez attempted to disentangle for me the relationship between the cartels and law enforcement officials in Mexico. He argued that sometimes drug smugglers are themselves the "victims" of law enforcement officials because they often extort criminal organizations, attempting to obtain a greater share of the profits than the cartel is willing to give up. Law enforcement officials and increasingly state and local politicians become extortion entrepreneurs and demand increasing amounts of money in exchange for allowing the cartel to operate freely within their jurisdiction or for offering protection. Many do not passively take what the cartel is willing to give. Instead, they set their own price. If the cartel does not deliver, its operations can be made quite difficult. Occasionally, there will be a police officer or even a politician executed because their demands on the cartel far exceed what the cartel is willing to pay for help or protection. The problem of corruption has now become a political problem as well. As crime has expanded its activities within Mexico, governors and mayors now participate in it with little or no restraint from the Mexican federal government. Many of them not only embezzle public funds but demand additional payoffs from organized criminal groups. The relationship between former Coahuila governor Humberto Moreira, now in prison in Spain, and various criminal groups that operated in that state is a complex connection that is still being investigated. The relationship between organized criminal groups in Tamaulipas and politicians in that state are also legendary.[46]

VIOLENCE AND THE DRUG-TRAFFICKING BUSINESS

For a long time, the border's image has been that of a violent place. This reputation was further consolidated by the atrocious violence that plagued Tijuana, Ciudad Juárez, Nuevo Laredo, Matamoros, and smaller cities that dot the Mexican side of the border. Although hardly any of this violence spilled across the border—for reasons not yet fully explored—Mexican cities became very dangerous. Ciudad Juárez in 2010 came to have 3,600 murders or about 10 per day. It became in fact the most deadly city in the world with the highest murder rate in the world, more than 200 homicides per 100,000 people. The U.S. State Department issues severe warnings against traveling to Mexican border towns. The six major border towns in Mexico remain on that list.[47] This hike in border violence over the last 10 years—even if it has come down considerably—has led many to believe that the war on drugs is a general failure, not only because it has failed to stop drugs coming across the border but because it has now produced hundreds of thousands of deaths with no end in sight. In Mexico, over the 10-year period, it has certainly meant almost four times as many deaths as American soldiers perished in the Vietnam War.

Even so, drug-related violence is not random. It is possible to discover patterns when looking at violent trends. Illegal drug–related border violence occurs under certain circumstances and for specific purposes—although at times it is difficult to understand it, especially the gruesome turn that it has taken in the last few years. But in fact, there are discernible principles that can help us understand illegal drug–related violence on the border.

When a government makes a commodity, such as psychotropic substances, illegal but the human desire for that commodity remains unabated, the result is the creation of a black market. In any market, disputes inevitably arise; so also in a black market. But in a black market, the dispute resolution procedures that there are in a legal, regulated market do not exist. Those who participate in an illegal market, such as drug dealers, have an acute awareness of the risks involved and know that all kinds of procedures might be used, even illegal practices, up to and including violence, in order to resolve disputes among the participants. Sometimes nonviolent procedures, such as negotiations, are used, even as a first instance of dispute resolution. But then, sometimes, the dispute escalates to the use of illegal practices. They may only threaten the use of violence, but sometimes they may actually use it. Often, violence is used not only to regulate competition but also to adjust accounts. Illegal drug–related violence for the most part is not random. It has a purpose and even a meaning. This is somewhat counterintuitive, given the extraordinary levels of violence that we have witnessed in the last 10 years in Mexico; but we want to argue that even those levels of violence follow specific patterns and have attendant cycles. Let us explore further the two specific reasons why a cartel would resort to violence: competition and adjustment of accounts.

Competition: Violence between Cartels

As explained earlier, the border was divided into four great territories or smuggling corridors up until around 2010: the Tijuana Cartel, the Sinaloa Cartel, the Juárez Cartel, and the Gulf Cartel. Every so often, there was a breakdown into violence because the lords of one or more cartels decide to compete with another for control of a given drug-smuggling corridor. This competition, as in Nuevo Laredo in the summer of 2005 and in Ciudad Juárez in 1996, can lead to extreme and sometimes very public intercartel violence. Nuevo Laredo is a highly profitable corridor because nearly 3 million trucks coming from southern Mexico (Mexico City, Guadalajara, etc.) and from Monterrey take the Nuevo Laredo-Laredo POE route. It is not surprising that the Gulf Cartel and Sinaloa Cartel were vying for control of this corridor. Competition between them resulted in a violent summer in 2005. It is also not surprising that after 2007, when Los Zetas broke off from the Gulf Cartel and became a major criminal organization, they fought hard for control of Nuevo Laredo. Much of the violence there can be attributed to the clash between Los Zetas and their former bosses in the Gulf Cartel.

Similarly, much of the violence in Tijuana in the period of 2005 to 2009 and in Ciudad Juárez in 2007 to 2012 was attributed to fierce competition among cartels. During that time, the Sinaloa Cartel, the most powerful of the four original organizations, was challenging both the Tijuana Cartel and the Juárez Cartel for control of those profitable corridors. The fight was so brutal that both cartels ended up dismembered and weakened, particularly after 2007, when the Mexican government decided to declare a war on drugs on all drug trafficking and organized crime. Worse, when these cartels broke apart—as did the Gulf Cartel—the different groups continued to fight among themselves for control of various criminal activities, which expanded beyond cross-border drug smuggling to many other mafia-style activities. Indeed, this is the period that saw nearly 120,000 bodies strewn about in Mexico, especially border towns, and an added 23,000 people disappeared. The intercartel struggles were violent, but still followed the principle of territorial control of smuggling routes and their profitable local drug markets.

Interestingly, another phenomenon made its appearance during the worst of the border violence. There were public executions and also individuals kidnapped and tortured and, once killed, their bodies were hung from bridges and overpasses in various border towns. Heads were also placed over the hoods of vehicles, and body parts appeared in several places. As already explored, much of this violence, however gruesome, followed this one pattern: to give a lesson and send a message to other groups fighting for control of a particular territory. The psychological, or the terrorist effect of this kind of violence, was indeed to try to deter the other group from continuing its violent acts to take control of a particular territory. Many of the banners that appeared unfurled throughout the city with very explicit threats and often accompanying those dead bodies were directed at an opposing group.

In 2007, when the Calderón administration decided to go against all drug-trafficking organizations in what is now known as one of the most violent periods in Mexican history, some of this violence was also inflicted on Mexican police and military personnel. These were fewer of these cases, however. Some American personnel were also attacked by these groups. Such is the case of Jaime Zapata, an American investigative agent, who was shot and killed on February 15, 2011, in the state of San Luis Potosí. Most of the most ghastly violence, however, was bestowed on the members of other cartels and organized criminal groups.

Competition: Intracartel Violence

At times, a kingpin or the head of a criminal group is killed or captured and jailed or outright extradited to the United States. These events can also provoke a struggle among his potential successors for control of the territory or the organization. Sometimes this intracartel violence becomes very public, and in the last few years it also became a ghastly spectacle as they exterminated each other and displayed the bodies for others to see. This competition can indeed lead to outbursts of public violence that often involve dozens if not hundreds of dead and disappeared, as in the Nuevo Laredo case in the summer of 2005, the Tijuana case in 2006, Ciudad Juárez starting in 2007, and Monterrey in 2010. Since then, many other cities have periodically succumbed to this kind of slaughter. Still, it is rare when a person who has nothing to do with the drug cartels gets killed. Most violence in these cases is intracartel, although it nevertheless projects a negative image of the border and there are, of course, sometimes victims among passersby. It is very controversial in some circles to state that this violence is mostly criminal-on-criminal violence, but upwards of 90 percent is just that. When Osiel Cárdenas, the head of the Gulf Cartel, was imprisoned, competition among his potential successors, including his brother, became ferocious and this also contributed to the Nuevo Laredo violence of 2005. When the Arellano Félix brothers were becoming extinct in Tijuana, potential successors and breakaway factions also entered the competition for succession, and the bodies mounted in the streets of Tijuana. That too was the case when Los Zetas broke away from the Gulf Cartel and fought their former bosses for territorial control. Thus intracartel violence exacerbated the violence already in progress by intercartel competition for control of this profitable corridor. As groups fragmented, the violence grew exponentially because there were simply more groups competing with their former allies for control of profitable criminal enterprises.

TAKING SIDES: THE MEXICAN GOVERNMENT

The war on drugs in Mexico has to be understood in two periods—the pre-2007 period and the post-2007 period—particularly when it comes to the Mexican government's actions and how these mixed with the criminal world to produce what is surely the most violent period in Mexico since the Mexican Revolution in 1910. Prior to 2007, besides inter- and intracartel rivalries, what could exacerbate illegal drug–related violence at the border was the level of willingness of the Mexican government to cut an explicit or implicit deal with the drug cartels designed to maintain public order. Before Calderón came into office in December 2006, it was generally acknowledged that the Mexican government—federal or state— would favor one group over its competitors and use its agencies to enforce that agreement. The deal generally implied that the protected group would keep its executions and level of violence to a minimum and its operations out of the public's eye. This is what has been referred to as "managing crime" rather than fighting it.[48]

President Vicente Fox's administration (2000–2006) largely refused to compromise along these lines. Instead, he declared a war on the cartels, making it very difficult for any group to establish most-favored status anywhere. The cartels had to defend their corridors with increased violence, not only against opportunistic violence from their competitors but also from a government, which did not let up the fight against the cartels.

The capture of several capos by the Mexican federal government created instability inside the cartels and between them. The result was increased violence. Indeed, violence began to rise in Mexico between 2000 and 2006, partly because of the refusal of the Mexican federal government— the first by the PAN party—to negotiate with criminal groups. But the Fox administration eventually demonstrated a relative lack of seriousness about fighting drug trafficking. In fact, Fox was eventually accused of letting up on the war on drugs and even going as far as neglecting strengthening the police and even dismantling the intelligence agencies. During this time, organized crime in Mexico grew and diversified into ruthless mafias that began to prey on Mexican citizens and businesses. Moreover, while the federal government refused to negotiate with criminal groups, many governors carried on in their dealings with different organized criminals, offering local protection for them in exchange for vast amounts of wealth. The cohesiveness that had characterized the Mexican government during the twentieth century came undone, and, in fact, the federal government and the state governments operated at odds with each other, enabling the worst wave of crime Mexico has ever seen to emerge and grow. In the end, Fox was derided as having paid no attention to crime in Mexico. This was the legacy that Calderón inherited at the end of 2006 and eventually had to contend with.

President Felipe Calderón took office in December 2006. According to many interviews I and a colleague conducted over the last year, President Calderón immediately diagnosed the state of Mexico as critical. He viewed the growth and diversification of organized crime to have come to the point of threatening the very survival of the Mexican government and the very effectiveness of Mexican institutions to function well. He made fighting drug cartels and other groups his main priority. This all-out drug war, which he later labeled war on organized crime generally, produced the most violent period in Mexican history since the 1910 revolution.

THE RESULT OF THE 2006–12 DRUG WAR IN MEXICO

There is an enormous debate on the results of the Calderón administration's efforts to confront organized crime in Mexico, particularly drug cartels. Volumes are still being written on this dark period. But in general, there are two camps in this debate. On the one hand, there are those who argue that it was a useless war that provoked an enormous bloodshed without necessarily ending drug trafficking into the United States and certainly without making a dent on organized crime within Mexico. After six years, tens of billions of dollars spent fighting drug-trafficking and other organizations, and nearly 150,000 dead and disappeared individuals, Mexico's institutions are no stronger than they were—even if the police is more effective and the intelligence agencies have been reconstructed—and crime has not let up. In fact, they argue, by nearly all measures, drugs in the United States are just as available, just as inexpensive, and perhaps even more varied in their type. Moreover, crime in Mexico has spread to the entire country, whereas before it was largely confined to border towns and states. On the other hand, there are those who argue that President Calderón correctly identified the problem as a matter of survival for the Mexican state. Mexico needed to rescue its institutions from the claws of drug cartels and other criminal groups and at a minimum restore the institutional capacity of the country to confront them. His major mistake may have been that he never had a plan to gain public support for his actions and to hold governors and mayors accountable for both their incompetence and often outright collaboration with crime. The Peña administration has not been able to do this either, even though his party holds most of those political posts.

AND THE WINNER IS . . .

Interestingly, three of the large drug cartels (Tijuana, Juárez, and Gulf) were severely weakened by the efforts of the Calderón administration. The remnants of these three cartels are still around, but in very loose coalitions of various criminal groups without the organizational capability to control their allied gangs or even their own members. They have been reduced to some extent to labels that offer passageway to other groups in exchange for a fee, known as "derecho de piso" or right of way. The one cartel that emerged unscathed and perhaps even stronger from this war on drugs was the Sinaloa Cartel. This organization remains untouched. It has made inroads into controlling the territories of the other three organizations. It has grown to have smugglings operations in well over 10 countries—to the point that it is hardly a Mexican organization any longer. And it now supplies more heroin, cocaine, confection drugs, and even marijuana than all the other organizations combined. It has adapted well, even to the new marijuana market in the United States and the relative decline in the cocaine markets by expanding its operations to heroin and confection drugs. Its profitability is greater than ever. And not even the capture (February 2014), escape (July 2015), and recapture (January 2016) of "El Chapo" Guzmán, its leader, has damaged the organization in any way. In fact, the saga of "El Chapo" Guzmán has probably shown that he is no longer the indispensable capo. His organization has transcended the Sinaloa Cartel. The criminal group can now operate and go on without its major capo.

Given the exceptional survival and prosperity of the Sinaloa Cartel, even in the middle of a massive onslaught by Mexican and American authorities, there were some questions on whether the Calderón administration favored that cartel over others, engaging in organized criminal group management, much as some of his predecessors had done. He was accused in fact of siding with the Sinaloa Cartel. This is a very controversial point. But I conclude that there was no such favoritism. The Sinaloa Cartel suffered the same kind of pressure that other cartels did. But there is an important difference that most analysts fail to consider. First, the Sinaloa Cartel, unlike the other three cartels, never turned against its own social base. Sinaloa and the Golden Triangle continued to be its base and the group continued to show a certain degree of loyalty toward the terrain and the people in that region. It continued to count on the support of the population and the local politicians. And it continued to funnel resources to that region, much in the way that it was in the past with all cartels. This gave them a lot of traction and protection.

Second, the Sinaloa Cartel did not confront the Mexican government head on. Unlike the other cartels, whose confidence in their ability to fight the government exceeded their capability, the Sinaloa Cartel seems to have preferred to skirt the conflict with the government, preferring to spend its resources in smaller but more effective operations into the other cartels' territories (especially Tijuana and Juárez) in order to gain control of corridors that the other criminal groups were leaving behind as they fought with the government, with each other, and within their own group. Sinaloa made enormous inroads, and today their operations are vast in the territories formerly under the control of these cartels.

Third, they also preferred not to confront the other criminal groups head on. They would use something akin to Apache raids or blitzkrieg operations—going in, exterminating a number of members of the other cartels, and pulling back quickly, with almost no losses. This smart way to fight the drug war enabled them to survive, prosper, and even grow stronger in spite of all of Calderón's and the American government's efforts to fight organized criminal groups everywhere and at once.

"PLATA O PLOMO": SILVER OR LEAD

The fundamental modus operandi of a cartel vis-à-vis the government and its officials in Mexico is "plata o plomo" (silver or lead). When a cartel requires the protection of a law enforcement agency, or at least needs it to stay out of its way, the officials are both incentivized and threatened at the same time. You either take the bribe (silver) or get killed (lead). Simply staking out a neutral position is not always a prerogative allowed to

Mexican government officials by the cartels—although there are those who have managed to remain somewhat neutral and not be bothered by the cartels. However, when an official decides to stay away from the criminal organizations and not take their bribe, the result is that he or she becomes mostly ineffective in combating drug trafficking. More often than not, officials take the money. The sums are too tempting and the alternative, dying, is just too extreme. Neutrality of course means becoming ineffective at doing one's work. Over the last few years, it has become evident that this kind of practice has spread to politicians. Many of them receive money from the cartels or criminal groups and they can hardly refuse. There is also increasing evidence, however, that in the new, fragmented political landscape in Mexico, many governors and mayors are now active collaborators with crime, taking money willingly. Corruption by Mexico's political class has become perhaps the most serious threat to the Mexican state—greater perhaps than crime itself. The early January 2016 death of the mayor of Temixco, Morelos, Gisela Mota, is one instance of a politician who refused to take money from an organized criminal group and she was simply shot. Dozens of mayors and city council members have fallen victim to drug traffickers in Mexico in the last few years.

Taking money from a cartel or criminal group always creates a liability for a government official—police officer, politician, military, or entrepreneur. Drug cartels sometimes will not kill an official who remains neutral or even who harasses their operations somewhat but who has never taken anything from them. Their ruthlessness, however, has increased and hardly anyone is safe these days. Executing a government official who is not involved with a drug cartel at all is a step capos prefer to avoid, but they will do it if need be—or at least that used to be the case, given that Los Zetas trumped all those rules and many other criminal groups followed suit.[49] They prefer instead to neutralize the incorruptible official by buying off those around him or her. But if someone has taken money from a cartel and then turns on it, death is the certain payback. Their bodies are often found tortured in back alleys or empty lots and lately exposed in ghastly ways for all others to see and understand what can happen to them. The criminal underworld in Mexico has gotten so competitive that anyone can now be killed, even for petty offenses. It used to be that small theft was sometimes taken as a teaching moment; today it is certain death.

DISCIPLINING THE WORKFORCE

A lot of day-to-day illegal drug–related violence, however, originates in the cartels' tactics used to discipline the workforce. Nearly all the bodies found scattered around the border cities, tortured and dead and sometimes gruesomely displayed, have to do with "ajuste de cuentas" (account adjustment). This is an issue of justice among drug lords, criminal groups, and their "employees," suppliers, or clients. Account adjustment occurs because in the clandestine business of drugs there are no legal mechanisms for the resolution of disputes, particularly between the capos and their employees, suppliers, and clients. That is still true in every black-market business. Thus, when employees, suppliers, or clients cheat the cartel, they are usually dealt with swiftly. They are tortured, killed, or "disappeared." Cheating cannot be allowed in an illegal market, and because it cannot be dealt with legally, it is generally punished severely. Sometimes, their bodies are displayed with signs of torture as a lesson to others. In a formal economy, these relationships have law enforcement and judicial systems to resolve this kind of cheating and maintain labor relations relatively peacefully. Such mechanisms are not available in a black market, and threats and violence are nearly the only way that cheating is resolved.

The violence, with its torturing and death and gruesome spectacles, can happen for several reasons. A few instances are illustrative. First, a member of the cartel may "shave off" a portion of the drugs from a bundle in his care. He may then try to sell it on his own to make a profit on the side. Similarly, an employee of the cartel may try to dilute a drug load by adding other substances to it in order to keep a certain amount of the drugs and either consume or sell them. Someone may also make off with a load of drugs or cash—a type of activity known as "bañarse" or "to take a shower." A client can also feel tempted to do this. An employee, supplier, or client may become an informant of the law enforcement authorities as well, usually the DEA. Sometimes a "bocón" (big mouth), someone who "talks too much" and blabs unnecessary information, can also get in trouble. Even taking unnecessary risks in crossing a "clavo" that is captured by the inspectors at the POE can be a reason for punishment by torture or death. Punishing cheating or mistakes sends a strong message to the cartel's employees and keeps the workforce, suppliers, and clients disciplined. At the same time, however, it projects an image of extreme violence along the border. Because so much criminal activity is about territorial and market control, increasingly, even petty crimes are punished with this kind of violence. If a dealer, for example, does business in enemy territory, he is subject to being abducted, tortured, killed, and then displayed as a lesson for others. Similarly, some criminal groups may recruit among the most vulnerable—the very poor or undocumented migrants traversing through Mexico—for their cartels or criminal groups. If they refuse to collaborate with the group, they too may be assassinated. Such was the case in the August 2010 massacre of San Fernando in the state of Tamaulipas. There, 71 mostly Central American migrants were found in a mass grave, presumably killed because they refused en masse to join Los Zetas in their criminal operations, thinking perhaps that they would not dare kill so many of them at once. But the cruelty of groups such as Los Zetas has no limits. They killed them all and perhaps several hundred other migrants who refused to be recruited by them. Mass graves are still being found scattered throughout the migrant routes from the Guatemalan border to the U.S. border.

RANDOM VIOLENCE: THE EXCEPTION TO THE RULE

Discerning patterns in criminal violence is itself difficult. It may seem nearly impossible when violence proliferates and new forms of violence emerge in the middle of a conflict between a government and drug cartels and criminal groups—a new type of nonstate actor that often resembles a terrorist group rather than a criminal organization motivated by profit. But it is not impossible to understand that kind of violence or discern the factors that sustain it. Seldom will drug lords and their lieutenants employ strictly senseless violence. Although sometimes passersby may become victims of illegal drug–related violence, their wounding or death is nearly always accidental or collateral damage—as it has been callously named by U.S. drug agencies. A cartel's violent act is always related to a target because of treason, cheating, whistle-blowing, competition, etc. Almost always, violence follows a specific logic, even if it appears random because innocent people may fall victim to it. Nevertheless, from time to time, a drug lord emerges who is particularly brutal and does not care to be discreet. The Arellano Félix brothers in Tijuana were particularly brutal and often killed for the sake of killing or because they felt annoyed at someone. Ramón Arellano Félix in particular was well known for using unnecessary violence, for being particularly cruel, and for avenging petty peeves. Blancornelas recounts, for example, how Ramón shot a neighbor dead for complaining that the music was too loud; or how he shot the son of a prominent Tijuana family for arguing outside a bar with a young man who happened to be his friend; or how he shot a waiter for warning him that he could not take the drink outside the bar building. But this seems to have been his personality trait more than the regular modus operandi of the cartel capos.[50] Most prefer to do their business quietly, including their most violent actions. The same seemed to be the case with Vicente Carrillo Fuentes, who took over the Juárez Cartel after his brother Amado Carrillo Fuentes died on the operating table while undergoing surgery to change his appearance. Vicente was particularly violent, and as recounted by a witness, one night he had several of his rivals brought to his hotel room where he personally tortured and killed each one of them, ending the night with a total of nine people executed. Los Zetas seems to have been one of the most violent and cruel organizations.

Their violent behavior, from 2003 through 2012, was such that the Mexican government made it a point to exterminate them. The military was deployed to do just that.

Incidentally, someone told me that Los Zetas were such an obnoxious organization that the Mexican marines picked them off, one by one, and even flew them out to the Gulf of Mexico, dropping them into the water in the hope of weakening the organization quickly. Whether this is true or not will be hard to find out, but what we do know is that Los Zetas no longer exist as such.

INCREASING IMPUNITY

One of the major problems in fighting crime is the growing level of impunity in Mexico. Impunity is defined as the ability to escape punishment, harm, or loss for one's action. In Mexico, the level of impunity is simply too high. There are several reasons for it. The government has a relatively weak institutional capacity to fight these well-organized, determined, and well-armed groups. It lacks a clean police force to go after them; it requires additional investment in investigative resources; it has a prison system that is practically in shambles; its judicial institutions are easily intimidated by criminals; and it has a political class that is implicitly or explicitly complicit with organized criminal groups. Additionally, after the Calderón administration's experience with high levels of violence because of the drug war, the Peña administration decided to abandon a full confrontation with criminal groups and has spent most of its efforts capturing top drug lords and high-value targets—the famous drug kingpin strategy that may create dislocations that lead to more violence and has ultimately no impact on overall drug trafficking and criminal activity. All of these issues prevent Mexico from having a strong state to confront organized crime. Most participants in drug trafficking and other criminal activities go unpunished and perhaps even protected by the political powers that be. Without a serious change in this, the country will continue to be the drug-trafficking and criminal haven that has been in the last 15 to 20 years.

THE *SICARIOS*

The executioners for a cartel are known as *sicarios*. These are death squads that the drug lords hire to do their dirty work. They are in the business of abducting, torturing, killing, and disposing of the bodies. Their work is gruesome. They sometimes dismember the bodies and display them in public for others to see. In the more classic period of drug smuggling, up to about 2003, they disposed of the dead by burying them clandestinely, which was generally the case, or in times of greater turmoil by leaving them in a public space in order to send a message to the cartel's employees, to the government, or to society in general. With Los Zetas and La Familia Michoacana, their work actually became quite ghastly. These groups had a paramilitary style of execution and had practically no concern for life or the spectacle of death. As the war on drugs picked up after 2006, the competition for territory and drug markets obliged many of them to engage other groups' *sicarios* in a head-on collision. The result was almost too graphic to describe here, but a quick Internet search on gang and cartel violence in Mexico during that period will yield thousands of pictures that are just hard to look at.

Up until the early 2000s, *sicarios* were men hired elsewhere, often squads put together for a single job. The men were brought to the place where they were to carry out their executions and then moved out or kept away from public sight as much as possible. Their mission tended to be narrow and well specified in advance. They lived together, usually in houses, and came out only when the job was to be done. Their work often took place at night, although they sometimes also worked during the day. Most of them were drug addicts and operated under the influence of some drug in order to mitigate any emotional reactions of remorse or revulsion while abducting or torturing or killing someone or disposing of the body. When they were finished with their assigned task, they were sent back to their hometowns elsewhere in Mexico. Occasionally, an American citizen with specific skills, such as sharpshooting, would also be hired for a specific job. In general, only a cartel could afford a death squad. The small-time smugglers could not. If they were cheated out of their merchandise or cash, they lost it all; they were left to take revenge with their own hands. All this changed after the mid-2000s.

Beginning with the Gulf Cartel, the use of violence became much more systematic and even merciless over time. The Gulf Cartel created an armed branch, Los Zetas, which they trained specifically to carry out violent operations, with unparalleled brutality. They often wore a uniform; they had insignia to identify themselves; they trained as military; they carried heavy weaponry and drove intimidating vehicles; and they operated as a professional military. They were also vicious. They made Mexico a very violent country. In time, Los Zetas broke away from the Gulf Cartel and became a criminal group unto itself, but with paramilitary characteristics, and diversified its activities, going from drug smuggling to kidnapping for ransom to human trafficking and smuggling to extortion, and so on. The Juárez Cartel too had an armed branch, La Línea, which operated in the same paramilitary fashion and exercised quite an incredible amount of nasty violence over the city. These groups emerged all around and they were nearly fearless, to the point of engaging the Mexican military and federal police in outright street battles in many cities and towns, which most of them knew how to do because they were recruited from the ranks of the military. During the Fox administration, for example, thousands of soldiers were reputed to have left the ranks of the armed forces and joined criminal groups and drug cartels. The appearance of these paramilitary groups gave the war on drugs the look that it had during the 2006–12 period. Such groups still operate today, but they are somewhat diminished, and many less disciplined—read less soldierly—individuals have joined them.

These developments worried the Calderón administration considerably and many of the resources went to fight these paramilitary groups that emerged throughout the country. This new phase of the drug war, unfortunately, resulted in brutal violence, partly encouraged and financed by the United States. At the end of the Calderón administration, the traditional cartels, except Sinaloa, had crumbled; multiple new criminal groups had emerged; 120,000 bodies and 23,000 disappeared were the human cost; the violence had only increased and spread to many more areas of the country; and the drug war's end was nowhere in sight—failure, by many standards, although many officials insist that it had to be done if crime was to be stopped from overrunning the country (See Figure 2.2).

We will never know if the Calderón administration's efforts were effective or not. Only history will tell. But we do know that the fragmentation of the cartels appears to have been by design. It was a matter of breaking those large organizations down so that they would not overtake the

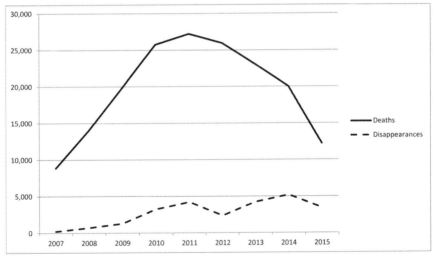

Figure 2.2

Number of deaths and disappearances as a result of Mexico's war on drugs between 2007 and 2015. (INEGI Conjunto de Datos, Defunciones por homicidios; CNN Español: Los desaparecidos en México)

government, in the hopes that the remains of them would be easily swept up by the military and federal police and then the state and local police forces. This much has been argued by some.[51] But 10 years later, it is hard to see the end to the violence of the drug war in Mexico and it is hard to see an end to the drug war.

HANDLING THE DISLOYAL

Another common feature is the brutal violence that now characterizes many of Mexico's cities and towns. Hundreds of dead bodies are found randomly here and there, usually tortured and sometimes displayed for others to see. There has been a shift in the kind of violence that the border has witnessed, however. It used to be that there was a clear method to the use of violence. Once an individual had been identified by the drug lords as a target for torture or death, the *sicarios* were brought in and prepared to do the job. Intelligence was gathered on the whereabouts of the target. A propitious moment was chosen to execute the target or to kidnap him and take him to a chosen place for torturing—sometimes houses rented or bought for that purpose. If the house was purchased, after it was used it was cleaned out and sold. It used to be that it was almost always preferable to kidnap the target and conduct the ghastly task of torturing him or killing him in a house where there were no witnesses. Many of the bodies were never actually found. Quite a few of them are buried in these same houses, under concrete slabs in back patios. Other times, the bodies were buried under the floors of the house. According to my guide in Ciudad Juárez, there are hundreds, possibly thousands of bodies buried under the backyards and patios and rooms of houses all along the border. This particular interviewee told me that he could personally point out several houses where bodies are buried, very often unknown to the current occupants of the house.

Those buried in houses constitute "los desaparecidos" or "the disappeared." Sometimes, and more often the case now that there is much greater competition for territorial control of drug smuggling corridors and local drug markets, the cartel needs to "send a message." In this case, the body disposal is public. The signs of torture are quite visible. Sometimes the bodies are beheaded. Other times, they come accompanied by a very threatening message, using vulgar language and generally bad writing and awful spelling—perhaps a testimony to the level of education of most of the *sicarios*. To send a message, the bodies of "cheaters" (employees, clients, or suppliers) are disposed of in a public place, as are those of rival group members. These are usually found by some passerby early in the morning of the next day. For a long time, there were several well-known methods to dispose of a body. One is known as "encajuelados" or "en-trunked" because they are generally found in the trunks of stolen cars. There was in fact an ongoing business of stealing cars in U.S. border towns to sell them to the drug dealers for needs such as this one—more recently someone told me that given the financial drought of these criminal groups, cars are no longer used because they are too expensive to abandon. Thus bodies are just thrown out in some ditch or lot, if not used to send a macabre message. Another disposal method is "encobijados" or bodies found wrapped in a rug or a blanket, just thrown out in the desert, empty lots, drainage ditches, or back alleys. Another method is the "entambados" or men who are stuffed into an empty oil barrel and disposed of anywhere in the city. Almost always these men show signs of torture and sometimes specific signs that reflect their "crime" or "mistake." A man with his finger cut off and stuffed in his mouth was probably an informant. A man with gunshots in the palms of his hands probably stole drugs or money ("took a shower"), and so forth.

A particular way of disposing of bodies made its way to the border in Tijuana. The bodies were submerged in oil drums full of chemicals that would quickly corrode the flesh and the bones until nothing was left. In mid-August 2014, "El Pozolero" ("The Stew Maker") was arrested. His name is Santiago Meza López. He is reputed to have dissolved more than 300 bodies. All over the border, however, most bodies are disposed of in mass graves, many of which contain dozens of bodies of immigrants, criminals, and regular citizens who refuse to submit to the demands of criminal groups. Many of these mass graves have been discovered in Coahuila, Nuevo León, and Tamaulipas. Others exist in Chihuahua, Sonora, and Baja California.

MONEY AND DRUGS: NORTH AND SOUTH

On a weekday afternoon, Juan, a 30-something Ciudad Juárez resident, got out of a taxi at the Santa Fe Bridge and ran across the border. He went straight to a U.S. official and asked for his help. He claimed that he was about to be killed by a *sicario* from the Juárez Cartel. Juan's job had been to collect the cash coming from the sale of drugs from all over the United States and to then transport it across into Mexico. He was paid $20,000 to $30,000 for every $1 million that he transported into Mexico.

That fated day, Juan thought it harmless to take his mother along on his trip. When he drove to the house where he was to deliver the money, the Juárez Cartel members waiting for him saw him as an undisciplined worker because he had been instructed to always ride alone. They took him outside the house to the backyard. As he was pacing, guarded by the *sicarios*, he could see through the window that his mother was lying in a pool of blood. She had been killed inside the house. He kept his cool and on the first opportunity made a run from the *sicarios*. He managed to make it to a major street and to flag down a taxi, which took him to the border.

The American appetite for illegal drugs is enormous; it constitutes a huge, northward pull. The border is caught in the drug war as the passageway for drugs to satisfy this insatiable demand. But what happens to the money gathered in the millions of daily illegal-drug transactions that occur in bars, clubs, restaurants, street corners, houses, and elsewhere throughout the United States? A ton of cocaine may produce "tons of cash." How is it possible to hide and transport all this money? How does the money make its way down to Mexico and on to Central America and on to Colombia? How is it distributed among many different individuals and spent and invested—indeed, whitened or laundered?

This is a complicated and increasingly dangerous process as well. Cartels send drugs north, accepting the risk of not being paid after delivery. There is a small chance of this as the local dealer can lose his or her client. There are disciplinary measures that are taken in these cases as well. My Ciudad Juárez interviewee told me about three African American women who failed to pay the cartel for the drugs sold to them. They were kidnapped and brought to Ciudad Juárez in the trunk of a car to force them to pay. Losing money is just as dangerous as losing drugs and the punishment is just as severe.

Most drugs move across the border and then north to the rest of the United States, an enormous majority of them in trucks and other vehicles—given restrictions at airports, it is likely that these are not used at all, even if occasionally there is an arrest of airline employees for attempting to build a distribution network inside an airport. The money collected in those areas where the drugs are sold is warehoused in homes in major U.S. cities and then carefully packaged to be smuggled south. The money is concealed in trucks and vehicles traveling south. These same vehicles move the cash over the interstate highway system and take it across the border into Mexico. Just as drug lords worry about packaging their drugs so that they are not detected, they also worry about packaging the money so that it is not detected by U.S. or Mexican authorities, who can confiscate it. The money must then be warehoused in places scattered along the border and prepared for money laundering. Cartels today have sophisticated finance and accounting divisions, which find creative ways to hide the cash and to launder it. Professionals are hired for that purpose. In addition, the networks of entrepreneurs that help invest that money—mostly in real estate and small businesses—are quite dense and very hard to detect. It has in fact been acknowledged that if there is no frontal attack on the financial assets of illegal-drug and other criminal groups, they will continue to operate and finance their own operations without end.

However, although both Mexico and the United States are slowly beginning to tackle the issue of drug financial assets, their efforts are not yet sufficient enough to have an impact.

Sometimes, when the cash makes it to the U.S. border town, it is then crossed in smaller amounts into Mexico. Individuals are often hired to cross the cash into Mexico. They make trips south with cash hidden in various compartments in their vehicles. Moving cash south is increasingly as delicate as moving drugs north. Cheating by cash smugglers is just as likely to be punished as cheating by other cartel employees. Treason, shaving cash off the stashes, or stealing are punishable by torture and death as well. A person is paid up to $30,000 for crossing anywhere between $500,000 and $1 million south in his car, truck, or van. Increasingly, public relations specialists are hired by the cartels to find people who can cross the cash south without raising anyone's suspicions. Millions of cars cross the border every year and some of them do so with cash stashed inside. This is made somewhat easier by the fact that the Mexican customs system relies on random checks where only about 1 in 10 or 20 vehicles is checked—if it triggers the red inspection light upon crossing. Most vehicles simply cross right through into Mexico without being bothered. This enables the drug lords to cross tons of cash going south.

More recently, the U.S. government began to cooperate with the Mexican government in trying to detect money going south. Traveling in any number of POEs in Texas, it is easy to see that CBP simply stationed a number of agents and additional scanning machines as well as random stops of vehicles as a way to "check for cash" going south. It has not really worked. In spite of small successes—a few hundred thousand dollars here and there—the only thing that has remained clear is that these new obstacles have made the lives of borderlanders miserable because the traffic going south slows down to a crawl and sometimes even comes to a standstill. At certain hours, it may take up to two or more hours to cross from the United States into Mexico. Legitimate border crossers—shoppers, students, tourists, workers, etc.—must now wait in line almost as long to get into the United States as to go out of the United States. CBP has yet to justify in dollars and cents the utility of these outbound checkpoints.

Even so, financially, little has been done. Efficient money smuggling contributes to the maintenance of the large cartel operations in Mexico and beyond. The cartels can take losses. They can bribe a considerable number of people. They can invest in R&D to go around the use of technology by U.S. law enforcement officials. In general, the enormous amounts of cash have created formidable criminal groups that can operate massively and turn a profit, even when the United States steps up the pressure on their organizations.

GUNS: FAST AND FURIOUS

Just as cash going south presents a huge problem for everyone, guns flowing from the United States to Mexico are even a bigger issue—at least for Mexico. During the Calderón administration, in the middle of the violence, it became clear that Mexico was flooded with weapons coming from the United States. These weapons quickly fell into the hands of drug traffickers and other criminals, who used them to execute people, kidnap, rob, extort money from businesses, traffic in human beings, etc. The problem of weapons became an even greater problem after the assault weapons ban in the United States expired on September 13, 2004. Very quickly after that, semiautomatic rifles, pistols, and shotguns began to appear in the streets of Mexico. Although many American gun distributors and others argued that many of Mexico's weapons were coming from the remaining stockpiles of the Central American civil wars of the 1980s and 1990s, the reality is that most guns came from the United States and fueled the war on drugs in Mexico. This led President Calderón to formally protest this flood of weapons and to erect a huge billboard right at the edge of the Bridge of the Americas in Ciudad Juárez that read "No More Weapons." The sign was made of melted guns that had been confiscated from various drug-smuggling groups. The sign irked the Americans, but they could not do anything about it, and it drew much attention to the problem of guns flowing south.

On that score, one day sometime in 2010 a student came to see me at the UTEP. He wanted my advice on a good lawyer in El Paso. The student had been caught with a weapon in his car's glove compartment as he was crossing into Ciudad Juárez from El Paso. A random check had revealed that he was smuggling that weapon into Ciudad Juárez. I recommended a good lawyer to him. In the end, he was accused of attempting to smuggle one weapon into Mexico and given 18 months' probation. Once the ordeal was over, he came back to my office to thank me. At that point, I personally asked him if this was true. And he said yes. He had smuggled a few weapons into Ciudad Juárez, where it was easy to sell them. He made some cash on each weapon and used it to pay tuition. He said he was not the only one. This was a common practice, even among "decent" citizens. This case showed to me, firsthand, that weapons smuggling was a huge problem, but clearly there is not much the United States can do about it, given the acrimonious debates on guns going on in this country. There simply is no appetite to restrict guns in any way or to hold gun owners accountable, and Mexico will continue to be the recipient of many of these guns, which will continue to fuel the violence.

THE MEDIA AND THE DRUG WAR

Most Americans get their news regarding the drug war from the media. The media not only choose the content of drug war stories, but they frame the issue as well, providing the general public with a certain view of the border. Sometimes the media focus on the number of overdoses that end up in hospitals, the ups and downs of drug use, street-level drug dealing, the ravages of drug consumption in U.S. cities, and law enforcement drug busts. Other times they focus on the actors of the drug war: the criminals, the organizations, the capos, the tunnels or spectacular caches of drugs or money, or the law enforcement officials. But when the media focus on the drug war on the border, they generally tend to sound a note of doom. Often, the portrayal of the border is a largely lopsided view of how the drug war and the border relate to each other. The words of Antonio O. Garza, the U.S. ambassador to Mexico, on June 9, 2005, regarding the Nuevo Laredo violence of that summer could be the words of nearly any story covering the drug war on the border. His declarations received extensive coverage in both the U.S. and the Mexican media. He said:

A few weeks ago, I asked the State Department to re-issue a public announcement about the on-going violence in the border region. This violence, combined with previous murders and numerous kidnappings involving U.S. citizens, remains a priority concern for state and municipal leaders and U.S. citizens along the border. And while I have no interest in criticizing the Mexican Government, given my responsibility to promote the safety and security of U.S. citizens, I will not shy away from speaking out when their safety is at stake . . . As friends and neighbors, we should be honest with each other about the rapidly degenerating situation along the border and the near-lawlessness in some parts. I absolutely recognize that the security of the border region around Nuevo Laredo is a shared responsibility and we are committed to doing our part. The bottom line is that we simply can't allow drug traffickers to place in jeopardy the lives of our citizens and the safety of our communities.[52]

Then coverage of the bloody 2005 summer of Nuevo Laredo died down by the fall. But soon after that, in 2006, Tijuana emerged as a very violent place. And then it died down there as well. And then by 2007, Ciudad Juárez fell to a huge wave of violence. And then Tamaulipas after that, where violence has not let up since and where corruption is so endemic that it is nearly impossible to separate it from everyday life. Coahuila, another border state, also fell to a wave of violence that to this day comes and goes. And then Nuevo León in 2010 experienced a period of brutal violence. And so on. Thus the media's sporadic, incomplete, and largely scandal-driven coverage of illegal drugs contributes to this generalized, partial understanding of illegal drugs and the drug war, particularly on the border. It also contributes to the largely negative image that the border has among both Americans and Mexicans. Media coverage completely ignores the positive aspects of what is going on all along the border, including, for example, that most people continued living their daily lives worrying about the same thing that everyone else does: work, school, and so on. But the general decay of the border, particularly on the Mexican side, is undeniable. Urban poverty continues to fuel both violence and the workforce for drug smuggling and other crime. The infrastructure of almost all cities is crumbling. Investment in human capital is very low. Economic development appears to be stuck in the maquiladora era and wages are abysmally small and insufficient to support a family. This leads many to turn to a life of crime. Living on the border has become very difficult and crossing it ever more dangerous. It is truly surprising that people continue to cling to the border as a resource, when it sometimes appears to be more of a curse.

Worse yet, for the bulk of the population, the border and its relationship with the illegal drugs that some 27 million Americans consume regularly and many more consume casually is a problem others focus on. Most Americans do not frequently think of the border and illegal drugs, and they seldom connect the appetite for illegal drugs in major U.S. cities with the smuggling operations of criminal organizations on the border. Even border residents have learned to live with the drug war as part of their communities. Even in the midst of all the violence of recent years, borderlanders have struggled to live normal lives. On the border, the drug war is part of the landscape.

THE WEALTH OF DRUGS: ON NARCO-MANSIONS AND NARCO-JUNIORS

Rio Grande City, the county seat of Starr County, is one of the oldest settlements in South Texas. It is located on the Rio Grande 100 miles from both Brownsville and Laredo. It is an international POE connected by bridge to the town of Camargo, Tamaulipas. Driving through Rio Grande City, visitors can easily be surprised by the various mansions that sprawl around the area. Speaking with a native of Rio Grande City, I was "confidentially" told that some of these houses, like many in Laredo, Brownsville, and McAllen, are narco-mansions. There are many other similar houses placed along otherwise poor areas throughout the border and beyond. A narco-mansion is defined by the locals as a house that belongs to someone who is making his money in the drug business. It can be a mansion that belongs to a drug trafficker, to his family, to a partner working in money-laundering operations or in another capacity. Often, the wives and children of various capos and lieutenants live in those narco-mansion compounds, some of which even have chapels within the compound itself. And more often than not, locals avoid even talking about them. It is simply "known" to whom these houses belong; no one dares to acknowledge this reality in public. Strangely enough, this penchant for luxury extends to narco-tombs. There are cemeteries in some cities, such as Culiacán, the capital of Sinaloa and the home base of the Sinaloa Cartel, where there are veritable mausoleums that resemble huge mansions. They are built big and well maintained. These are the tombs of the capos and lieutenants.

Interestingly, however, the children of the powerful drug traffickers study and travel extensively throughout the United States and Europe. They attend colleges and universities and shop at the most expensive malls in global cities. They drive luxurious cars and spend money lavishly. None of them seem to have trouble obtaining visas to enter the United States or Europe. This is partly because of the fact that the visa-issuing process in American consulates in Mexico places an inordinate importance on the number of zeros that the bank account of the visa applicant has—to this day one hears complaints that visa officers pay attention to the income of applicants in granting or denying visas. It is nearly always sufficient to show a bulky bank account to obtain a visa to travel and study in the United States. This has allowed a number of relatives of drug traffickers to live in relative safety inside the country that is waging war on their fathers! These privileged offspring of cartel capos and lieutenants are better known in Mexico as narco-juniors, the children of those who smuggle drugs today and send their children to a posh liberal arts college in California or Texas. One finds enormous paradoxical situations, such as the fact that "El Chapo" Guzmán, formerly the most wanted international drug trafficker, had his twin daughters born in Los Angeles, to a young woman who is an American citizen. And they cannot do anything about the fact that this woman and her babies go back and forth, even as the U.S. government has engaged in major efforts to have Guzmán extradited to the United States.

THE BIG CARTELS VERSUS THE SMALL-TIME PLAYERS

The large cartels used to do most of the illegal-drug smuggling. But there were also a number of small, illegal-drug entrepreneurs. I interviewed one of them in Parral, Chihuahua, Mexico. Every so often, he went up to the mountains of Chihuahua and bought marijuana by the kilogram. He recruited the occasional worker to help him bring it down from the mountains and drive it to the border. There he generally hired a "clavo" entrepreneur or a truck driver to bring it across the border.

He also went out to the nightclubs and recruited someone to help cross a load, often a few dozen pounds at a time to minimize losses and to protect the smuggler, whose sentence might be lighter if caught with a smaller load.

The small-time smuggler sometimes paid a few hundred dollars to a naïve teenager or barfly to hide the drugs and sneak them across the border in his vehicle. Sometimes, imprudent partygoers were also willing to do so as they return across the border from "clubbing" in Mexico. It was not uncommon to see late-night drug busts and young people being led away in handcuffs for trying to cross a load of illegal drugs in their car in exchange for a few dollars.

For some time, the favorite group to recruit was Hispanic single mothers who were U.S. citizens and sometimes had their children with them to distract the inspection officer. Once the border inspectors caught on to this trend, this modus operandi disappeared almost entirely. To these women, the few hundreds of dollars earned smuggling drugs often made a big difference in their personal or family finances.

In an ironic twist, the Homeland Security strategy of the post–September 11 era hurt these small-time smugglers in higher numbers. As new technology was introduced, as border law enforcement resources and personnel increased, and as inspectors got savvier at finding the drugs hidden in "clavos," the small illegal-drug entrepreneurs were being more easily detected and caught in higher numbers. This still happens, of course, but less and less so, particularly after the huge wave of violence that ensued after 2007 and completely shook the drug-smuggling field.

During the golden era of the large, territorially based drug cartels, however, they had the wherewithal to invest heavily in corrupting truckers and U.S. and Mexican officials, and to invest in more sophisticated technology to get around Homeland Security tactics. They also invested in building better "clavos." If caught, they could also take larger losses, given the volume of drugs they handled. Unlike the small-time entrepreneurs, they enjoyed an economy of scale that afforded them higher risks. Thus Homeland Security effectiveness contributed to strengthening veritable oligopolies in the drug cartels. This was further evidenced by the kinds of cases that come to the federal court along the border. Most of those arrested and hauled to court for smuggling were, or worked for, small-time smugglers. Seldom was someone working for a large drug cartel arrested crossing a "clavo."[53] The testimony of many of those that end up in court shows that they were often hapless, inexperienced smugglers hired through a friend, at a bar, or on the streets. A quick analysis of court cases and testimony corroborated this consolidation of large cartels along the border because of enhanced Homeland Security tactics.

All this changed after Calderón took office. The war on drugs represented an all-out confrontation with the major cartels and their paramilitarized branches—such as Los Zetas, who split from the Gulf Cartel, and La Línea, which remained loyal to the Juárez Cartel to the bitter end. This meant that the cartels were being hammered and eventually fragmented into splinter groups that controlled smaller corridors and cities and towns separately. They were cells that attempted drug trafficking on a smaller scale and also rented their territory to the Sinaloa Cartel and other criminal groups for a fee. Thus the drugs confiscated at the border either belonged to new and emerging but smaller groups or belonged to the Sinaloa Cartel, which could afford to push its way through these newly liberated corridors available for a fee—or "derecho de piso" (right of way), as it was known. The smuggling industry became much more chaotic and there was a breakdown into many different actors, trying to cross drugs in many different ways through many different entry points. The scenario became much more chaotic and it has remained that way thus far, although Sinaloa continues to be a force to be reckoned with, in spite of the arrest (for the third time) of its major capo, "El Chapo" Guzmán.

THE BORDER GEOGRAPHY OF THE DRUG WAR

Traveling along Highway 2 in Sonora, going west through the high-desert reserve, I wondered at what point I had crossed over the territory that the drug lords agreed to as the line between their great cartels back when territory was the basis for organizing drug smuggling in Mexico. The U.S. drug market is vast and the borderline long, but there were clear lines in the sand in regard to who had the right to smuggle what through where. It is nearly impossible for anyone to build an empire that can control the entire border and the entire market, but it is possible to achieve agreements among different cartels so as to divvy up the profits. Thus, just like the U.S. drug warriors are divided into two groups— prohibitionists and permissivists—the Mexican drug lords had to make their own arrangements, corporate-style, to divide the borderlands and create peace among them. That was what a cartel consisted of: a series of providers who agreed to coordinate their actions in order to organize and maximize the profit for all. Because no corporation can survive if it has to defend its assets from the violence of others, the Mexican drug lords met to divide the border into what are essentially four large drug suppliers. The Gulf Cartel operated out of northeastern Mexico and supplied drugs going to the east. The Juárez Cartel operated out of northern Mexico and supplied drugs to the Midwest and east of the Rockies, with some smaller drug markets in California. The Sinaloa Cartel operated out of western and southern Mexico, except for Baja California, and supplied drugs from west of the Rockies to the California border. The Tijuana

Cartel operated out of the Baja California peninsula and supplied drugs mostly to the West Coast. The negotiations occurred mostly among the great lords in the 1990s, when the drug trade began to flow through Mexico rather than the Caribbean, which became unprofitable due to effective interception of drugs by the U.S. drug war troops. One of those great meetings occurred in Ciudad Juárez. There, the capos agreed to respect the boundaries of each cartel. This consensus no longer exists. Most capos have been arrested and jailed, killed, or extradited. Most of the large cartels, except Sinaloa, have been fragmented into smaller groups, and most territorial control has essentially disappeared. This is no longer about territory but about who has the ability to control the passage through a territory. Sometimes, groups will settle for a fee to allow drugs to go through. Other times, they may settle for victimizing Mexican citizens themselves through various criminal activities. Others will definitely engage in drug trafficking, but always subject to being challenged by a different group. The situation is by far much more chaotic than it used to be.

CONCLUSION

There is a dire need to understand how the drug war interacts with the border, particularly under a continuously changing market and criminal landscape. The study of drug-trafficking organizations—their motivations, their operations, and their strategies—is still highly underdeveloped because just as we thought we had understood how the world of drug smuggling was put together, a huge war ensued and upset and unsettled the entire criminal world. It has in fact transformed it in ways that may be more difficult to both understand and control. Yet criminal organizations and their operations are not outside the reach of our study. In spite of their complexity, it is possible to understand and make sense of how these criminal organizations interact with the other dynamics of the border. Several things have to be kept in mind to make sense of this: the economics and geography of the border, the nature of underground businesses, the entrepreneurship and creativity of criminal organizations, the escalating character of U.S. antidrug policy and its ability to force Mexico into a war on drugs in its own territory, the use of violence and corruption by drug cartels and the collaboration of the Mexican political class with these criminal groups, and the attention of the media to the issue. Similarly, we have to pay attention to the institutional capacity and political will of the Mexican state to confront these criminal groups—both of which may continue to be too low for what is truly required. Without considering these crucial pieces of the puzzle, it is nearly impossible to understand how drug-smuggling organizations work and why the border is such a propitious place for them to prosper, even when they have suffered an ongoing war that made them crumble and reemerge as criminal cells and even as they too face a more uncertain and unpredictable future. And I say to prosper because up to today drug cartels and especially the many criminal groups that now inhabit the border continue to do their business as usual along the border, even as the U.S. government continues to struggle to eliminate them.

From an academic perspective, combining the study of the border and drug-smuggling organizations and now other types of criminal groups that interact with them after three of the major cartels fell apart is an exciting prospect. As this chapter demonstrates, all of these elements, put together, can help describe and explain the "problem of the border" and then propose potential solutions to the issue of illegal drugs on the border. Doing the hard work of studying these criminal organizations' modi operandi and classifying their work is an indispensable element if we are to succeed in "cleaning" the image of the border—although admittedly, cleaning the image of the border should be a by-product of cleaning the border and not the other way around. Of course, this kind of work has, undoubtedly, enormous implications for policy makers in Washington, DC, and Mexico City as well. Clearly, the interplay of the drug war and the border is not easy to disentangle, and much less so now. But the major conclusion of this chapter is that over time, the U.S. drug war on the border forced the cartels to consolidate their operations, to make their practices more efficient, and to make use of economies of scale. Cartels became flexible hierarchies, capable of responding to the contingencies of the drug war. And they generally succeed in doing so. The border drug war waged by the United States consolidated drug smuggling into four large oligopolies that continue to send massive supplies of illegal drugs to the country. Similarly, the next lesson is that a major confrontation with the cartels has essentially fragmented them, created numerous cells of criminal groups operating sometimes together and sometimes apart and against each other. This has made it more difficult to eliminate them and has made the drug-smuggling business much more chaotic and difficult to control. These people have little respect for the lives of others and they cannot be easily intimidated. They are essentially unafraid of death—in fact this may be the reason why they pray to *La Santa Muerte* or Holy Death, a makeshift saint that is heavily worshipped among drug traffickers and other criminals. What is clear is that there are no strategic successes in the drug war, and the tactical successes of the drug war have change the face and nature of drug smuggling but not made it disappear. It is an ever-shifting arena, and they will continue to evolve and adapt to whatever the U.S. and Mexican government bring upon them, as long as we refuse to deal with the demand. Such conclusions, which should be important to everyone, can be drawn only if we dedicate the time and energy to a careful consideration of all the forces that interact across the border to make drugs the profitable business that it is and to make the U.S. drug war the great failure that it is.

CHAPTER 3

Immigration and
the U.S.-Mexico Border

THE NEVER-ENDING STORY OF IMMIGRATION

Immigration is a controversial word in the United States. In reality, it has always been so. This is surprising given the profound tradition of migration to the United States from many different parts of the globe. Many new arrivals suffer exclusion, discrimination, and sometimes outright racism. Yet immigrants have proven quite resilient. They stick around; they prosper; and they leave new generations of patriotic Americans after them.

The latest wave of migration is from Latin America. The second half of the twentieth century and the first decades of the twenty-first century have witnessed one of the largest surges of migration to the United States. Most of these immigrants from Latin America come from Mexico, although there is new evidence that Central Americans are now a larger number of migrants than Mexicans,[1] and Asians are now the single largest source of new migrants to the United States.[2] Mexicans, however, have always been part of the U.S. immigration landscape, especially in the Southwest, although lately Mexican migration has become much more controversial. This chapter is concerned with immigration but not with immigration broadly speaking. Here we will focus specifically on immigration at the border.

LEGAL AND ILLEGAL IMMIGRATION

Unfortunately, there seems to be very little appetite in the American political debate to make a true distinction between legal and illegal immigration. It is true that after the mid-1960s, there was an increase in undocumented immigration, but it is also true that most immigrants are largely legal, law-abiding, and contribute enormously to the prosperity of the United States. Illegal immigration, however, came into focus in the United States after the mid-1980s, when President Ronald Reagan signed into law a broad immigration act granting amnesty for undocumented migrants but also beefing up security at the border. By the 1990s, American public opinion viewed undocumented migration negatively and the rhetoric became increasingly harsh.[3] Many legal migrants also paid a price for undocumented migration. The border, however, became associated with illegal or undocumented migration, and Mexicans came to be viewed as largely undesirable immigrants; so that by the mid- to late 1990s, the border was perceived as chaotic and being overrun by hordes of undocumented migrants. The border has not been able to shake that image, even though the numbers hardly justify it. Reputation is a lagging indicator, and although the border is largely secure and the number of migrants has decreased by well over 60 percent, the border continues to be perceived as a lawless region, overrun by mobs of migrants.

THE SCENE AT THE BORDER

At the peak of the immigration crisis, in the early 2000s, I found myself driving along the border from Columbus, New Mexico. A little away from the town, one runs into James Johnson's farm right next to the U.S.-Mexico border. Every night, several hundred migrants used Johnson's farm to make their way into the United States from Mexico. These undocumented migrants were generally dropped a few feet from the border by a yellow school bus that they caught at the main square in Palomas, Chihuahua, across from Columbus. Like Johnson, many farmers and ranchers in New Mexico and Arizona complained continuously that the undocumented migrants tore their fences, spoiled their desert crops, and fouled their water wells. In addition, a lost sense of security woke them up in the wee hours of the morning. These complaints eventually surged into a broad movement against migrants that swept the entire state of Arizona[4] and made it increasingly difficult for migrants to cross through these ranches. Several thousand would eventually die in the desert seeking alternative routes.[5]

Driving on New Mexico's Highway 9, going west and hugging the border, I came back to the town of Columbus. The town's claim to fame is the armed invasion by Pancho Villa on March 9, 1916. The first thing that strikes any visitor to Palomas is the dust. It is very fine and clings to everything. I often wondered why anyone would want to live there—Columbus or Palomas. There is hardly anything there—although there is a very good restaurant and curio store called The Pink Store, where the food is quite good. I drove around and found numerous hotels in the rather small town—although most were really run-down or just houses turned into makeshift hotels with signs outside that read "Se rentan cuartos" (Rooms for rent). Tourism could not be the main reason for so many hotels or doss-houses. The annual memorial occasioned by Pancho Villa's "raid" on Columbus never really attracts any large crowds, but the lodging industry seemed disproportionately large. I set out to talk to the townsfolk about this mystery.

Several men standing around explained to me that Palomas has become a major crossing point for people to enter illegally into the United States. This was particularly true, said one, since they began to "put the squeeze" on the Arizona border, and the "sharpshooters" (referring to the Minutemen) began to guard the line there. While in town, these immigrants rent rooms and stay five or six to a single room, while they make contact with the "coyote" (human smuggler) who is going to lead them across the border.

The one thing common to the dozens of men waiting around in the streets and the squares of Palomas was their knapsacks. They carried the minimum, as recommended by the coyotes and those who have made the trek before. Several of these men were waiting for the yellow school bus that would drop them right up against the border, perhaps on the Johnsons' farm, or any other trek through any other farm, that night. By around the year 2000, about 1.5 million immigrants were being detained annually by the Border Patrol, although that number had been cut back to 479,000 by the year 2015—of which only 188,000 were Mexican. Strangely, the migrant flood has been stemmed in Arizona and New Mexico, but has moved to South Texas, and more than 50 percent of those apprehended today are Central Americans, not Mexicans.

But going back in time to Palomas, after talking to that group of men I saw in the street, I made my way to the main square, which was nearly as dusty as the rest of the town. There, lying on a patch of grass, was another group of men. I approached them and asked some questions. The most outspoken of the group told me that they were from Chiapas, a southernmost state in Mexico. (These days many are likely to tell you that they are from Guatemala, Honduras, or El Salvador.) They had just arrived that morning and were waiting for a "contact" to take them to the coyote, who would to charge them $2,000 each to guarantee their way to Phoenix, where they would work on a farm or in the construction industry. These men were lucky—it was relatively cheap to cross the border. That $2,000 has now turned into $7,000. More recently a Salvadoran in Silver Spring, Maryland, who had just arrived told me that the family paid $10,000 to get him across. As the U.S.-Mexico border has become more difficult to cross, the risk premium for crossing these migrants has gone up. And many coyotes simply lead them to the borderline and then let them loose to fend for themselves. Most are now caught by the Border Patrol very quickly.

Visits to the New Mexico border with old Mexico offered firsthand and early views of the political battle that was brewing over undocumented immigration in the United States. Visiting the border in 2006 was like visiting the frontlines of the coming war over immigration in America—one that is not yet over, since we have not resolved the issue of immigration. Immigration reform has in fact been a broken promise several times already over several presidents. Politicians, bureaucrats, the media, the public, the local ranchers, and farmers in California, Arizona, New Mexico, and Texas, U.S. businesses, the American consumer—everyone has a stake in undocumented migration. That we have such broad interest in resolving the issue but have not been able to do so speaks to the dysfunction of the American political system. But when talking about immigration and the border together, the issue looks pressing, chaotic, and in need of much more attention than anyone was willing to give it beyond the border at least until the summer of 2006. And that image has stuck in our head, 10 years later, even though the border is much more secure and much harder to cross, and undocumented migration, especially from Mexico, seems to have collapsed drastically.

My investigations have led me to the borderline time and time again. Ten years ago, while driving along the rugged road between Sonora and Arizona, just before Ambos Nacos I got out of the car and walked along the fence. I saw numerous water bottles, clothing, and other personal items that surely had belonged to men and women trying to make their way across the border without documents. Most striking was a pair of toothbrushes, one blue and one purple. These were scattered right along the fence, next to other items. My mind flashed to the people to whom these items belonged and I wondered who they were and even whether they "made it." On the frontlines of the war on immigration, even these small items can give us the frames to put together the puzzle that is the border.

A decade later, this flood of migrants has become a trickle of migrants. There is a huge wall built between the two countries—more than 700 miles of walls and fences; there are many more border agents stationed all along—18,000 on the U.S.-Mexico border alone; there are many more sensors and cameras and flood lights; there are many more vehicles ready to react and helicopters and now drones watching the borderline. It is nearly impossible to cross the border without being detected. Few now make it across that once porous border in the Arizona desert. Recently, I drove off Highway 9 in southern New Mexico right up against the borderline. As soon as my car stopped against the barrier, I was already surrounded by two different Border Patrol vehicles. The same thing happened in

Texas, near Los Ebanos. As soon as we approached the river, several agents were already on us. This does not mean that people do not try to cross illegally or that some do not manage to cross the border—clearly a few hundred thousand are still trying—but the chances of success are so low now that only a fraction manage to avoid getting caught and fewer and fewer are trying to cross the borderline without documents in the first place. Central Americans may now be the exception. Their numbers have been climbing for the last decade.

THE BEGINNING

The problem of undocumented immigration on the U.S.-Mexico border is relatively recent in the history of the two countries. From 1848 to 1929, Mexicans crossed the border freely. In this period, it was not illegal to cross the border without papers. It sufficed to declare one's citizenship, if there was anyone even guarding the POE. The immigration acts prior to 1929 included provisions that allowed Mexicans to cross without papers, perhaps in deference to the fact that the southwestern United States were Mexican territories and many Mexican citizens remained there after 1848 and 1853. These acts were designed to exclude people of nationalities other than Mexican—some actively targeted Asians, particularly the Chinese. But the 1929 Immigration Act made it illegal, for the first time, to cross the border from Mexico without papers. A simple declaration of citizenship no longer sufficed. This was, in some ways, a response to the economic hardship of the 1920s. With unemployment at 25 percent during the peak of the Great Depression, jobs were needed and Mexicans were perceived to be taking jobs from Americans. With this 1929 legislation, open immigration was drastically curtailed. And hostility to Mexican migrants grew as well. Hundreds of thousands of Mexicans, even many born in the United States, were in fact repatriated to Mexico in the 1930s.[7]

Slowly but surely, the United States recovered from the Great Depression during the mid to late 1930s. By the 1940s, the United States entered World War II and, with an enormous number of people occupied by the war effort, its labor needs skyrocketed. At the same time, Mexico began an aggressive program of industrial development, but its population outpaced its ability to provide jobs for all the new entrants into the labor market. This was a match made in heaven. The United States needed labor and Mexico had a surplus of it. To tap into Mexican labor, the U.S. Congress created a guest worker program known as the Bracero (literally "Arm") Program in 1943.[8] This program would bring about a somewhat privileged status for Mexican laborers. Many Mexicans who came to the United States under that program were poor peasants but also very hard workers and their labor quickly filled the gap left by the mobilization of Americans to the war effort. The Bracero Program inaugurated an exodus of economic refugees from Mexico to the United States. And although they were supposed to leave when their contracts expired, many of them would eventually settle in border towns, many of which began to see their Hispanic population explode. Many others made it to other southwestern cities, and to Chicago and eastern Washington State. The Bracero program continued until 1964. In 1956, the *El Paso-Herald Post* wrote, "More than 80,000 braceros pass through the El Paso Center annually. They're part of an army of 350,000 or more that marches across the border each year to help plant, cultivate, and harvest cotton and other crops throughout the United States."[9] Some 4 to 5 million Mexicans worked in the United States between 1943 and 1964, when the program was canceled.

On a side note, the U.S. and Mexican governments made some promises to the Bracero Program workers that they would put aside some of their funds for their retirement. Many of these old men are often seen protesting in the streets of border towns because they never received any pension monies and they do not know what happened to the taxes that were deducted from their paychecks for this purpose. The U.S. and Mexican governments do not know either what happened to these funds.[10]

With the cancellation of the Bracero Program in 1964, the state of affairs on immigration that prevailed through 2005 began. Many Mexicans could not find work in Mexico, a rapidly urbanizing society in the 1960s and 1970s, with an exploding population growth. Many came back to the border and continued to cross, this time without a guest worker visa, to work in the farms and other industries in the United States. Many succeeded in crossing a relatively open border and settling in various parts of the United States. Many others simply took their families and moved to the United States to continue to work with their previous bosses. Others made it to cities as varied as Chicago, Los Angeles, San Antonio, Houston, and Dallas. At that time, unlike today, it was easy to get a job and to live without papers in the United States. Much of this migration, however, was circular migration—workers came to the United States, worked for a period of months, and returned home to Mexico, only to come back the following year. By the early 1980s, the problem of undocumented migration reached new levels, but circular migration kept it a relatively moderate problem. By 1986, there were an estimated 4 to 5 million undocumented migrants in the United States.

Thus the current undocumented-migration "problem" on the border is about half a century old, because the cancellation of the Bracero Program forced Mexicans to attempt access to the U.S. labor market without documentation. Between 1965 and 1985, the pace of Mexican undocumented migration on the U.S.-Mexico border grew steadily albeit still slowly. Although many settled in the country, others simply came and went—in a circular migration pattern. The major debate around undocumented migration during this 20-year period focused on the idea that undocumented migrants displaced American workers because they worked "hard and scared." There is evidence of course that undocumented migrants worked in sectors where most Americans simply refused to work and at wages that most Americans would not take. The agroindustry, construction, and services industries benefited enormously from this labor.

THE BREAKING POINT: 1986

By 1986, the problem of undocumented migrants was picking up political steam in the United States. It was part of the presidential debates of 1980 and 1984. By 1986, Congress passed the Immigration Reform and Control Act, granting amnesty to nearly 3 million undocumented migrants, many of them Mexicans. The act would regularize the situation of those already in the United States and put them on a path to citizenship, increase border patrolling to prevent more workers from coming in, and penalize employers who hired undocumented workers to the tune of $10,000 per worker. The combination of these three would, in the eyes of Congress, solve the problem of undocumented migration across the U.S.-Mexico border.

But the 1986 act did no more than focus on the problem of undocumented migration as a border problem. It did nothing to solve the issue of migration between Mexico and the United States beyond reinforcing patrols along the border, mostly because it never acknowledged the quiet labor integration that had been going on for decades, since the 1940s, and did not seek ways to institutionalize the inevitable labor market forces that still push for labor integration. The first sign of this border reinforcement was more boots on the ground. From 1986 to 2006, the Border Patrol grew from 2,000 to about 12,200 agents and its budget expanded from $200 million to $1.213 billion This trend has not let up. Ten years later, in 2016, the Border Patrol has more than 20,000 agents and a budget of some $3.5 billion a year. Most of these agents (about 18,000) guard the 2,000-mile U.S.-Mexico border. The rest guard the Canadian border and other POEs. The Border Patrol today, with all its staff and resources, represents where American immigration controls have gone wrong.

Interestingly, the Border Patrol is today more a symbol of a broken border than even the undocumented migrants. The Border Patrol has been given enormous power, with very little accountability.[11] The agency is today a victim of its own success, and the sign of bureaucratic imperialism now affects all aspects of the agency. As recently as September 2015, the National Border Patrol Council president, Brandon Judd, said that they needed another 5,000 agents.[12] He continued to portray the border as a very dangerous place, even as border cities and counties remain some of the safest in the country, including El Paso, Texas, and San Diego, California,[13] and the number of detentions has collapsed by more than 60 percent from their peak in the year 2000.[14] Most of the violence is on the Mexican side of the border—and it cannot be downplayed—but the Border Patrol refuses to be accountable for its own infractions. A recent report published by the American Immigration Council argues that Border Patrol abuses of migrants, including physical and sexual abuse, have risen, with hardly any action taken against abusers.[15] The agency has also bucked the national trend for police to wear body cameras in order to better investigate incident complaints. Several members of Congress have also acknowledged that the Border Patrol plays by its own rules. This is unfortunate, as accountability is probably good for both migrants as well as the Border Patrol itself. And most Americans would not tolerate from their own police agencies the kind of abuse that goes on at the border.

By 1986, undocumented immigration from Mexico was conceived as a border law enforcement problem rather than a general labor policy problem—a definition that would have implied economic and labor market solutions to cross-border human mobility rather than more boots on the ground. Thus the United States made the Border Patrol a new "army" in its new war on undocumented migration, and the agency fully engaged in a logic of escalation, much like with the war on drugs. As some critics of bureaucratic imperialism have said, there is no agency that ever says that the problem it was created to solve is over or that it has had enough resources to do so. It was also in the 1980s that the U.S. Congress forced the military to aid the Border Patrol in guarding the border. A reluctant military conducted various operations along the border with relatively little success beyond what the Border Patrol could effectively do by itself. Thus the U.S. government's war on undocumented immigration was based on a logic consisting of throwing more people, more resources, and more vehicles, and now more planes, helicopters, high-tech gadgets, and drones at the problem. This has created dire conditions for migrants at the border. Deaths have skyrocketed; human rights abuses have increased; and poverty is on the rise. Most efforts against undocumented immigrants centered on the international borderline rather than in the major metropolitan areas where undocumented immigrants lived and worked. They focused on the undocumented workers rather than on those who employed them. They focused on the problem of law enforcement on the U.S.-Mexico border rather than on the issues of increasing economic integration in North America. There is as of yet no stomach in Washington, DC, to acknowledge that there is a quiet economic integration that involves labor flows, not just commerce in goods and services and financial movements.

This law enforcement bent on the problem of immigration had two important consequences. First, among undocumented workers, it is well known that the most serious danger is on the border. Once they make it to Chicago, Denver, or Atlanta, they are relatively safe—although less and less so as living without documents in the United States is becoming more difficult. Still, once in the United States, it is likely that no one will go after them. This situation also benefits U.S. employers, who profit from relatively inexpensive and flexible labor, although this too has been changing as of late, as the Border Patrol and U.S. Immigration and Customs Enforcement have staged major raids throughout the United States to expel migrants who have been here for a long time. In fact, most migrants now live in outright fear due to the uncertainty of their situation. They never know when they are going to be detected and deported. These raids have in fact been very effective from a law enforcement perspective. According to the Pew Hispanic Center, the number of undocumented residents has actually gone down under the Obama administration, from 12.8 million in 2009 to 11.2 million in 2015—a dramatic drop considering that undocumented migrants continue to cross, albeit in much smaller numbers.[16] Second, increasingly strict law enforcement on the border has discouraged many undocumented immigrants from returning to Mexico. Instead, they prefer to stay put in the cities, thereby increasing pressure on many local governments around the country and causing a political firestorm.[17] The huge anti-immigration sentiments in Arizona, Alabama, Pennsylvania, and other states, all of whom passed very hostile legislation and ordinances against undocumented residents, were largely fueled by the burden on local governments, which have to provide services to these migrants. SB1070 in Arizona was one of the most punitive bills, authorizing local police forces to detain any individual who could not at the moment provide proof of legal residency or citizenship. This effectively turned police and sheriff departments into immigration law enforcers. This made it very difficult to live in the United States without documents, to obtain jobs, and to circulate without fear in many cities and towns. And although there has been a slowdown in these hostile efforts against migrants, the status of longtime undocumented residents has not been resolved and their presence continues to fuel very acrimonious positions against immigration to this day.

Law enforcement, rather than smart immigration policies, has been the default position. This is fueled by a political gridlock in Washington, DC, which has made it impossible to pass immigration reform. The 2007 and 2014 efforts to pass an immigration bill failed, largely because there was little willingness to negotiate an agreement between the two parties.

They were really not far apart; but in Washington, DC, any small gap between the two parties is magnified into a major disagreement and positions are hardened to the point of gridlock.

A FAILED LOGIC FOR A FAILED WAR

The U.S. government, with all its Border Patrol agents, its drones, planes, and helicopters, its trucks and jeeps, its fancy night-vision goggles and flood lights, its underground sensors, and all its operations on the nearly 2,000-mile U.S.-Mexico border, has made no inroads into the problem. This is not to say that undocumented migration has not stalled—it has; or to say that the flood of undocumented migrants has not slowed—it has. This is really about discerning how much the Border Patrol and law enforcement has made a difference and how much the economic conditions themselves have taken care of the problem. Congress continues to trust that its law enforcement strategies on undocumented immigration from Mexico works and it has given the Border Patrol nearly everything it has asked for. Yet there is plenty of evidence that shows that the 2008 financial crisis, during which many of the economic sectors in which millions of undocumented residents work, including construction, agriculture, and the service sector, collapsed and lost a disproportionate number of jobs. The first to be let go, of course, were undocumented migrants. Thus, although law enforcement is probably part of the equation, as the border is more secure than ever despite all the rhetoric to the contrary, it is very likely that the pull factors, such as the dynamism of the American economy or lack thereof, have also affected the willingness of many migrants to make the trek north if there are simply no jobs to be had. This hypothesis will be tested as the U.S. economy makes a full recovery in the next few years and so-called pull forces increase. If so, however, the border may become quite a difficult place given that law enforcement has increased so dramatically, organized crime is increasingly brutal in its tactics, and migrants will be pressured to continue advancing. A crisis looms if we do not solve this issue soon through comprehensive immigration reform.

Curiously enough, Congress continues to call for repeats of the strategies already in place—just more of the same, even though most of the evidence shows that we are missing an important opportunity to overhaul the immigration system. There are calls on Capitol Hill to strengthen the Border Patrol with more agents, to increase its budget by hundreds of millions of dollars every year, and to introduce new high-tech gadgets to "guard" the border. The strategy of the Border Patrol today, according to its own documents, is to stop terrorists attempting to cross between POEs, to stop illegal entries through improved enforcement at the border, and to detect anyone smuggling drugs, humans, and other contraband.[18] In other words, instead of looking at the immigration issue as a comprehensive policy issue occasioned by globalization and North American integration forces, the U.S. Border Patrol insists on looking at it exclusively as a narrow law enforcement issue, focused on the border, and as an action against undocumented migrants and their smugglers. However, the statistics show that the number of undocumented workers in the United States has stabilized and even decreased. The numbers have dipped to about 11 million and the border is much more secure, so it is very likely that we are now catching upwards of 80 percent or more of all those who attempt to cross—479,000 in 2015. Fewer and fewer undocumented workers make it into the country every year. Not to fix the immigration system along the lines of orderly and legal labor market integration would be a mistake, as the issue of undocumented border crossers could grow again if the U.S. economy does well and the conditions in Central America and elsewhere continue to deteriorate.

THE BALLOON EFFECT

In considering my next point regarding the war on undocumented migration, my mind returns to my visit in Columbus and Palomas. Back in 2006, walking across the dusty town of Palomas, two things struck me immediately. The first one I mentioned already—the number of hotels and the number of "Rooms for rent" signs everywhere. Palomas is a small town. Who could possibly need so many hotel rooms? Second, there was the large number of idle men hanging around the Main Square and surrounding streets. They were obviously not local men. Most carried a knapsack with them. I approached another group of them, lying on the grass, and struck up a conversation with them. They were very reluctant to talk to me at first. But after a while, I managed to gain their trust and they opened up. Their honesty about what they were seeking surprised me. Bulmaro, the most outspoken of them, told me that all five of them came from the same town in Oaxaca. They were heading to Denver where jobs in the construction industry were waiting for them. They were patiently waiting for the border runner who would take them to Las Chepas, a dusty, mostly abandoned town 20 miles west of Columbus, New Mexico, where they would make the run into the United States walking long hours in the wilderness. A yellow school bus, whose driver refused to talk to me, would take them to Las Chepas. Eventually, someone would pick them up on the other side, well into the United States, and smuggle them to Denver. The undocumented-worker smuggling rings are well developed and there are certain routes and routines in place to convey humans across the border and into the United States. These smuggling rings are now veritable international criminal organizations, with their own networks of contacts on both sides of the border and with their flexible systems for transporting undocumented workers, sometimes from the worker's hometown all the way to a major metropolitan area in the United States. Their operations around the New Mexico-Chihuahua border had increased, particularly since the U.S. government "put the squeeze" on undocumented migration through Arizona. Undocumented migration in Arizona had increased, of course, since the squeeze was put on the California border with Mexico.

Today, a more common story would be that of a Central American family making the choice to send their child or teenager north, on a dangerous trek, and have them present themselves to a U.S. border agent and ask for asylum in the hope that they would be reunited with some relative already living in the United States while their case is resolved in an immigration court. This is what caused the unaccompanied minor crisis of the summer of 2014. Tens of thousands of unaccompanied minors continue to travel to the U.S. border to this day.[19]

Over the last decade, the U.S. government has built a massive wall, extending through much of California, Arizona, and New Mexico and even some parts of Texas. Driving east from El Paso, Texas, I took hundreds of pictures of the wall extending down the Rio Grande, at times resembling a fence and other times an intimidating metal mesh wall, always watched by Border Patrol agents on either side of it. Though not completely a deterrent, the wall together with the high-tech gadget deployment and the added monitoring by agents have channeled much of the undocumented migration flows to other places. And that is still the case. Whereas Arizona bore the brunt of illegal migration around 2005, 10 years later South Texas has become the favorite place, largely because it is nearly impossible to build a wall there. Thus, instead of dying in the Arizona desert, migrants are now drowning in the Rio Grande. This undocumented-migration flow redirection is clearly what we call the balloon effect. People will not stop coming altogether just because the border has become a tough place and difficult to cross. People will simply seek new routes. What is worse, criminal organizations that profit handsomely from illegal migration will also seek new routes and new expertise on dodging the border obstacles, and of course they will charge more and more for leading migrants to the border and across.

The 2014 unaccompanied-minors crisis in South Texas is one example of the balloon effect. During the summer of that year, there was a considerable spike in the number of children who came right up to the border and, instead of trying to cross illegally, presented themselves to the

Border Patrol and asked for asylum. These children were sent by their parents in hopes that they would make it to the United States and benefit from President Obama's Deferred Action for Childhood Arrivals (DACA), an executive order that gave undocumented residents who were brought to the United States as children respite from deportation. Many in Central America interpreted this as a kind of amnesty for children and sent their kids with coyotes to the U.S.-Mexico border. The numbers went from roughly 25,000 in FY2013 to more than 65,000 in FY2014, most of them in the Rio Grande Valley sector of the Border Patrol. As it became more difficult to send children to the other sectors, by now heavily fortified, South Texas, the remaining sector difficult to guard, was overwhelmed. This unaccompanied-minors crisis roiled the American immigration system and public opinion. Eventually, the U.S. government took several actions to stem this tide. First, they began a campaign in Central American to "warn" potential immigrants of the danger of making the trek north. Second, they cajoled the Mexican government to establish a program to begin to close its southern border with Guatemala—this came to be known as Programa Frontera Sur and it has had many negative consequences on migrants. This program makes it difficult for Central American migrants to cross, exposes them to extortion not only by criminals but also by Mexican immigration and police agents, and forces them to seek new routes through the country, in what is really another instance of the balloon effect. But what the Programa Frontera Sur has not done is stop Central American migrants from moving north. There is in fact wide agreement that all this program does is fuel the violence on migrants.[20] The narrow law enforcement focus on immigration at the border by the U.S. government has perhaps slowed down the flow of undocumented workers, but we will not know this until the U.S. economy recovers and there is renewed interest in their cheap, disposable labor. Undocumented workers will likely keep coming in greater numbers, taking greater risks. What the various U.S. law enforcement operations on the border have done is simply push undocumented migrants from one place along the border to the next and from one route in Mexico to the other. It has also increased their vulnerability, making them more susceptible to rape, theft, assault, and extortion. Many will never complain and we will never know the magnitude of the problem. In 2005, U.S. agents made 1.5 million arrests at the border, in more and more isolated areas, away from the well-guarded urban centers along the border. In effect, the squeeze on undocumented immigration at major cities and towns pushed the crossing routes into the dangerous desert.[21] Today, it has pushed them into the dangerous waters of the Rio Grande. This has brought about some ghastly consequences.

THE DEAD

The war on undocumented migration on the border is producing an increasing number of casualties. As the U.S. government has escalated its efforts against undocumented migration at the border and as Mexico's corrupt officials prey on Central American migrants, the men and women, and increasingly children, who want to make it to the United States take greater and greater risks on their lives by trying to cross, first through the hostile deserts of Arizona and New Mexico and more recently through the dangerous waters of the Rio Grande Valley in Texas. The hostility toward migrants is causing more and more undocumented migrants to perish, as they lose their desperate gamble to make it into the United States under the very harsh conditions. In 2004, according to the Border Patrol, 464 undocumented workers perished in the Arizona desert. A more comprehensive recent report by the International Organization for Migration shows that more than 6,000 migrants, at least, have perished trying to cross the border since the year 2000.[22] The number of disappeared is simply hard to calculate.

Back in the mid-2000s, the Pima County Medical Examiner's Office, in Arizona, received the bodies of hundreds of undocumented migrants who lost their own war against the desert to make it into the United States. The bodies were kept in the morgue for a certain period of time. If no one claimed the body, the medical examiner sent it to be buried, but kept a small sample of the bones in order to conduct DNA tests if someone ever came to claim the person. In fact, a man from Hidalgo came looking for his sister once. He gave a specific description of her to the medical examiner. The description matched the characteristics of a body found just a week before. The Mexican consulate paid for transporting her body back to her hometown so that at least this one young woman came to rest closer to her family.A more recent report shows that as the flow of migrants has moved from Arizona and New Mexico to South Texas, the number of deaths in that sector has gone up. Hundreds of migrants have perished in the Rio Grande or walking very long distances, lost in the wilderness in the South Texas terrain. The numbers now reach several hundred, beginning in 2012 and into 2016.[23] Very often, migrant remains recovered are disposed of in mass graves in South Texas, sometimes buried by the Border Patrol and the Rangers, without any reports. In the summer of 2013, a team of experts from Baylor University and the University of Indianapolis found the skeletal remains of hundreds of migrants in Falfurrias, Texas. The mass graves were not marked, and the Texas Rangers simply said that no laws were broken in disposing of the bodies without making any effort to identify them.[24]

The stories of the casualties of the war on undocumented migrants on the border can be found all along the border from the Pacific to the Gulf of Mexico as the number of undocumented workers perishing in the desert, the dangerous mountains of the Southwest, and the Rio Grande has increased to several hundred a year. In the town of Holtville, California, lies a cemetery where about 150 undocumented workers are buried. Their tombstones line a patch of land and read only "No Olvidado" (Not Forgotten). Sacred Heart Cemetery in Brooks County, Texas, is another example. Such tombstones now dot the border counties of the Southwest and are a clear sign that stricter enforcement has slowed down but not stopped the flow of undocumented workers. It has only made it more dangerous to cross, costing thousands of lives in addition to billions of dollars in enforcement. Another casualty is of course human rights and due process rights. The balloon effect is at work. The squeeze in California pushed the flow to Arizona and New Mexico, and the more hostile conditions of the Southwest deserts only cause more people to perish. And the push to seal the Arizona segment of the border has only pushed migrants to Texas, with similar consequences. Where will the flow go next?

BUILD IT AND THEY WILL COME

The border is a paradoxical place. It is at once a place of opportunity and hope but also of suffering and entrapment. It is a place of wealth and poverty. It is a place of freedom and violence. And it is the opportunities it offers, the wealth it possesses, and the freedom it provides that have attracted millions of immigrants from all over Mexico to its border. The past three decades have witnessed fast population and economic growth in northern Mexico. The combined population of the U.S. and Mexico border counties and *municipios* (the Mexican equivalent of "county") is 15 million residents. The border acted as a magnet and for decades had some of the fastest-growing counties and cities in the United States and in Mexico. The total projected combined population could grow to more than 23 million by the year 2030—although the violence and lack of rule of law has slowed down the growth of the border population in recent years. The border, however, will continue to grow and the majority of this growth will be people of Mexican descent. (To some Mexicans, the Mexicanization of the border is part of the "reconquista" or reconquest of the Southwest—to which many Mexicans feel a sense of connectedness.[25] But the images of the border that today dominate the U.S. media are the stories of entrapment, poverty, and violence—and that may be having a negative effect on the attractiveness of the border. With this terrible image of the border, it is a puzzle that so many people still want to come to there. Why do they see opportunity, wealth, and freedom where the rest of America (and even many Mexicans) sees entrapment, poverty, and violence? This is a puzzle that needs explanation. And history may

be giving an answer to this question: central Mexico now enjoys phenomenal growth, both economic and demographic, while Mexico's north has
buckled under a wave of violence, poverty, corruption, and waning
opportunities.

THE BACKSIDE OF ECONOMIC DEVELOPMENT

The growth of the border to its current and projected dimensions, in
spite of its troubles, was caused largely by a fundamental shift in the
Mexican economic orientation that began with the establishment of a virtually free-trade border zone in the 1970s. U.S. manufacturers were able to
settle just across the border to take advantage of cheap Mexican labor,
bringing their own supply materials free of import duties into Mexico
and then returning them as finished goods to the United States. These
plants came to be known as "maquiladoras," which to this day dot the
entire border on the Mexican side and have expanded to all of Mexico
since NAFTA went into effect in 1994. The maquiladora program stimu-
lated rapid population growth along the Mexican side of the border.
The population in cities like Tijuana, Ciudad Juárez, and those by the
Rio Grande Valley (Matamoros, Reynosa, and Nuevo Laredo) grew exponentially because the jobs generated by the maquiladora industry
attracted hundreds of thousands of people to them. Ciudad Juárez, for
example, went from 425,000 people in 1980 to 1.3 million in 2000. Tijuana
went from 460,000 in 1980 to 1.2 million in 2000. This rapid growth did not
permit local and state governments to keep up with the infrastructure
needed to sustain those levels of population growth. This eventually
would give the Mexican side of the border its chaotic, underdeveloped
look and would cause the creation of *colonias*, some of them veritable
shantytowns. The growth of some Texas border counties, particularly in
the lower valley of Texas, was similarly fast and nearly equally chaotic,
causing some of these shantytowns to spring up along the Texas side of
the border as well. It would surprise many a visitor to the border to see
so many of these *colonias* without basic services, such as running water,
sewage, garbage collection, or paved streets in the Texas counties abutting
Mexico.[26] Arizona and New Mexico have similar conditions in various
border counties.[27]

For many of these workers coming from the interior of Mexico to the
border, it also became a goal to cross over into the United States where
they knew wages and the quality of life were considerably much better
than even in the better-off Mexican border towns where there were jobs
to be had.

In fact, whereas the Bracero Program was composed of mostly poor,
hardworking peasants being pushed off the land by Mexico's rapid

industrialization and urbanization, undocumented migration to the United States during this period of rapid growth (1970–2005) was increasingly composed of the urban poor, leaving behind the economic and social stress of the rapidly expanding Mexican cities. Much has changed since 2005. A recently published Pew Hispanic Center poll found that this desire to migrate north has not waned, but the clarity of the opportunities that lie in both northern Mexico and across the border in the United States is not as crystal clear as it used to be. Of course, still half of all Mexicans would leave Mexico today for the United States if they could,[28] but many are now afraid of both the dangers of the border as well as living in the United States without papers in an increasingly hostile environment. The proof is in the demographics. Since 2005, Ciudad Juárez has not grown and still has 1.3 million people as of 2015. Tijuana has barely grown, and now counts 1.4 million people—quite slow compared to its past fast growth. And other cities along the border have also stagnated and are now crumbling under the weight of their own violence and crime, with little if any escape north. Many have simply opted to move south. Several young men I met in Ciudad Juárez—Eduardo, Alejandro, Fernando, and José, all of them no older than 30 years of age—have chosen to go to Guadalajara and Mexico City, acknowledging that the border has nothing desirable to offer. This exodus is now evident in nearly every state of the Mexico side of the border. Even U.S. cities, with the exception of San Diego, have failed to attract talent. Some of them, like El Paso, Nogales, Brownsville, and McAllen, export natives to other cities from Los Angeles to Phoenix to Dallas, San Antonio, and Houston. The opportunities for youth along the border are simply too low. Over half of my former students at the University of Texas at El Paso now live elsewhere. It is revealing that the best-paid jobs on the border are often associated with law enforcement and the military.

AGAIN: IT'S ECONOMICS, STUPID!

Mexican migration to both Northern Mexico and the United States is almost entirely motivated by economics, although not exclusively. Mexicans, like nationals of other countries, move mostly in search of economic improvement. Inside Mexico, one can detect a push force. But there is also, within the United States, a pull force. Together, these push and pull forces motivate hundreds of thousands to move toward the border every year. On the push side, undocumented workers leave Mexico, in part pushed out by the depressed economic conditions of certain areas. On this, it is worth keeping in mind that Mexico creates just over half a million jobs a year, but more than 1 million of its young people enter the job market every year. More recently, a new debate has ensued on Central

American migration and push forces—which has now surpassed Mexican migration to the United States.[29] Many argue that migration from the northern triangle of Central America is also largely motivated by the economic conditions and the lack of opportunity. Others argue that the exodus is largely due to the public safety and security crisis that today affects those countries. Speaking with a Jesuit friend of mine who is well versed in the conditions of Guatemala, Honduras, and El Salvador, during a conference in San Salvador on the same issue, he told me that it was economic conditions that were pushing people out. Over the course of the conference in September 2015, it became clear that most migrants could adjust to the lack of security, but they could not adjust to the inability to feed their families. If we fail to examine the real push factors and create public policies to deal with them, we will fail to stem the flow of migrants and perpetuate a migration crisis that affects us all in Central America, Mexico, and the United States.

For years, there was also some evidence that Mexican undocumented migration had a lot more to do with the labor market conditions in the United States than with unemployment in Mexico—that is, the pull force.[30] An enormous number of undocumented workers are still pulled to the United States by their own migrant networks already existing in U.S. cities—although fewer and fewer make it as their labor markets contract. The construction sector in the United States, for example, collapsed after 2007, and jobs became scarcer. Workers already in the United States used to inform people in their hometowns in Mexico (and increasingly, other countries) that there were jobs waiting for them. Those already here received the new migrants and got them jobs in the industries where they worked. This network theory of migration has been relatively well studied by sociologists and anthropologists. Because of these networks, some workers even left their existing jobs in Mexico—it was not only the unemployed who migrated—and followed their networks in the United States. Thus, although there are criminals that migrate, the overwhelming majority of undocumented border crossers were economic refugees or economic migrants—and they still are, providing researchers with an amazing constant. Interestingly, the U.S. labor market seemed to be able to absorb somewhere between 300,000 and 400,000 undocumented workers every year before the 2008 financial crisis. A study in *The Economist* showed that the U.S. market continued to have a shortage of labor in spite of that additional labor from undocumented migrants. There were, the magazine argued, some 161 million employments in the United States and only about 156 million workers. The capacity of the U.S. economy to absorb large numbers of economic migrants, documented or undocumented, remained formidable. And the border is where all these forces came to a head. Every day, bus terminals in Mexican towns all along the border received busloads of men, women, and some children who were willing to risk life and limb to make a run into the United States for the sake of economic progress. Standing in any bus terminal in Nogales or Agua Prieta, I could easily identify these migrants because they carried little and knew even less about the perils of the border towns they came to on their way to the United States. They often looked disoriented and sometimes scared. Many refused to talk to me, nearly always a sure sign of distrust and fear of exploitation.

The financial crisis of 2008 brought all this to a halt. The U.S. labor market hemorrhaged jobs at an unprecedented pace. Unemployment would eventually reach nearly 10 percent of the labor force. As of 2016, the U.S. economy has not yet recovered. As jobs were lost, undocumented migrants were often the first to go, particularly because they occupied positions in industries highly sensitive to economic crisis—construction and services such as garden care, the prepared-food industry, etc. The number of migrants seen in the parking lots of stores in places like Phoenix, selling their labor for a day and a few dollars, increased, causing further moral panic in the American public, which began to pressure its politicians to do something about it. The environment became very hostile. In some places, such as Arizona, it even sparked vigilantism, and some heavily armed groups went to camp along the U.S.-Mexico border, arguing both that the U.S. government had failed and that border towns and cities were being overrun by what they saw as hordes of individuals trying to cross into the United States.[31] This made the situation of migrants so hostile that many chose to move to other states, less unwelcoming than Arizona.

What is clear today is that we have failed to take advantage of a lull in the flow of undocumented migrants to the United States to pass immigration reform—dealing with those who have already been in the United States for years and even decades and providing for a broader and more efficient flow of labor between the United States and Mexico, and perhaps Canada, so as to create over time a single labor market or at least a better integrated one. What is sometimes surprising here is that the U.S. government often promotes free-trade agreements and aggressive moves to globalize the economy—Republicans appear to be all in favor of it— but often refuse to deal with the consequences of trade promotion and globalization, such as displaced labor, integrated labor markets, and the human ability to find opportunities and go after them—Republicans appear to be all against it, although Democrats do not seem to have a much better record on the issue.

THE LEGAL SIDE

But Mexican immigrants to the United States are not just undocumented immigrants. There are also many legal immigrants who come from Mexico every year. American consulate employees in Ciudad Juárez process tens of thousands of permanent resident cards for Mexicans to move to the United States. Some 10 years ago, a student of mine who worked in that consulate, at that time the only green card processing center for Mexicans, told me that in 2006 they granted some 260,000 legal residencies a year; the numbers have since become about half of that.[32] The history of the United States shows that the motivations for allowing immigrants into the country have changed over time. In the latter part of the twentieth century, family reunification and skills became the primary and secondary criteria for allowing new legal immigrants to enter the United States. Family reunification is crucial to understanding Mexican legal migration not only to the United States but also to the border counties. A quick but representative count of the reasons why Mexican legal entrants into the United States come is family reunification, although increasingly entrants come in because of their professional or technical skills.[33] Cross-border social life also makes up an important component of Mexican legal migration. Many U.S. citizens marry Mexican citizens who eventually come to live with their spouses in the United States, many of them in border counties. These cross-border intimate networks are largely responsible for much of the growth of the Hispanic population in U.S. towns and cities along the border. The percentage of foreign-born residents in border counties is extraordinarily high due partly to these familial ties. Unless family reunification ceases to be a criterion in judging who enters the country, Mexican legal migration will continue at a healthy pace given that many Mexicans in the United States have family in Mexico. Between 1985 and 2010, some 5.5 million Mexicans migrated legally to the United States.

The flow of goods and people across the border, except for a very brief hiatus during the days following September 11, kept growing through 2005; then slowed down after 2007, but has picked up since. Approximately 41 million pedestrians crossed the U.S.-Mexico border in 2014, as well as 70 million vehicles, 5.5 million trucks, 10,000 trains with goods and passengers, and 214,000 buses with nearly 3 million passengers at POEs.[34] Mexicans buy billions of dollars of goods every year and sustain tens of thousands of U.S. businesses all along the border. These crossers return home to Mexico every day as well. The border thrives with this flux of tourists, shoppers, workers, and other daily crossers. And all of these are legal border crossers. Compared with the roughly 250,000 detentions of Mexicans trying to cross the border illegally that the Border Patrol reported in 2015, the problem of illegal immigration is negligible today, in spite of what the rhetoric may imply or what the Border Patrol may report. The proportion of those adhering to the law is many times greater than those trying to cross the border without documents. And yet, in the eyes of the media and the public, it is that small minority that gives the border its image of lawlessness and chaos.

MEXICO'S LOSS

More recently, there has been another trend that has affected not only the U.S.-Mexico border but all of Mexico and the United States. The number of Mexicans who are highly educated, are extremely skilled, or are entrepreneurs has increased enormously. After 2007 and through today, there is an exodus of Mexicans to the United States, most of them fleeing the underwhelming economic development conditions within Mexico and the worsening public safety and security situation. Many of them bring with them their families and their resources. A recent study showed that some of the reasons for this new class of migrants' flight are lack of credit to open and expand businesses, red tape, excessive taxation with few and bad government services in exchange, and lack of public safety and security.[35]

This migration is of course the kind of migration that the United States has always sought. But it is bad news for Mexico. Too many of its brightest and entrepreneurial minds are leaving the country, probably setting Mexico's development back, as human capital is an indispensable input for any country's economic, social, and political development.

MOTHERS AND THEIR BABIES

Alejandro was a student of mine in the mid-2000s. He spent his childhood in Ciudad Juárez and some years in the seminary, studying to be a priest for the Diocese of Ciudad Juárez. Alejandro left the seminary and moved to El Paso to attend UTEP. Alejandro was learning English as fast as he could when I met him, even as he was trying to study the subject matter of his core classes. Fortunately for Alejandro, the university offered introductory sessions of several of its classes in Spanish and he could eat away at the curriculum, even as he tried to become proficient in English. Alejandro is a U.S. citizen. He was born in El Paso, even though his parents are Mexican and still live in Ciudad Juárez. Alejandro is not a unique case.

Alejandro is an example of another form of legal-migration phenomenon, largely hidden but increasingly controversial, in border counties. Many Mexican mothers prefer to come across the border to have their children born on U.S. soil and ensure them access to the "American dream." Many Mexican women take advantage of this unique opportunity to give their children the gift of dual citizenship. Universities along the Texas border, including my own, UTEP, for example, have a considerable number of students who are Mexican in their cultural makeup and grew up in Mexico, but carry a U.S. passport by virtue of the fact that they were born in U.S. border towns. Few studies have been made of this phenomenon, but it is clear that Mexican mothers are increasingly taking advantage of this to ensure access to a "better future" through dual citizenship.

All along the border, hospitals and maternity houses aid this process by offering deals and plans to Mexican mothers who can pay the birth services fees in installments throughout their nine-month pregnancy period. Although this was a service mostly used by upper-middle- and upper-class families in the past, increasingly this opportunity is being taken advantage of by lower classes as well. As recently as two years ago, an assistant of mine at the Autonomous University of Ciudad Juárez went to New Mexico in the last two months of her pregnancy and stayed until her baby was born. For hospitals and maternity houses, these are business opportunities to make hundreds of thousands of dollars. For Mexican mothers, this is a way of ensuring access to the United States for their children.

This is becoming more controversial now. There is a whole new debate about "anchor babies," a pejorative term used to define these newborns, who are often thought to be the way their parents intend to migrate to the United States eventually. Of course, almost two decades will go by before any of these young U.S. citizens can even attempt to claim their parents, but the fact that people are taking advantage of birthright citizenship is irking many conservatives in the United States. It has certainly been an important component of the presidential debate in 2016. Moreover, it has brought many to question the meaning of the Fourteenth Amendment of the U.S. Constitution. One presidential candidate in 2016 has even argued for ending birthright citizenship, effectively repealing the Fourteenth Amendment.[36] This is not likely to happen, and the border will continue to produce many U.S. citizens; but the issue will continue to be controversial—as controversial as it is relatively easy to cross the border and give one's children citizenship by birth.

Finally, to be fair, Mexicans are not the only ones that are doing this. It has become increasingly common for both Asians and Middle Easterners to use this strategy to make their children U.S. citizens. Many mothers travel to the United States during the months of their pregnancies and stay until their child is born on U.S. soil. Chinese birth tourism, for example, is booming, but the focus of the debate is almost exclusively on Latin Americans.[37]

HOW THEY COME

On March 13, 2005, the *New York Times* reported a harrowing story. A truck driver, Tyrone M. Williams, was carrying a cargo of 74 illegal immigrants hidden in the box of his 18-wheeler. Unable to breathe, 19 of them died before Mr. Williams abandoned the truck in Victoria, Texas. He was paid a flat $7,500 fee for that fated trip. Two weeks earlier,

Mr. Williams had carried another human cargo of 60 undocumented migrants to Houston.[38] Stories like this are, unfortunately, all too common on the U.S.-Mexico border. Hundreds of undocumented workers have lost their risky gamble to make it to the United States and died in the river, the desert, or caught in train cars or cargo trucks in the deadly heat of the Southwest summers. It is still hard to believe that such inhumanities happen on the soil of what is presumably the most advanced nation in the world. And yet they do happen and are still happening.

Reading this story, my mind zoomed into that 18-wheeler cargo box and went through the faces of each man, woman, and child, lethargic and fading out, unable to hold on to their lives. The questions that came to me were: Who are they? Who comes? Why do they come? Why would they risk their lives like that? What do they want? What are the routes they follow? What are the contacts that help them cross? How much do they pay? These are the questions that, as simple as they may be, can shed light on the problem of undocumented migration on the border.

More recently, we know that tens of thousands of undocumented migrants, particularly women, children, and entire families, are being transported through Mexico and then driven right up to the borderline. They are instructed to run to Border Patrol agents and present themselves, asking for asylum. The reality is that few are truly granted asylum in the United States—upwards of 80 to 85 percent of them will eventually be deported, as a lawyer for Catholic Charities told me recently—but at least for a while they can enter the United States and escape the horrid economic and public safety conditions in their countries. Additionally, according to this same lawyer, some of them are given a date to appear in court but choose to skip it altogether and instead get lost in the population at large, enlarging the ranks of undocumented residents. Given stories like this, it would appear that it is nearly impossible to truly control the flow of undocumented migrants.

THE OVERSTAYS

Another issue that has been detected in the United States is the so-called overstays. These are people who are granted a visa and a permit to come and visit the United States. Once inside the country, they simply throw away the permit and settle wherever they went. We do not really know how many overstays there are, but it is possible to guess it fairly accurately by calculating the number of I-94s (permits) that are granted against those that are returned, especially because every person that receives an I-94 card must return it upon exiting the United States.[39] Of course, not returning an I-94 on time may exclude a border crosser from eligibility to reenter the United States, but many are less concerned with that than with the opportunity to come and stay in the United States.

There are few ways to solve this problem. The United States has moved to install an "exit" program, but it has not yet completed it and will likely need enormous resources, as a whole another army of law enforcement agents will be required to find the overstays and capture them for deportation. That just seems prohibitive in terms of both civil liberties and an already overburdened law enforcement budget.

THE OLD CROSSERS: HOW TIMES CHANGES

In the 1980s, when I used to travel to El Paso, Texas, as a teenager to visit relatives, the sight of tire inner tubes floating on the Rio Grande carrying undocumented border crossers was quite common. Almost anyone could make a run for it and be in the United States in no time. Hapless Border Patrol agents would randomly chase one or another person on fields along the Rio Grande or on the downtown streets of El Paso on the suspicion that they had crossed the borderline illegally. Often they would be right, because most undocumented border crossers used the major urban centers in Texas and California to come across the border. Most of them wanted work. Cities like Tijuana and Ciudad Juárez were growing fast and received hundreds of thousands of Mexicans from all over. Not every one of them could have a job. Conveniently, many of the undocumented border crossers were afforded the opportunity to come across as day laborers, return to Mexico at night, and come back the same way the next day. Some of these daily undocumented border crossers were agricultural workers, others were women who worked as maids and babysitters, and others were construction workers, repairmen, gardeners, and mechanics. All of them would come and go nearly as they pleased across the border. The moving force? Economics.

It was simple economics: they needed a job. The border was, for all practical purposes, a wide-open border, and the U.S. labor market craved the cheap labor undocumented border crossers provided. This breed of daily crossers who used the urban centers of the border to come across for daily employment is now pretty much extinct. As the U.S. government gradually closed the border around these urban centers, undocumented border crossers were forced to ever more rural, more hostile areas, often risking their lives. And many, once they crossed, stayed permanently because the risks of coming and going were increased considerably. Hardly anyone today crosses at urban centers illegally, although some do it legally and still perform some clandestine work as maids, yard and lawn workers, day laborers, etc. Still, it was the closing of the border that had an unforeseen effect: as the United States made it difficult to cross the border illegally, many more who actually made it ended up staying and inflating the population of undocumented within the United States. Ending this circular migration phenomenon that had been part of the border had as a consequence the swelling of undocumented migrants who were now trapped inside the country. This is what made the undocumented-resident population go from some 5 million in 1986 to over 12 million by 2006, of which 6.7 million were Mexicans and the rest of various other nationalities.[40]

In addition to day laborers and workers, there were also those who came to the United States seasonally. They would make it well beyond the border and settle in cities and rural areas. Many were agricultural workers in the orchards, groves, and fields of California, Arizona, Texas, and beyond. They would work for low wages and settle for living in rather squalid conditions. They were willing to move quickly from field to field as the harvests required it. These undocumented workers would often go back to Mexico when the agricultural season was over. Many would return the following year. Other undocumented workers labored in the service industry, construction, etc. What motivated every single one of them were the economic disparities between Mexico and the United States. Even the worst wages in the United States were much higher than what they could make in Mexico. In regard to undocumented migration, even more than in regard to illegal drugs, it is possible to say with certainty that it is economics, stupid! These seasonal workers too ended up staying once it became more dangerous and expensive to cross the border back and forth. Many of them, once settled, sent money for their families to come to the United States. That too added to the ranks of undocumented permanent residents. The border enforcement strategy had failed.

It is very surprising that given this historical and current evidence of the fundamental economic motivation of undocumented migration to the United States and recognition that border enforcement may have actually added to the problem of undocumented permanent residents in the United States, no American political leader has recognized this as another element of the economic interdependence between Mexican workers and the U.S. labor market and attempted to find a more permanent, mutually beneficial solution. The acknowledgment by former president George W. Bush, Senator John McCain, and the late senator Ted Kennedy that a guest worker program might be a better, long-term solution was a step in the right direction, but it was a long shot. The failure of the House of Representatives to consider S.744, a comprehensive immigration bill that did pass in the Senate by 68 to 32 votes, was another sign that the United States remains ambivalent about immigration.[41]

HUMPTY DUMPTY AND THE BORDER

The punitive, law enforcement approach to undocumented migration on the border is a typical American story. Let me illustrate. Nearly every American child is familiar with the story of Humpty Dumpty:

> Humpty Dumpty sat on a wall.
> Humpty Dumpty had a great fall.
> All the king's horses and all the king's men
> Couldn't put Humpty together again.

The approach of the U.S. government to Humpty Dumpty's problem would have been that putting Humpty Dumpty together again would simply require more horses and more men. And so it is with the border. The approach of the U.S. government is that undocumented migration would be solved with more Border Patrol agents and more resources. More law enforcement has been the general answer to what is fundamentally an economic issue. This decision in fact is made against all the evidence gathered on immigration so far and, worse, against the fact that the U.S. economic system itself promotes free trade and globalization processes that destroy traditional economies, displacing millions of people. We want the benefits of globalization, with very few of the human costs that it brings with it. In a recent book, *Expulsions: Brutality and Complexity in the Global Economy*, by Saskia Sassen, the central argument is that globalization is producing "elementary brutalities" created by what is beginning to look like chronic unemployment and inequality accelerated by processes that are destroying the land, water, and the environment, in addition to the ability of ordinary people to make a living in the face of the world system's depredations.[42]

Thus Congress and the American public have adopted an increasingly more punitive, law enforcement–oriented approach to the border. And political parties do not matter here. President Obama has come to be known as the Deporter-in-Chief—sending away an average of 400,000 undocumented migrants and devastating Latino communities throughout the country. Throughout the 1980s, the border-patrolling bureaucracies became a "growth industry." The Border Patrol saw enormous quantitative and qualitative improvements. Between 1980 and 1988, the Border Patrol personnel nearly doubled, reaching 5,500 positions. Since then, it has nearly quadrupled, with about 70 to 80 percent of them assigned to the U.S.-Mexico border. And there are calls for as many as another 10,000 agents, as already pointed out. The high-tech gadgets of the Border Patrol were also improved. There are sensors and cameras and night-vision goggles, and new, sturdier jeeps and other vehicles, and thousands of floodlights and a much greater budget. There are now planes and drones and intelligence centers producing actionable data on migrants, and holding facilities reminiscent of science fiction movies, and even bigger budgets. Tougher sentences too have been created. The first arrest of an undocumented border crosser means summary deportation. By the second arrest, there are prison sentences, usually months. By the third arrest, there are stiffer prison sentences—sometimes years. In effect, this phenomenon has begun to fill American prisons with undocumented workers as well, placing an added burden on the American taxpayer. The number of illegal aliens sentenced in federal courts has risen dramatically.[43] The crime these people were charged with was unlawfully entering the United States. In 2016, the third-largest contributor to the federal prison population is immigration.[44] And in 2014, undocumented migrants accounted for 37 percent of all federal sentences, according to the U.S. Sentencing Commission.[45] This does not consider all the hundreds of thousands being detained in other facilities and county jails on any given day, waiting to be processed. The cost is truly overwhelming.

Interestingly, the statistics all around are not always reliable. Looking at the number of undocumented border crosser arrests, for example, does not make clear that all the additional efforts of the U.S. government to wage war on undocumented migration at the border have paid off at all. The number of arrests went up considerably in the early 1980s, peaking at 1.7 million in 1986, but dropped dramatically to less than 1 million after the 1986 Immigration Act legalized the status of nearly 3 million undocumented workers living in the United States. Then it went back up somewhat to reach close to 1.5 million apprehensions in the mid-2000s. But the numbers are tricky. The number of arrests does not faithfully reflect the number of people that crossed the border, given that a person can be arrested several times in a given year. Many workers caught and deported simply turned around and tried to cross again—that is a double count, although more careful record keeping is now making it clearer who tries to cross two or more times and it is possible to tell how many individuals actually attempt crossing without papers.

Moreover, it is difficult to calculate how many undocumented workers actually make it to the United States—by definition, we do not know how many do so. A larger number of arrests could mean that there are more workers trying to make it across or it could mean that the Border Patrol's effectiveness has increased. Which is correct is nearly anybody's guess. In my own estimation, the border is considerably more secure today than it used to be. Thus the rate of undocumented migrants trying to cross and are caught has gone up, getting closer to the actual number of individuals trying to cross. And if the number of detentions has gone down from 1.5 million at its peak in 2005 to 479,000 in 2015, then clearly there are fewer people trying to come. Let me put it this way: if we are

catching most of them now and even so only about a third are still coming, then we have had some success in securing the border, although it
will never be 100 percent shut. And yet, this level of success is not making
Congress act to both fix the immigration system and provide for a flexible
system that can attract temporary workers to the United States when
needed and reduce that rate when the economy is not doing so well.
We prefer instead a Border Patrol that is even more militarized in its
approach with a series of military-style operations to "stem the illegal
alien invasion" on the border. There is hardly anyone more blind than
he who does not want to see.

THE MORE THINGS CHANGE, THE MORE
THEY STAY THE SAME

By the early 1990s, Americans' attitudes toward undocumented
immigration began to change rapidly once again. In 1992, 42 percent of
Americans held a negative view toward foreign immigration in general.
By 1993, two-thirds felt that immigration should be stopped altogether.
There was particular outrage toward undocumented migration, although
the reasons for opposing it had changed since the 1980s. Whereas in the
1970s and 1980s, undocumented workers were blamed for displacing
American workers, in the 1990s and 2000s, the belief was that undocumented workers were placing an inordinate burden on the local taxpayers
because of the services that they consumed. Everyone agrees in fact that
many of the tax dollars coming from undocumented workers flow to the
federal government, but the costs of the services that they consume are
paid by state and local taxes.[46] This localized outrage in the 1990s led to
major efforts to prevent undocumented immigrants from coming across
the border and some strong anti-immigrant movements in California
and then in Arizona and Texas. Some propositions on the ballot in
California and Arizona attempted to deny basic services to undocumented immigrants because of the burden that they constitute to the local
taxpayers. This anti-immigrant sentiment has even extended to many
other parts of the country, from Hazelton, Pennsylvania, to Birmingham,
Alabama. What is relatively new in recent years is the volatility of public
opinion on immigration. From the 1960s to the early 1990s, views on
immigration shifted slowly, but starting in the mid-1990s, Americans'
views on immigration varied wildly from relatively hostile attitudes in
the mid-1990s to relatively welcoming attitudes in the early 2000s to very
hostile attitudes in the 2010s.[47] The reality is that the U.S. relationship
with immigration has been complicated. There is a deep understanding
that the country's own prosperity depends on immigration and the free
flow of people, ideas, and capital, but at the same time, every new group

that comes in suffers discrimination and rejection. That has been the history of immigration for more than 200 years and it is not likely to change and public opinion on immigration is much more volatile today than ever before.

For nearly a century, all the attention to the issue of immigration has given the Border Patrol even more leverage in Washington and greater leeway to implement aggressive operations on the border. In the 1920s, for example, the Border Patrol was created to stem the tide of illegal-alcohol smuggling into the United States from Mexico. When Prohibition was over, however, the Border Patrol reconfigured itself to tackle the issue of illegal border crossers. Starting in the 1990s, the Border Patrol became even savvier at lobbying Washington, DC, for additional resources by portraying the border as a chaotic, lawless land. Operation Hold the Line, Operation Gatekeeper, and Operation Safeguard were three such efforts by the Border Patrol in Texas, California, and Arizona respectively to build a narrative around the border that would benefit its own bureaucratic prosperity and to obtain more resources and support from politicians. These operations marked a definite turn in the war against undocumented migration on the border and gave it its distinctive look today. After September 11, the Border Patrol added terrorism to its list of responsibilities, further consolidating its operations on the border and justifying an increasing use of brute force and lack of accountability. More recently, a special report on the Border Patrol alleged that the agency was violating the human rights of migrants and refused to even provide information so others could understand what it was doing.[48] This is happening even as the number of arrests by the Border Patrol along the border is going down, showing decreasing returns on investment. Flying a drone along the border, for example, costs $28,000 for every single undocumented migrant detained in addition to the $12,500 that it costs to process and deport him or her. As the number of migrants trying to cross the border decreases, the costs of border patrolling per undocumented migrant obviously rise.

OPERATION HOLD THE LINE

In El Paso, Texas, in the mid-1990s, the chief of the Border Patrol, Silvestre Reyes, had had enough of the border chaos. He was also a very astute bureaucrat who knew how to create a crisis to benefit his agency. In 1994, he set up Operation Hold the Line, which began in El Paso (soon followed by Operation Gatekeeper in California and Operation Safeguard in Arizona). Operation Hold the Line consisted in beefing up the Border Patrol and laying siege to the U.S.-Mexican border by posting Border Patrol agents every quarter mile, within sight of each other, for 20 miles east and west of El Paso, Texas. This heavy military-style operation was later extended into New Mexico and beyond. Reyes, who later became the Democratic congressman for the 16th district of Texas (El Paso), thought that this type of operation would plug all the empty areas that the Border Patrol was unable to guard at all times. This was of course futile, because the number of undocumented crossers continued to rise into 2006, when it finally dropped for reasons that are still puzzling many academics. In California, Operation Gatekeeper included building a wall between Tijuana and San Diego County. In Arizona, Operation Safeguard built a similar fence between Ambos Nogales (Sonora and Arizona). The wall-building component of the border, however, was to become fashionable, and by 2007 the U.S. Congress authorized the Secure Fence Act, allocating funding to build a 700-mile wall along the U.S.-Mexico border.

THE WALL

Driving along the Nogales, Arizona, portion of the border, and turning south toward the borderline, one very quickly comes to the border wall. It is a 12-foot fence, made of different materials and shapes depending on the portion of the wall that one visits. But it now extends on the California, Arizona, and Texas borders. Curiously, the wall drops into the sea along the Tijuana-San Diego region. The wall has created much controversy because it splits asunder the environmental ecosystems of the region, doing them much damage,[49] it is an eyesore that extends for hundreds of miles, and it symbolizes the final affront in the war against the border. Moreover, although it has deterred some undocumented crossers, it clearly has had little or no effect on drug trafficking and has punished migrants because it has made them go around it to more remote areas, risking life and limb. The balloon effect has also come into the picture, with migrants looking for additional areas to cross where there is no wall, including South Texas, where they sometimes drown, and the Big Bend region between Texas and Coahuila, where they have to walk for hundreds of miles before reaching any population center. Moreover, as the wall has gone up in Arizona and California, tunnels have sprung up everywhere—some of which are dedicated to drug trafficking but others also to undocumented-worker smuggling.[50]

Additionally, the wall has done very little to stem the tide of overstays. There are many Mexicans who obtain a visa and then an I-94 permit, the kind the Mexicans are required to have if they are to travel beyond the first 25 miles from the border. After they obtain the I-94, many simply overstay their permits. Although there is very little sign that this is a huge issue today, some are using this over-the-bridge way of getting into the United States and then staying in the country. CBP is now enforcing the requirement that tourists and other travelers return the I-94 before it is expired, in order to have a clearer picture of who is overstaying their visa, but as stated earlier, this exit control system is still incipient.

ESCALATION OF THE WAR ON MIGRANTS

This unprecedented law enforcement effort on the border at first led undocumented workers to move to more isolated areas and away from the urban centers, a situation that continues today and has made it increasingly dangerous to cross the border. And although these operations eventually became permanent fixtures of the border and may have contributed to a decrease in the number of crossers in the long run, the reality is that they also raised the number of migrant deaths and ultimately do not deal with the other variables that pull migrants into the United States—better-paying jobs, or the other variables that push them out from their own countries such as poverty, violence and lack of public safety, and a dearth of opportunity. Even so, these measures did make the number of detentions at the border drop dramatically in the urban areas they covered. After 2007, the number of undocumented workers crossing dropped likely as much due to the harsher conditions of the border as to the collapse of the U.S. economy. Thus the up to 12 million undocumented workers that today live in the United States, most of whom made it through the U.S.-Mexico border in the 1990s and 2000s, are still here but have not increased dramatically and in fact have probably become a smaller number, given the mass deportations of the Obama administration.[51]

The operations, however, represented an escalation of the war on undocumented migration across the U.S.-Mexico border. The personnel, the budgets, and the technology, along with the raids on migrant communities and the mass deportations, all escalated in an attempt to prevent these "economic invaders" from coming across the border and from staying and feeling at home. Hardly any undocumented migrant today feels at home. Fear has become a permanent component of their daily lives, even if some in the United States insist that they have a comfortable life in this country. Migrants today live in the shadows. The precariousness of their lives is evident everywhere. They live in fear of detection and deportation at all times. Their daily lives are far from normal.

EMPOWERING THE COYOTES

Ten years ago, walking down the Santa Fe Bridge between El Paso and Ciudad Juárez, I was struck by the number of idle men hanging around the streets and corners of the main drag in Ciudad Juárez. My "guide," who met me at the end of the bridge, took me to one of these idle bystanders. He was leaning against a telephone booth. My guide told him that we had two "pollos" (people hoping to cross the border illegally) in a hotel. The man promptly told us that he would charge $300 each to take them to El Paso. My guide then added that they were Cubans. The coyote said that he did not deal with Cubans at all. They were too difficult to cross—something I never understood given that Cubans are readily granted asylum to this day as soon as they step on American soil. But at that time, he told us that he could take us to someone who would take that risk. However, it would cost a lot more to cross them into El Paso and probably about $6,000 each to take them all the way to Miami, Florida. The price to cross a Central American to El Paso was $600 at that time. An Asian or a Middle Easterner would be upwards of $1,000 to El Paso alone. It would cost much more if they wanted to go farther up into the United States. Almost any immigrant today pays up to $10,000 to a coyote to smuggle him or her into the United States—as the risks of crossing have gone up, so have the coyote fees. If one were to multiply the hundreds of thousands of clients by the thousands of dollars that each is willing to pay, it becomes obvious that this was and is even today a multimillion-dollar business every year. The rewards are obviously worth the risks, and the forces of supply and demand impose themselves again.[52]

As the United States has beefed up its law enforcement activities along the border and as more walls are built, more agents are hired, and more high-tech gadgets are deployed to guard the border, its efforts seem to have contributed to empowering and enriching the coyotes or human smugglers. Undocumented migrants, who previously made runs across the border by themselves, with little or no guidance, now have to rely on very well organized smugglers to help them across the border through more dangerous desert areas of the Southwest and across the river in Texas. This reliance on coyotes has in turn created well-greased networks of human smugglers (coyotes) and undocumented workers (pollos) that play a dangerous game of cat and mouse with U.S. law enforcement forces in some of the roughest terrain of the United States. Very few undocumented workers today make a run on their own anymore, empowering the coyotes and giving them the means to watch the moves of the U.S. government and draw their own conclusions as to where the best opportunities are to smuggle undocumented workers. When the numbers reach the hundreds of thousands of workers and hundreds of millions of dollars, the game becomes one of risks and rewards, much like any other U.S. business makes its calculations. And now that half of the migrants detained are from Central America, the costs have gone up even more. And yet there are people willing to pay these exorbitant amounts of money to make it to the United States.

In effect, it is very difficult to obtain data measuring the number of undocumented entrants. By definition, no one really knows how many migrants make it across the border illegally. It is also very difficult to assess how many coyotes there are who help people cross the border and make it to U.S. cities for a fee. Even so, in my estimation fewer undocumented workers are now making it across for two reasons: fewer are coming, in spite of what incendiary politicians may say, and of those that are coming, more are being apprehended. Let me explain. In 2005 and 2006, at the peak of detentions at the border, about 1.5 million migrants were detained, but the border wall did not exist and the human and technological capabilities of the Border Patrol to detain migrants were not yet what they are today. One can assume that many migrants were coming and many actually made it through. Today, the Border Patrol has increased its ability to detain migrants trying to cross the border and even so, apprehensions in 2015 were 479,000. This can only imply that fewer migrants are coming and of these, more are being caught, especially given that the ability of the Border Patrol to detain more has increased exponentially. Moreover, of those apprehended, just over 50 percent were Central Americans, then Mexicans have, for the most part, ceased to come across illegally in large numbers.

What we know for sure is that undocumented immigrants can no longer cross on their own at all. With the beefed-up law enforcement along the border, the reliance on coyotes to cross them and guide them is greater than ever. Migrants rely on coyotes who have greater knowledge of the routes to take, can measure the probability of apprehension, etc. Of course, coyotes demand more money if the risk of apprehension is greater. Throughout the 1990s and into the 2000s, the coyote rates kept escalating, signaling the higher risk of crossing the border. Several factors influence the rates, but there is some evidence that the number of coyotes offering their services to smuggle people across the border has increased considerably. All this was revealed in a study done by the Federal Reserve Bank, which also states:

Despite increasing coyote use rates, coyote prices were in steep decline until 1994. Median reported smugglers' fees fell from $941 in 1965 to $300 in 1994 (constant dollars), suggesting that increases in the supply of smugglers outpaced the increase in demand. Several factors contributed to the rise in smuggler supply. First, the border's improved accessibility through the building of roads and expansion of bus, rail and airway service significantly lowered transportation costs. Second, free entry into the industry by experienced migrants also increased supply. Third, the growth of the illicit drug trade during the 1980s attracted more smugglers as well.[53]

By the 2000s, however, the risk of apprehension went up exponentially, making the price of smuggling a migrant go up again and reaching in some cases $10,000 per person—as reported by a Central American I spoke with in a Washington, DC, Maryland suburb in the spring of 2016. All that indicates that smuggling human beings is subject to the same economic laws of any other black market—higher risk means higher prices, and higher prices means more market entrants to offer those services, and so on.

In all, the business of law enforcement on the border has created its own new enemy: the criminal organizations dedicated to beating the mechanisms for law enforcement on the border and to keeping the U.S. labor market duly supplied with cheap labor. In the process, hundreds of millions of dollars change hands from the undocumented workers and their families to the criminal organizations they hire, enhancing the ability of the coyotes to circumvent U.S. law enforcement. It is hardly surprising then that sophisticated criminal organizations, such as Los Zetas, got in the business of immigrant smuggling. The business was just too profitable, incentivizing new entrants. Unfortunately for the migrants, human rights abuses by the coyotes have also increased, as the same kinds of abuses by the Border Patrol have risen as well.

The issue of the business of smuggling human beings—and even trafficking with them—deserves slightly more attention now, as the signs that this is a growing industry are everywhere. One of the unintended consequences of the escalation of the war on immigration is that we may be contributing to building strong criminal networks dedicated to the smuggling of humans across the U.S.-Mexico border and then incentivizing their falling victim to human trafficking as well. As it has become harder to cross the border, more migrants have to rely on the expert scouts—coyotes—for their services. Migrants are often sexually abused, their money extorted, recruited for organized criminal activities, and so on, without any recourse to law enforcement because they are afraid. Thus we have a community of migrants trapped between criminals and law enforcement. And as the risk to both migrants and coyotes has gone up, the premiums have also gone up. In the late 1990s, it may have cost $900 to hire a coyote. Today, it can cost up to $10,000. Any economist would argue that these fees are enough to incentivize new "entrants" into the coyote services industry. And sometimes, these coyotes actively advertise their services to get migrants to the United States. Although they do not always deliver, they charge thousands of dollars per migrant to serve as a guide and increasingly they abandon their cargo or lead them to the borderline and push them across, leaving them to their own devices in the middle of the desert or the river waters. After that, migrants are often caught but do not necessarily know who their coyote was and what happened to their money. This in turn leaves their families back home—increasingly in Central America—with an enormous debt as they have to pay the money borrowed to help their relative get to the United States.

In the end, there seems to be a direct correlation between criminal activity and enforcement effectiveness. We often assume that crime is static and criminals do not have a learning curve or that their incentives are not elastic. These are all erroneous assumptions. Very often, they adjust and innovate and their own incentives to participate in smuggling humans also change. As I have said elsewhere, better bureaucrats also make better criminals.

GOOD FENCES MAKE GOOD NEIGHBORS

I want to return to the issue of the border walls, particularly because it has been such a traumatic experience for many border communities that now have to live with a wall right up against their streets, parks, and even homes. Robert Frost wrote his famous poem "Mending Wall," thinking perhaps about borders. As I walk along the steel wall that divides Naco, Arizona, and Naco, Sonora, I think of Robert Frost and recite his poem in my head:

> Something there is that doesn't love a wall,
> ....
> "... Before I built a wall I'd ask to know
> What I was walling in or walling out,
> And to whom I was like to give offence.
> Something there is that doesn't love a wall,
> That wants it down." ...
> ....
> And he likes having thought of it so well
> He says again, "Good fences make good neighbors."

A few days later, hiking on the rugged hills of north Tijuana, I can look down across the steel wall and see a Border Patrol agent sitting inside a truck looking in my direction with his binoculars. I am talking to two men who are surveying the hills in search of an opportunity to make a run into the United States. It is a long shot for them. There is a steel wall—in some places a triple wall, many Border Patrol jeeps, sensors, and the marshes between Tijuana and San Diego. It is nearly impossible to cross there today. And they know that. But they will try nevertheless.

These miles of walls that now mark the U.S.-Mexico border in towns in Arizona and California were part of Operation Safeguard in Arizona and Operation Gatekeeper in California. Steel plates that served as makeshift airport landing strips during the first Iraq War were flown to the Southwest and used to build walls along the borderline. The plates are rusty and unwelcoming. And they have contributed to pushing undocumented crossers to more isolated and hostile areas of the Southwest desert.

Whether they make good neighbors or whether they reinforce the separation between the two countries, even against all the economic forces that point to integration, is a matter for discussion. But the walls are there. They are a daily reminder to all that the U.S. government intends to fully enforce the border, even if they have yet to deter the determined workers bent on making it to the U.S. labor market. As with increased patrolling, the walls also have contributed to a perverse secondary effect: the creation of organized, strong networks of human smugglers.

Ironically, North American integration is unstoppable. Local communities continue to find ways to collaborate. Driving along the *Frontera Internacional* highway in Tijuana, hugging the U.S.-Mexico border, one runs into the Tijuana International Airport. This airport is now considered a binational airport. The Tijuana airport now provides airport services to both the U.S. and Mexican sides. The San Diego airport, enclosed by the sea and the downtown area in that city, cannot expand and the two communities found a way to collaborate to expand Tijuana's airport operations to serve the international needs of the entire area. In a recent visit to CBX, as the terminal is referred to, I could personally see how the new airport terminal on U.S. territory works. Passengers arrive, check in, and then move on to a skywalk to cross into Mexico and board their planes. Upon return, passengers deplane, cross the skywalk bridge back to San Diego, and go through immigration and customs. These innovative efforts, while important to the local communities and their economic development, often find resistance from law enforcement agencies, who appear to prefer a border shut tight and frozen in time. CBP, for example, refused to staff the CBX terminal unless the investors paid CBP for its personnel—and now CBX pays CBP $6 million to staff the facility. Local communities will continue to fight these uphill battles against the law enforcement apparatus that we have built all along the border.

THE CROSSING CARD TRICK

In the mid-2000s, a human-smuggling guide took me to a seedy hotel in the middle of downtown Ciudad Juárez. In a dark upstairs room, we were shown a box containing perhaps 5,000 U.S. crossing cards. Crossing cards (B1/B2 visas that look much like a driver's license) are given to residents of Mexico and allow them to come across but only within 25 miles of the border. To travel farther up, border crossers holding a crossing card need to also have an I-94 card. The man we talked to in that hotel was told that I wanted to cross into the United States and I needed a crossing card. He had me sort out through the box to find a "look-alike." The process is fairly simple. I would find a card whose picture looks like me. I would pay $250 for the use of the card. I would cross the bridge into El Paso with that card. Someone from the criminal network would follow me and take the card from me once I was safely across the border in the streets of El Paso. Most of the cards in that box are stolen or lost cards. If I were to find a lost passport, I could also sell it to him. I would get $150 for it. If I lost a passport, however, and I found it in his box, he would sell it back to me for $500. Smarter technology and biometrics put an end to this, but it demonstrates that the border is a strategic field, with actors always seeking innovative ways to accomplish their goals—the criminals as much as law enforcement.

Such is the creativity of the human-smuggling rings that have flourished as the U.S. government border enforcement efforts create a class of people still desirous of entering the United States but who must now rely on "experts" to do so. Like drug lords, these criminal networks become ever more creative, but also take more risks with the lives of their "clients," resulting in an increased number of deaths.

Ten years later, technology has been implemented so that this is now impossible. RFID technology alerts agents to who is coming; they pay more attention to the individuals that cross; the patterns of behavior are evident on their screens so that they can detect who crosses what, when, how, through where, with whom, in what vehicles, etc. Information gathering on individuals is now much more intense and has made it very hard to operate at POEs. The environment is one of fear. In fact, it is quite evident that CBP agents are a very intimidating presence even to legal crossers. They yell orders; they push people around; they display their authority; etc. In general, they have the power to stop anyone, to bring anyone in for further questioning, to harass anyone even if they eventually find nothing suspicious, etc. People live in a constant fear of being detained for no reason. CBP has an incentive to create this environment of submission, fear, intimidation, and even humiliation. Even a minimal sign of disobedience can be quickly punished, with no explanation. The face of CBP is not the smiling, attentive, courteous face that the U.S. government promises in its advertising. It is the face of fear, intimidation, and humiliation. It is certainly not a welcoming attitude.

But smugglers are terribly creative and they too know how to manipulate their own situations. The latest method they employ is to run migrants from Central America up to the U.S. borderline and then to let their cargo loose on the Border Patrol. In fact, they often advise migrants to present themselves before the Border Patrol and ask for asylum. This is exactly what happened in the summer of 2014, when human smugglers actively recruited migrants, and especially minors, in Central America and drove them up to the U.S.-Mexico border. That summer, the number of unaccompanied minors increased from some 35,000 to nearly 70,000. These minors were let loose at the borderline and told to present themselves to Border Patrol agents and ask for asylum.

The Border Patrol was overwhelmed during that summer, accused of housing these minors in squalid conditions and other sundry abuses. The reality was that they were simply unprepared to receive as many children as they did.[54] Although the crisis has subsided, there is still the danger that coyotes will continue to incentivize minors and entire families to make the trek north for thousands of dollars at no risk to them as they no longer cross them themselves but take them right up to the Border Patrol and advise them to request refuge.

NAFTA AND UNDOCUMENTED IMMIGRATION

As with drugs, NAFTA has had an enormous impact on the U.S.-Mexico border. Again, truck traffic on the border has increased exponentially. In a given year, 6 to 7 million trucks cross the border. Millions more travel from and through the booming border towns north, east, and west to the rest of the United States. The story told earlier of Tyrone Williams and his deadly cargo point to the primary way that undocumented workers, like illegal drugs, are transported into and throughout the United States to this day. Truck drivers are today responsible for carrying most of the undocumented workers deep into the United States where they meet friends or relatives and acquire the connections to begin working in the numerous industries that employ undocumented labor. But the American truck flotilla is over 20 million vehicles, moving all the time all around the country. It is impossible to control their cargo. They are a veritable conveyor belt for illegal drugs and migrants.

The networks are also very convoluted. There are individuals working with the coyotes who dedicate much of their time to recruiting truckers who are willing to hide their human cargo in their 18-wheelers. In El Paso, like in many other border towns, there are truck centrals, where drivers can get a hot meal, a shower, and some rest before continuing on their trips. On I-10, just east of El Paso, there is one such central. I saw many of them in Laredo and Nuevo Laredo, which together handle about 45 percent of all land trade between the United States and Mexico, overwhelmingly by truck. In those places, there are often recruiters who approach the drivers trying to gauge their vulnerability to the trade of both drugs and human beings. And many drivers often fall for it. It is a good deal for many of them to supplement their income with a few thousand dollars for hiding a few people in their truck box.

Trucks are the most convenient means of transporting smuggled undocumented workers to the urban centers of the country, not only because it is very hard to detect every person hiding in every box of every truck but also because at the internal checkpoint, usually between 50 and 80 miles from the border, the Border Patrol is looking closely at cars and vans but not necessarily inspecting the large trucks that come through. Even with all the new inspection gadgets, including the X-ray machines, it would still simply be a logistics nightmare and very expensive to open every one of the millions of 18-wheelers that travel the major highways along the border. Such exhaustive inspections are impossible, even at the international POEs between Mexico and the United States; it would be prohibitive to add yet more costs of inspecting trucks once they are circulating inside the United States. Generally, Border Patrol agents at the internal checkpoints use their intuition to pick the trucks they will inspect. A sign that something is wrong, for example, would be an exceedingly nervous driver.

OTMs: OTHER THAN MEXICANS

Some years ago, a colleague of mine at UTEP, who travels to Poland frequently, mentioned to me that he had seen some posters outside travel agencies in that country announcing packages for travel to Ciudad Juárez, across from El Paso. He and I laughed at the idea that Ciudad Juárez would be such an attractive place for Polish people to go to on vacation. We both suspected that there was something else to the poster. And yes, there was. I discovered this standing on a field just east of Nogales, Arizona. There, a Border Patrol agent radios his colleagues telling them that he had detained some OTMs (Other than Mexicans). He then explains that they are two Brazilian nationals. They will need translators. The agent will have to fill out an additional number of forms on that report. OTMs distract an agent from his daily work activities because they require much more paperwork than Mexicans. And they cannot be deported to Mexico. The whole process of detention and deportation is much more complicated and costly for OTMs.

Walking into El Paso's Border Patrol detention center, the visitor is struck by the various languages other than English and Spanish spoken there. The number of nationals attempting to cross the border without documents and who come from countries other than Mexico is growing exponentially. There are now, as I mentioned, more non-Mexicans than Mexicans attempting to cross the border. Because so many OTMs are coming to Mexico to make their way into the United States, the detention center in El Paso has a whole host of interpreters available for the detainees held there and they often ask for volunteers in the community who can translate between English and other languages. More recently, a wave of Cuban nationals crossed to the United States through El Paso.[55]

The number of apprehensions of OTMs, particularly from Central America, but also from Europe, the Middle East, and beyond, is growing at a fast pace. By the end of 2005, the estimated OTMs apprehended

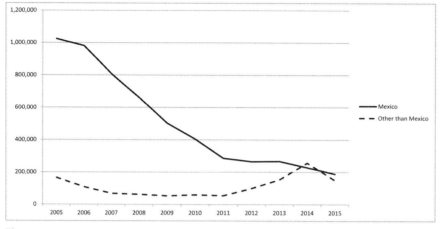

Figure 3.1

Number of apprehensions on the U.S.-Mexico border by nationality. (CBP Stats and Summaries)

reached 150,000, up from 65,000 in 2004, and about 35,000 in 2002 and 2001. Today, OTMs apprehended on the U.S.-Mexico border number 250,000, above the number of Mexicans apprehended for the first time (See Figure 3.1). OTMs, however, though they make their way through Mexico, cannot be sent back to Mexico when they are apprehended. They are generally detained by the Border Patrol and then held in detention centers in the United States until they can be sent to their country of origin. Often, the detention centers are full and these OTMs are released on their own recognizance to report at a later date at an immigration center or in court. Half of them never do. In fact, a DHS Inspector General 2006 report stated that about 85 percent of all detainees released never come back to court—they simply abscond.[56] However, fewer OTMs are now being released as detention centers have grown, but sometimes overcrowded conditions and new rules regarding children and family detentions mean that many, especially children and women, are still being released and some never show up in court. They disappear into the mass of the population and hide from U.S. law enforcement authorities among undocumented residents everywhere.

It is somewhat disconcerting that Mexico and the United States have not found a common agreement on how to deal with OTMs who break immigration laws in both countries. There is no real cooperation in dealing with this increasing problem between the two governments. Instead, Mexico becomes the passageway for these OTMs and the United States their final destination, exposing the flawed system of cooperation between the two countries and the increasing vulnerability of the Mexican law enforcement system itself, let alone the fact that there is a network of corruption that permits these OTMs to make it through Mexican territory to the U.S. border. OTMs are also abused throughout Mexico by both coyotes and law enforcement, with no one to complain to.

More recently, after the unaccompanied-minors crisis of 2014, Mexico implemented the Programa Frontera Sur, a five-pronged program to stem the flow of Central Americans through Mexico. However, this program, encouraged and supported by the United States, has had some unintended consequences that have added to the plight of migrants as well as the problem of human rights violations in Mexico. Given that the program authorizes Mexican authorities to crack down on Central American migrants, the country's police forces often extort money from the migrants to let them continue on their way instead, abuse the migrants sexually or physically, and even sell them off to coyotes. Migrants cannot complain because they are afraid of being detained in Mexico, where detention center conditions are awful, their human rights are violated, and deportation is certain in any event. The program has only made it worse for migrants and added incentives for corruption of the police and immigration authorities in Mexico. This has also made migrants look for alternative routes in Mexico, given that they cannot travel through the traditional paths, where both cops and criminals are waiting for them.[57] In the end, Mexico's own immigration crisis is the product of the failure of the two countries—Mexico and the United States—to deal with the program of immigration on a regional scale, one that includes the Northern Triangle of Central America.

OTHER MODI OPERANDI

That many coyotes lead hundreds of thousands of undocumented workers through remote areas of desert land in Arizona and New Mexico and now Texas, let alone through Mexico, does not mean that creative ways are not found to smuggle people at POEs. In El Paso is the National Border Patrol Museum, where there is a display of the many creative ways in which people attempt to cross right under the noses of the border inspectors. People are stuffed in second gas tanks; they are hidden in small compartments in vehicles; they are found inside washing machines; they are sewn inside the seat of a van; or they may use fake or stolen documents. They now use tunnels and of course scale the U.S.-Mexico border wall to make the run across or come legally and overstay their visas. Looking at the many creative ways that there are to smuggle migrants across the border, the visitor to the museum gains insight into the desperation of the many willing to risk their life and limb to seek better economic opportunities across the border. This will continue to be the story of the border until we recognize that the economic forces that we ourselves promote demand that labor too be freed to integrate as another important input of our economies. If we continue to align political citizenship with economic rights, we will continue to drive people to criminality in order to partake of economic rights from which they are barred because they lack political citizenship.

THE MILITARIZATION OF THE BORDER

A book published in 2004 titled *Patrolling Chaos: The U.S. Border Patrol in Deep South Texas* makes the argument that the border is chaotic and utterly poor.[58] Along these lines, other authors even speak of "loss of control over national borders." They sound as if the state were about to collapse under the weight of transnational crime. This is still the dominant border narrative today in many quarters.[59] This image has been recently reinforced by the violence that has enveloped border towns on the Mexican side, from Tijuana to Ciudad Juárez to Nuevo Laredo to Matamoros. And there is no doubt that at times, anyone standing on the U.S. side of the border looking across may think that the border is generally, as the Romans said, "ubi leones," where the lions live, the wilderness. But even a war is not chaotic. And the border and the wars waged on it by the U.S. government are not chaotic. Border "illegal immigration" has its own logic—just like the drug war and homeland security do as well. The border in fact has a certain order. The armies of "criminals" and the armies of "government bureaucrats" are playing a strategic game in which they respond to each other with some degree of predictability. It is a cat-and-mouse game, not a free-for-all. Someone deeply ensconced in either law enforcement or the "criminal" network who bothers to remove himself or herself sufficiently from his or her organization might just find that the cat-and-mouse border game on undocumented migration does have a certain logic: a logic of escalation *ad absurdum*. This logic becomes clear as one observes the Border Patrol do its work along the U.S.-Mexico divide.

LAW ENFORCEMENT AND ESCALATION

Along the U.S.-Mexico border, the only consistent feature of the war on undocumented immigration, especially since 1986, has been escalation. Escalation of law enforcement activities, with no real thought to long-term solutions beyond law enforcement, and no real thought to market and labor forces that feed the movement across the border or make people pick up in Central America and risk their lives going through Mexico and entering the United States illegally, has been the logic followed by the U.S. government responding to the so-called crisis on the border. Even as the

U.S. and Mexican economies become increasingly integrated and trade has grown 12-fold since NAFTA went into effect, the physical border has become more and more tightly controlled. It is hardly any coincidence that any new free-trade agreement and any economic liberalization effort comes accompanied by increased efforts to control the movement of people, instead of providing in these agreements for just such a thing. Additionally, almost any escalation on border enforcement is first followed by a wave of rhetoric about the chaotic nature of the border or about its lawlessness. It is almost as if politicians and bureaucrats primed the public discourse—manufactured consent, as Noam Chomsky would say—so as to end their efforts with new material resources to control ever-growing numbers of people, mostly pushed around by the very economic integration that we promote in our commercial agreements. Opponents of immigration add their voices and begin to speak of invasions, loss of sovereignty, devastation, vulnerability, etc. They use words that are sure to fire up fear and nationalism everywhere—often without realizing that real loss of sovereignty sometimes comes in larger wallops through the promotion of "free trade" and "economic liberalization." Sometimes the public discourse on immigration seems like a red herring, a distractor, to hide the real problem—that we are promoting economic policies that are devastating entire communities that are then forced to move.

The Federation for American Immigration Reform, for example, is a rabidly anti-immigrant group whose web page includes phrases such as "vulnerability of our borders," "border insecurity," and "terrorists will take advantage of the border."[60] This kind of language, if it catches the attention of the national media, presents the border and the issues around it as a matter of high politics and of national security. The media's preference for "crises" and "conflict" and "scandal" and its herd mentality eventually engulf the entire debate and give it a national emergency frame. This type of media frenzy is precisely what happened in the summer of 2005, and what occurred during the Arizona immigration crisis of 2010, which gave rise to SB1070, and what transpired during the unaccompanied-minors crisis of 2014 in South Texas. The national debate was intensely focused on the border, on illegal migration, invasions, and other such phenomena. There were thousands of stories about the loss of control on the border and the danger of this "alien invasion." Very little was said, however, except in academic circles, about the push forces—the economic and public safety conditions that kept expelling hundreds of thousands of migrants because of our own promoting of free trade and because of our own illegal-drug habits. With this, I do not mean to say that free trade is bad in and of itself. But free trade is never really free trade—it is more likely trade "managed" for the benefit of the larger corporations and hardly ever for the benefit of the small-time entrepreneur, and we hardly ever talk about the dislocations that it creates in local economies, thereby displacing people who then have to move. Fortunately, these crises do not last either. They fade away, just as they did when Hurricane Katrina struck New Orleans, making the issue of undocumented migration fade from the airwaves. Yet this "moral panic" is never really far away. At any moment, the issue of immigration can be quickly revived in the media, and fear stoked by those who would benefit from it.

Moreover, with the rhetoric and media attention also nearly always comes the attention of politicians. And with political attention over the border nearly always comes the aggressive lobbying of government agencies bent on a logic of escalation in resources, personnel, and border security technology. All law enforcement resources thrown at the border have increased considerably with every "border crisis." Curiously, the more they get, the more they like to talk about a "border crisis." It would appear that no one has a bigger incentive in preserving the border crisis than the CBP and its Border Patrol, precisely the agency that is tasked with solving it. The Border Patrol, for example, is the preeminent agency on the border between POEs assigned to stem the flow of illegal immigration. The Border Patrol has a long history. It began as a mounted border patrol as early as 1904. On May 28, 1924, the Border Patrol was created as we know it today. By 1950, there were more than 1,500 agents patrolling the Mexican, Canadian, and coastal borders of the United States. The Border Patrol had about 11,000 agents in 2005, and it has over 20,000 agents today, the overwhelming majority of them guarding the U.S.-Mexico border. Between 1994, the year when important law enforcement operations began in El Paso and San Diego, and 1999, the Border Patrol grew by anywhere between 1,000 and 1,900 agents per year. In 2005, some members of Congress proposed hiring 10,000 more border patrol agents to guard the U.S. borders.[61] Today, the agency is arguing that it needs another 5,000 agents to "solve" the crisis. They argue that they need this to "secure the nation," and no one can question security even on the back of a budget deficit. Overall, by 2015 the U.S. government was spending about $20 billion a year on border security, including the Border Patrol budget, with at best mixed results overall.[62]

DETERRENCE AND ESCALATION

Such is the logic of escalation. The theory behind escalation is one natural to American society. Americans tend to assume that individuals are rational actors, that they make ends/means calculations, that everyone freely chooses his or her actions, and that these actions are directly related to the pleasure/pain calculations of hedonistic human beings or the costs/benefits that the action can cause. The natural follow-up to this nearly universal assumption behind U.S. policy is that the swiftness, severity, and certainty of the punishment will deter individuals from violating the law. To ensure compliance with immigration laws, then, one must increase the swiftness, severity, and certainty of the punishment. The way to do it is to increase the possibility of getting caught; that is the reason for the law enforcement activities along the border.

Empirical evidence shows the failure of this cost/benefit or pain/pleasure analysis to explain what is happening on the border. On the border this logic is flawed—at least when applied strictly to the border alone. There are other considerations that defy the law enforcement escalation logic of the U.S. government at the borderline. The number of arrests and the number of undocumented workers in the United States appears to obey a parallel logic in spite of the increased swiftness, severity, and certainty of the punishment if you get caught trying to enter the United States without documents. Why? The explanation to the presumed "choice" of the undocumented workers who attempt to cross into the United States at the border without documents must involve individual "rational calculations" that extend beyond what can happen to them on the U.S.-Mexico border as they try to cross—e.g., the probability of getting caught. The rewards once inside the United States must be greater than the risk taken by an undocumented worker on the borderline. And hundreds of thousands still choose to cross precisely because the rewards far surpass the risks, even as the risks keep escalating.

This kind of cost/benefit or pain/pleasure analysis, however, reveals another flaw in the U.S. strategy to contain undocumented migration at the border. The U.S. government's strategy focuses on the border nearly exclusively, but its law enforcement against those who employ undocumented workers in the interior of the country is much lower and intermittent, although it has been growing in the last few years. Undocumented-immigration enforcement is still largely a border phenomenon, not something that occurs inside the United States, in spite of the raids that sometimes occur in neighborhoods and workplaces throughout the United States. American businesses and corporations who hire undocumented workers are seldom bothered or punished for their practices. The government is complicit because they implicitly allow thousands of businesses to operate by hiring undocumented workers. How else would some 12 million workers have jobs without a Social Security card, a driver's license, or a work permit? Undocumented workers know that once they have made it to Miami, Chicago, New York, or San Francisco, they are relatively safe from law enforcement efforts, for the most part. All they have to do is keep a low profile, obey the rules, and say very little. This obviously may be changing, and it is becoming very difficult to live in the United States without papers, but it is still the case.

THE ILLEGAL-DOCUMENT INDUSTRY

When I was living in Washington, DC, going to graduate school, I could count a Salvadoran family among my neighbors. At some point, their cousin Isaias came from El Salvador to join them in Washington. Isaias made the awful trek through Guatemala and Mexico, hiding wherever he could and guided by a coyote who charged Isaias and his family $4,000 to get him to Washington, DC. When Isaias arrived in Washington, there were certain things that had to be taken care of first. The family first taught him how to dress so as not to be detected, how to use the Metro system, where to go and where not to go. They taught him a few useful English words. One other thing was to get him a driver's license, a Social Security card, and a work permit. After that, he would be introduced to a friend of a friend who would get him a job as a busboy in a restaurant in Arlington, Virginia. Curious about how this document industry worked, I asked to accompany some of the family members as a mere observer. We took the Metro and got off at Mount Pleasant. We walked down Columbia Road until we came across a short, stocky man. Very quickly, the family members accompanying him informed the man that Isaias needed a whole set of documents. The man promised the documents would be ready in two days. Isaias was given new first and last names. His new name was Martin Olivares and for $150, he received all the new documents, which were picked up at the same corner where they had been ordered. It was that easy.

The kind of border-oriented war that the U.S. government is waging against undocumented migrants and workers at the border allows these same workers to live and work in the United States almost unfettered once they have "made it" to a metropolitan area in the United States. The border focus of this war against undocumented migrants has, as a consequence, produced another phenomenon worth mentioning, the emergence of this formidable fake-document industry. In fact, with fake Social Security numbers, undocumented workers function as legal residents—although this is becoming harder and harder. The *New York Times* reported on April 5, 2005, that the Social Security Administration received nearly $7 billion a year from taxes withheld on fake Social Security cards. These contributions continue, showing that they are an integral part of the health of the U.S. economy.[63] In February 2016, the Institute on Taxation and Economic Policy reported that undocumented workers paid some $12 billion in state and local taxes.[64] They also pay property taxes, directly if they own a home or indirectly if they rent. So it is not that undocumented workers do not contribute to the economy; it is that they are perceived as moochers, when they clearly are not. Their economic activity still counts, even if their income is less than a native household's income.

One issue is of course false filings. There are several million W-2s issued with incorrect Social Security numbers because, unless an undocumented worker is paid in cash, the employer must file a W-2 form with the IRS and the form must carry a Social Security number—which may be made up. Ten years ago, according to a study by the Government Accountability Office of the bogus W-2s, 17 percent came from restaurants, 10 percent from construction companies, and 7 percent from farm operations, the kinds of industry well known for the number of undocumented workers they hire.[65] The numbers are similar or even lower today because the undocumented population has not grown or maybe even decreased since 2005. Undocumented workers will never receive any of the benefits of Social Security that would accrue to a legal resident. Nor do they seem to want to claim such benefits. In fact, making use of government benefits is increasingly hard even for residents. Undocumented residents cannot even aspire to make any such claims. Moreover, most migrants, about 70 percent, are in their prime working age and ready to contribute to the U.S. economy and the United States has not spent a dime on their education.

These numbers should be considered when reforming the immigration system. But stripping the public policy debate of incendiary rhetoric is difficult. Politically, it pays more to blame immigrants for most social ills than to consider their contributions and their costs with a cool head.

THE ATTRITION ARGUMENT

There is an argument among government officials, conservative pundits, and others who would advocate tough law enforcement measures called the "attrition" argument. They justify the increases in law enforcement resources and efforts along the border because, they argue, the situation would be much worse if no measures were taken or no efforts were made to stop the "invasion" of undocumented workers. Somehow, they say, some will be deterred from making the trek to the United States by the sheer knowledge that it is increasingly difficult to cross and that the penalties are much higher.

This argument has some merit. Clearly, if we left the border completely unguarded, more people would try to cross and settle in the United States. There are important push and pull forces that would make more people move were it not for the reinforced border. Stiff law enforcement, in other words, tempers the effect of these push and pull forces. But the reader must be suspicious of the politicians, the bureaucrats, and even the groups of American civil society that present this argument. First, they do not really know if deterrence works. They simply assume that deterrence works, but no one has measured it yet. How many workers are prevented from trying to cross because law enforcement is tougher? No one can tell for sure. Clearly some, but that is an inherently very difficult question to answer. There is enough evidence to show, for example, that the economic conditions in the United States—such as the Great Recession of 2008—did more to deter people from coming than law enforcement itself. Second, politicians have their own incentives to profit electorally from taking tough stands against immigrants, particularly on one side of the aisle. And bureaucrats have their own organizational interests. I have yet to find a bureaucrat sitting atop an agency—or even a street-level bureaucrat—who will not say that "more is needed." A large agency means resources, prestige, perks, etc., for those who work for it. The unspoken agenda of every bureaucrat is to make her or his organization grow, not shrink it with "long-term" or "reasonable" solutions or by saying that the problem is finally contained. At a conference on border security that took place in El Paso, Texas, in August 2005, every government agent and member of Congress that attended spoke of the need for more resources, more agents, and more technology. These arguments have not ceased. In fact, border enforcement has become the sine qua non of immigration reform. Without shutting down the border, some politicians say, there will not be immigration reform—holding smart public policy change hostage to their own political interests. But are they to blame? They followed their own logic of escalation. The Humpty Dumpty effect is everywhere, from the speeches of politicians to the halls of Congress to the corridors of bureaucracy to the rugged terrain of the southwestern border, and down to the muddy waters of the Rio Grande in South Texas. Finally, the logic behind this argument has been partially exposed by the fact that a cost/benefit or pain/pleasure analysis of a border-oriented deterrence strategy does not seem to work well. Not a single undocumented worker that I interviewed seems to have thought much beyond making it to Los Angeles, Denver, Chicago, or Houston. This is not to argue that enforcement does not work. But how do we find the would-be migrants who decided to cancel their trip north because they thought that law enforcement is just too tough? Of course, it is now becoming more difficult to live and work, even in Los Angeles, Denver, Chicago, or Houston. The environment is hostile; the penalties are increasing; and fear of being detected now governs even micro-decisions by all immigrants.

THE U.S. MILITARY AND THE BORDER

The U.S. government has effectively increased the militarization of the border in two ways. First, the bureaucracies that work on the border are trained increasingly like a military body. They wear the uniform; they carry the high-tech gadgets that include infrared goggles, spray, batons, etc.; they bear their firearms, including powerful automatic weapons, quite visibly; etc. The Border Patrol has installed ground sensors to detect movement along the border. It has posted hundreds of cameras at various points along the international line. Each vehicle is equipped with high-tech communications equipment. There are floodlights everywhere. And now they use planes, helicopters, and drones all along the border. Sometimes, the border resembles a war zone. In terms of its personnel, it is now a force of over 21,000 agents of which about 80 percent work on the U.S.-Mexico border. There are also the vehicles that have gone from simple vans in the 1970s and 1980s to trucks with heavily welded steel cages, many resembling military jeeps. And of course, the Border Patrol is now within the Department of Homeland Security, not within the Justice Department. Their whole job has been redefined not as one of keeping "illegal aliens" out or enforcing the law but one of defending America against would-be terrorists who might use the U.S.-Mexico border to harm the country. Every single migrant is now seen not as a lawbreaker but as a potential terrorist. Crossing the border without papers has been magnified into something more akin to a crime against humanity.

Second, beyond militarizing the training, the look, the equipment, and the activities of the Border Patrol, Congress forced the military onto the border by demanding that the Pentagon get involved in providing "support" to the law enforcement agencies operating along the border. The military was initially very reluctant to do so. Throughout the 1980s, they resisted getting involved. They alleged that the military under the Posse Comitatus Act could not get involved in law enforcement activities. They were quite protective of this organizational tradition within the military. However, by 1989, they had to create an office for drug control support inside the Pentagon. They were also given a budget of roughly $1 billion for drug control support, mostly on the border.[66]

The military, which could no longer avoid participating in border law enforcement, even if only in a supporting role, decided to use that money differently or at least they viewed that money differently than law enforcement agencies did. The military began to pay for training for the military, although that training occurred along the U.S.-Mexico border. If any activity was detected along the border, it was reported to the Border Patrol, but in general the military was happy to have that money to get the soldiers "out there" in the wilderness to train all night using their high-tech equipment. And this is not a secret at all. The March 3, 2005, issue of the *Monitor*, the military newspaper for Fort Bliss, Texas, ran an article in which they praised Alaska's 414th Cavalry, which was "preparing for deployment" by "assisting the Border Patrol." The unit, according to the paper, was concluding "a 60-day joint training mission in support of the El Paso sector of the U.S. Border Patrol" in New Mexico.[67] Since then, the military has continued to resist participating in border activities, but they have supported the Border Patrol, particularly with training and infrastructure building.

Thus in reality, the military tends to use its participation in border law enforcement operations with an ulterior intent. They generally provide support for law enforcement agencies, not with a view to the law enforcement work of these agencies, but with a view to give their own soldiers the opportunity to practice in rough terrain and use their high-tech gadgets. If law enforcement is done on the border and they contribute, that is entirely coincidental. The military has long disagreed with using their own to enforce drug laws or immigration laws. They would have preferred to stay away. Besides, the Marine Corps had already been stung by their participation in border law enforcement activities. A Marine training in the Texas borderlands killed a shepherd boy, Ezequiel Hernández, when he mistook him for a smuggler. The killing caused an uproar against the participation of the military in border enforcement operations and the Marines pulled out.[68]

To add to this, the Texas government has gotten increasingly aggressive in regard to immigration. In fact, Texas has continuously argued that the federal government has failed to secure the border and now the state government must take charge. In May 2015, during the biennial meeting of the Texas state legislature, a bill was passed approving $800 million to deploy the National Guard and to fund anti-immigration efforts by the Department of Public Safety—all this against the evidence that fewer migrants are coming, that the border is largely secured, and that all 16 of Texas border counties are among the safest in the nation.[69] There is no evidence of violence spillover to the U.S. side either, but repeating this has become a useful mantra to profit politically in Texas and to spend money further militarizing the border.

ALL THE BORDER'S A STAGE

Before Hurricane Katrina hit New Orleans, the undocumented-immigration issue was picking up steam. A quick search for news stories on the issue yielded hundreds of pieces in the months of July and August 2005 alone from newspapers and news broadcasts all over the country. The punch of the debate was sucked up by news of a devastated New Orleans. The most radically conservative newscasters would place the responsibility for undocumented immigration squarely on the backs of the workers attempting to cross the border and secondarily on the U.S. government. However, it is worth asking the question of whether most of the "problem" can be simply blamed on these two groups. In reality, this constitutes a more complex issue, if blame is to be assigned anywhere. Let us examine the responsibility for the "breakdown" of the border where it belongs, item by item, piece by piece.

The purpose of this section, however, is not to assign blame in any moral sense. I have consistently made the argument that these issues are motivated, at a very deep level, by economics. The purpose of assigning blame is simply to uncover the insincerity behind the undocumented-workers debate and to answer the more neutral and eternal question: *cui bono* (who benefits)? And the answer is nearly everyone.

THE AMERICAN PUBLIC

Sometime in late 2003 and into 2004, a federal grand jury began an inquiry into the labor hiring practices of Wal-Mart. Wal-Mart executives were accused of knowing that their subcontracted janitorial services were using undocumented workers but ignored this because it was part of their strategy to lower the price of goods on its shelves. Wal-Mart, which is a major importer of cheap goods from China, has also been aggressive at cutting costs at home by paying low wages. This was all part of the bottom line for the company but extremely beneficial to Wal-Mart's customers who pay "Always Low Prices. Always."[70] The Federation for American Immigration Reform—an anti-immigration group—has published a list of all the businesses that over the last 10 years, like Wal-Mart, have been accused of *knowingly* hiring undocumented workers. They are in the dozens—although still a small fraction of all those that do or need to.[71]

Walking up Wisconsin Avenue in Washington, DC, I visited a well-known Mexican restaurant where some of my Salvadoran friends worked. I walked up to the kitchen window and said "Hi" to several of them. I also know their personal stories. They had come from El Salvador in 1998, making a fear-inspiring trek through Mexico, squeezing through the border after paying thousands of dollars to a coyote in the Sonora-Arizona corridor, and then taking a flight to Washington National Airport, where a waiting relative received them, housed them for a few months, and then got them jobs in the restaurant in which they worked. After saying "Hi," I proceeded to sit down and enjoy a meal they had prepared in the kitchen. According to the *Washington Post*, undocumented migrants are a life source for specific industries, including services, construction, installation and repair, transportation, and farming. Their representation in those industries is well above the average of all Americans. In some cases, those industries could not function without migrant labor.[72] Yet most people ignore the fact that there is no "line" in the immigration waiting list to occupy those jobs. The U.S. government provides for very few visas directed at those jobs. Without an immigration reform that will consider those professions and the need to widen the visa availability for them, we will continue to rely on undocumented labor to the detriment of both the workers and their employers.

Moreover, the tougher immigration enforcement system has also made undocumented workers more vulnerable to abuse, which they cannot report because they live in fear of deportation. In March 2002, Birda Trollinger, Robert Martínez, Doris Jewell, and Tabetha Eddings brought a lawsuit against Tyson Foods complaining that "all such persons have been victimized by a scheme perpetrated by Tyson to depress wages paid to its employees by knowingly hiring a workforce substantially comprised of undocumented illegal immigrants for the express purpose of depressing wages."[73] This clearly showed that undocumented workers are preferred because they work long hours, take lower wages, and do not complain at all. Employers use this labor because it ultimately makes their bottom line better. In some industries, like agroindustry, employers simply complain that natives would not do the job.

These three stories have something in common. When I walk into a Wal-Mart or I sit down at a restaurant to enjoy a meal, I generally am surprised and even smile when I acquire a good or service at a relatively low price. Often, however, the prices are kept low by the low wages paid to the workers behind the scenes. In fact, new immigrants, including undocumented workers, are overrepresented in the service industries (busboys and cooks, domestic help, janitorial services, security guards, etc.) and the farm and forestry occupations. The construction industry is also heavily populated by undocumented workers. All of them contribute to competitive pricing of goods and services, which the American public enjoys at large.

Yet the same people sitting at a restaurant in Washington, DC, or eating al fresco in San Francisco, or buying cheap goods at a store in Little Rock, or hiring a day laborer in Newark, or having their grass mowed inexpensively in Chicago or Dallas, are often the same people appalled at and angered by the debate on "illegal immigration." Few stop to think that undocumented workers often keep wages in check, thereby contributing to keeping inflation relatively low and the general goods and services consumed at relatively low prices. They also keep U.S. global competitiveness high. This might explain why law enforcement against undocumented workers is "thin," that is, focused on the borderline but almost universally ignored inside the rest of the country, where undocumented workers feel safe and businesses thrive on their cheap labor. The alternative is of course that we pay the right wages and ultimately the right price for what we consume.

Thus the American public is largely complicit on the issue of undocumented immigration because they are mostly unwilling to pay higher prices for the goods and services they consume. Instead, the American public places enormous pressure on businesses to cut their prices. Businesses are often obliged to do so upon the backs of undocumented workers who are generally loyal, hardworking, and quiet employees. The American public contributes by its demands that shape the pull force that draws hundreds of thousands of undocumented workers to the border every year. The public would be enormously upset if they had to pay prices that reflected the wages that American workers demand when they work the jobs that undocumented workers take for so little. To this day, most Americans refuse to pay living wages. And businesses are always looking for ways to keep costs down.

THE MINUTEMEN

A few days into the month of October 2005, as I was driving my car about 30 miles east of El Paso, Texas, near Fabens, Texas, I came across a pair of men patrolling the Rio Grande riverbank. These were, at last, the Minutemen—just the people I was looking for. They were the men "fed up" with the country being "overrun" by this illegal-alien invasion. It was a veritable spectacle to observe these men scanning the border, and the protesters watching them to ensure that they did not commit human rights violations on undocumented border crossers. It was also quite a sight to see the media give them so much coverage.

This operation east of El Paso was just like the operation in Sunland Park, Columbus, and Hachita, New Mexico, and elsewhere in some 25 spots along the border from California to Texas. It is not that civilian groups had not been unhappy before. They had. It is not that they had not patrolled the border before. They had. The reality, however, is that they were never more than a few hundred and, more often than not, just a couple of dozen men and women. But it was in 2005 that the Minutemen, led by Chris Simcox, decided to employ a different type of tactic to draw attention to the problem of undocumented migration and to "expose the incompetence of the federal government" to guard the border. They made an effort to recruit men and women angry at the "illegal-alien invasion" across the border. They called them to arms in Tombstone, Arizona. They made a conscious effort to attract the attention of the media. And attention they got, even if the numbers failed to be what they had announced. They knew consciously that they were now shifting tactics, from simple patrol work along the border to a war for the perception of the general public. It was now a media war. Throughout the month of April, the Minutemen patrolled in Arizona. They left at the end of the month, but they kept relatively sustained media attention throughout the summer. They announced that they would come back to various points along the border in the month of October. And this they did. They recruited people to spread along the 2,100-mile U.S.-Mexico border.

The two men I spotted east of El Paso packed up and left at the end of October, having done little more than report a handful of undocumented border crossers to the Border Patrol. They told of having been somewhat disappointed and even bored at the lack of activity on the sector they were patrolling. Similar operations had been conducted by civilians along the U.S.-Mexico border for quite some time.

This reaction continued for several years. By 2010, the movement was at its peak. There were all kinds of ersatz anti-immigration groups coming together all along the border. These civilian groups accused the U.S. government of having failed to do its job. They declared essentially a "state of exception" and promised to take the law into their own hands.[74] This vigilantism took hold and stayed on and off the media radar for several years, but eventually faded. What really took the air out of this movement was the Supreme Court ruling on SB2070—the very hostile bill passed in the Arizona legislature against immigrants. Once the Supreme Court declared some of the provisions unconstitutional in June 2012, the ongoing vigilantism faded and even public opinion changed somewhat, although none of this has resulted in immigration reform in the United States.

The Minutemen project is not hard to assess materially. Even at the height of the media and public attention, they drew no more than a few hundred people and never really lived up to the numbers they announced. It is nearly impossible for a small number to guard a large, rugged border through a civilian-funded and civilian-manned operation. They could not possibly make a real difference. If the Border Patrol, with over 20,000 members, has failed in stopping the flow of undocumented workers and illegal drugs completely between POEs, it is not likely that the Minutemen project could do so. It is also very expensive for a militia group to carry out sustained operations. For individual members and their families, it is simply too expensive. That it is materially impossible for the Minutemen to sustain an operation such as this one has become clear over time. But the Minutemen understood that they were not going to make a difference on the ground. They did not seek to physically stem the flow of undocumented workers across the border. They sought instead to draw attention to the problem. And this they did, until the Supreme Court took the air out of the movement by its decision on SB1070.

Nevertheless, the Minutemen polarized the debate on undocumented immigration. They also legitimized much of the anti-immigration rhetoric. And they paved the way for politicians' profiting electorally from the issue. Even if they were largely motivated by a sense of victimization and insecurity, they managed to expose the fact that the U.S. government had failed to stem the tide of both undocumented workers and illegal drugs. They also showed that there was neither political will nor vision on the border. They showed the vacuum that is U.S. border policy. They exposed a broken system. As such, their effect is mostly symbolic, not material. They drew attention to the broken border system—one that remains broken to this day, mostly because we have no coherent plan to manage the border for the benefit of all. That is perhaps their most important contribution to the debate on the future of the border. Still, as of 2016, Congress has failed to act on comprehensive immigration reform. Many of the efforts of vigilantes and pro-immigrant groups fell on deaf congressional ears. Washington has its own skewed logic for action, one that seems to be getting worse.

BORDER POLITICAL GRANDSTANDING

An additional word is pertinent when it comes to political grandstanding. Politicians are a major factor to consider in the border immigration debate. It is not only the national-level politicians that have entered the fray on this issue, but also local politicians. To hear Washington politicians speak about the border is to hear people speak of complete chaos, absolute disorder. John McCain speaks of "the scourge of human trafficking and smuggling." Other members of Congress have used similar rhetoric to draw attention to the issue. It is contradictory, however, to hear politicians talk about the border with that sense of urgency and then proceed to do nothing about it. Surely then, it must not be that urgent.

State and local politicians have also taken advantage of the situation to carry out their own political grandstanding. Former governor Bill Richardson of New Mexico declared a "state of emergency" over illegal immigration and stated that the federal government has been unable and unwilling to stop the crossing of undocumented workers.[75] That was promptly followed by former Arizona governor Janet Napolitano, who also declared a state of emergency in her own state. She said that she would tap into an emergency fund of $1.5 million from the state disaster funds to pay for law enforcement on the border. The grandstanding by both Janet Napolitano and Bill Richardson did not lead to anything really substantial. Instead, it was much hot air to score points with their respective constituencies, and then the issue was dropped entirely. Congress is full of such opportunistic politicians. The next governor of Arizona, Jan Brewer (2009–15), was even more aggressive. Even though the Arizona immigration issue was already fading, she fueled the fire by portraying the border as a lawless place, run by criminal aliens about to burn the state of Arizona down. She pushed for state legislation that included the controversial SB1070, and she enabled Sheriff Joe Arpaio of Maricopa

County to treat undocumented migrants as veritable felons. Arpaio has since been placed under federal investigation for civil rights violations and had to settle a lawsuit, and then was found in contempt of that settlement.[76] The human rights abuses by police increased and even the rights of citizens and legal residents were violated, as the police were deputized as immigration officers and relied on racial profiling in a state that is almost a quarter Hispanic. They could not detect undocumented from citizens and legal residents if they did not rely on the "look" of a person. This is precisely what created a pushback on these practices and eventually a Supreme Court challenge to the law.

OBAMA'S APPROACH

There were important attempts at passing immigration reform. Any immigration reform had to deal with two large issues: (1) what to do with the 12 million or so undocumented residents already in the United States and (2) how to reform the system in such a way that we could redefine who has the right to come to the United States and on what basis. There were at least two important attempts to solve these two questions. The Comprehensive Immigration Reform Act of 2007 was discussed in the 110th Congress. It did create a path to legalization for undocumented workers, and it did reinforce the budget for border enforcement—adding technology, agents, and vehicles to the already congested border. But there was no agreement. Congress could not come to a consensus, especially in regard to the 12 million undocumented residents already in the United States. President George W. Bush could not get Congress to act, the window of opportunity closed, and the 2007 bill went the way of the 2005 attempt. There would be no other chance to deal with immigration until the Obama administration.

There were important attempts to force immigration reform through Congress. Bills died in Congress almost systematically several times. The most notable is the DREAM Act (Development, Relief, and Education for Alien Minors), which would grant conditional residency to any undocumented residents who were brought to the United States as minors. Although the bill was first introduced in 2001, it was reintroduced in 2009, 2010, 2011, and 2012. It failed to pass every time. That these individuals—who were brought to the United States as minors, grew up in the country, and did not by their own will violate immigration laws—could not be given relief was in and of itself a sign that Congress was hopelessly deadlocked on the issue and there would be no progress on immigration.

FORCING THE DEBATE

Over time, President Obama grew frustrated with Congress on this issue. Although he himself had adopted tough stands on immigration, deporting more immigrants than any other president before him, and made concessions on border security, he too was unable to convince Congress to pass any legislation on immigration. So the president decided to force the debate by announcing on June 15, 2012, his own program on immigration. The program was essentially the DREAM act by executive order. Anyone who came to the country before their 16th birthday and before June 2007 would receive a work permit as well as protection from deportation. This executive order, known as DACA (Deferred Action for Childhood Arrivals), would cover nearly 15 percent of all undocumented residents or some 1.7 million people. DACA went into effect on August 15, 2012, and as of 2016, some 700,000 people have applied. The response by Congress, particularly the Republican Party, was one of outrage because, it was argued, the president did not have the power to waive immigration laws. Still, DACA went forward and the president invited Congress to pass immigration reform and even threatened to act even more aggressively if Congress failed to do so.

And Congress failed to do so, and so the president acted more aggressively. By the end of 2014, President Obama announced a new program by executive order, DAPA (Deferred Action for Parents of Americans and Lawful Permanent Residents). This granted a deferred-action status to undocumented migrants who had lived in the United States from before 2010 and who had children who were U.S. citizens or lawful permanent residents. Like DACA, DAPA is not full legal status, but it gives people a quasi-legal status, allowing them to obtain a work permit, travel, and in general "come out of the shadows." This new program could potentially cover as few as 3.7 million and as many as 5 million additional undocumented residents. Upon announcing this new program, the president told Congress if you don't like it, "well, my response is pass a bill." Unfortunately, the U.S. Supreme Court blocked DAPA on a 4–4 tie vote in June 2016. Millions of undocumented workers will now have to wait for the next administration to act.[77]

This does not mean that Congress did not try. S.744, the Border Security, Economic Opportunity, and Immigration Modernization Act, was a broad-based immigration bill that dealt with the undocumented population, refurbished the immigration system, and added resources for border enforcement. That bill passed in the Senate by 62 to 38, but failed to even be introduced in the House. Congress was hopelessly deadlocked on several issues, but the end result is that the bill died after the Senate vote. DAPA was the president's answer to congressional failure.

But the story was not over—or rather is not over. Texas, along with 25 other states, all with Republican governors, sued in the U.S. District Court for the Southern District of Texas, essentially asking the court to enjoin implementation of DAPA and any DACA expansion. In February 2015, DAPA was prevented from implementation by the court and is now in the hands of the U.S. Supreme Court, slated to be resolved in the summer of 2016.

The end result is that the immigration issue is resolving itself. The undocumented population is now smaller than it was 10 years ago. Deportations now match new arrivals. Undocumented border crossers are only about 30 percent of what they were at their peak 10 years ago, and more and more of them are being caught thanks to enhanced border enforcement. That means that Congress is essentially losing an opportunity of decompression on the issue to modernize the immigration system. There is, as of yet, no political will to solve this issue and Washington is hopelessly gridlocked on the matter. Today, not even a more restricted immigration system is likely to be approved in Congress. There is simply no stomach to debate the issue, and in the meantime public opinion remains frustrated with Congress on this and other issues but electorally locked in position due to gerrymandering and other political conditions that make a turnover in Congress nearly impossible.

A NEW APPROACH IS NEEDED

Undoubtedly, September 11 was devastating to the border. On the one hand, the response to it did bring a much greater law enforcement apparatus to the region, but it failed to figure out a way to manage the border more efficiently and for the benefit of the local population. In many ways, the problem with the bureaucratic restructuring that occurred after September 11 is that it was just that, a reshuffling of bureaucracies. Ultimately, however, it resulted in a much more hardened border, but one with enormous inefficiencies built into the system and unable to function in a way that distinguishes threats from nonthreats. In other words, there was no fundamental reform to the border immigration problem; there was no fundamental solution to American businesses' unquenchable appetite for cheap labor; there was no long-term agreement to aid Mexico in its transition to a more prosperous and democratic society; there was no answer to the many questions on immigration that the American public has to this day. The creation of the Department of Homeland Security, which was supposed to offer an answer to the problem of undocumented migration, turned out to be a dud—the problem of immigration continued to get worse and the border is now a sclerotic series of binational arteries compressed by an authoritarian bureaucracy that does not necessarily understand its context.

And there are changes that have made the border truly unlivable. There are new requirements on the human mobility front. As of December 2007, Americans traveling even across the border need a passport. The checks on immigration applicants are now deeper. Even though new technology was introduced to expedite crossing the border, the reality is that the lines are nearly unbearable, taking sometimes up to four hours to cross. New checkpoints have been built on the southbound lanes, and lines to leave the United States are getting longer and longer as well. The quality of life for borderlanders is deteriorating very quickly. And many are happy to just leave the region. Foreign students are more rigorously tracked. Penalties for visa overstays have been jacked up. Exit programs have been instituted slowly, penalizing those who fail to turn in their I-94s on time. The exit program is supposed to track all border crossers, not only when they come into the United States but also when they exit the country, but all this has done is overwhelm border infrastructure. The costs of all this have also gone up for the border user. And on the aggregate level, these are all expensive measures that have increased the cost of immigration enforcement. In effect, separating immigration application adjudication and immigration enforcement may or may not have been a good idea. Perhaps the Immigration and Naturalization Service (INS) deserved to be split into the Bureau of Citizenship and Immigration Services and Immigration and Customs Enforcement, but neither this move nor the added requirements on border crossers nor the additional layer of paperwork for all has resulted in a decrease in the number of undocumented workers employed in the United States or crossing the border every year. And this has only added layers of government to an already overwhelmed U.S.-Mexico border. In the future, the Department of Homeland Security is likely to come under pressure to ensure that it deals with the border—as well as all of its tasks—in a more efficient manner. To secure the border does not have to mean sapping the energy out of the local communities, decreasing local democracy and participation in border processing, and sacrificing economic prosperity. There has to be a better balance.

CONCLUSION

The debate on immigration in the United States is not an easy one. There are too many players, with too many ideologies and too many interests. Nevertheless, it is possible to make some generalizations regarding this debate because it is a phenomenon that occurs in a much greater context: the forces of globalization.

The U.S. society and economy are among the most open in the world. But its prosperity and competitiveness are increasingly dependent not only on the cross-border exchange of goods, services, and capital but also on labor, particularly less expensive labor—in fact, it would seem that we are now building an economy based on low-paid labor. In other words, the forces of globalization are knocking hard at the gates of the U.S. economy and society, which have benefited enormously from the globalization processes of the last two to three decades—through the production of unprecedented wealth and the creation of a dynamic, ever-changing society. To the creation of this wealth and the maintenance of a vibrant society, undocumented migrants, with their labor, have contributed substantially. The heart of many an American city has revived with the influx of immigrants. Mayors of cities as diverse as Miami, Baltimore, New Orleans, and Detroit understand that migrants contribute much to local communities. Immigrants work hard; they abide by the rules and they hardly complain. Their contributions have hardly been measured because they get lost in the debate of how much they "burden" the American society.

And it is precisely because the debate on immigration focuses on the "burden" that immigrants represent to the American society and economy that the natural reaction by many in the media, in political circles, and in some conservative segments of society—and not just American society, because the problem is a European problem as well—has been to deny that globalization is both beneficial overall and inevitable in the long run, and to denounce immigration as a major evil threatening the survival or the identity, or the whatever, of our society. This denouncement stems from a sustained focus on how painful the process is rather than its enormous benefits and the inevitability of immigration if the country is to remain competitive in the face of the growing economies of Asia in what could become known as the "Asian Century." (Curiously, China has now replaced Mexico as the major source of immigrants. Asians too are discovering the value of living and working in the United States and they are coming in the millions. But they have not yet drawn the attention of nativists. This may be only a matter of time, however, even if Asians are often perceived as more desirable immigrants, given their relentless pursuit of higher education.)

The year 2005 saw the ideological resistance to globalization take the form of opposition to an important—and in the long run inevitable—component of globalization: human mobility. Clearly, there are push and pull forces at work in regard to undocumented migration. Traditionalist Americans tend to focus on the dilution of their identity and even on the local economic "costs" of undocumented workers. Seldom do they talk about the contributions of undocumented workers to the U.S. economy. But the debate should be couched in the language of globalization.

Moreover, it should take place within the revival of the rhetoric regarding the North–South divide. Today no one talks about the North–South divide, that is, the discrepancy in wealth between the developed North and the underdeveloped South. This language died with the leftist movements inspired by communism. Yet it is at these junctures (whether on the Mexico-U.S. border, whether between Spain and Morocco, or whether between Italy and Libya or more recently between Syria and the European Union) that we find the great human push from south to north. Undocumented migrants are pushed north to pursue opportunities and the wealthy North pulls them in so as to remain competitive, keep inflation in check, enjoy the fruits of cheap labor, etc. But migration is no longer limited to south to north. According to the World Bank, soon there will be 250 million people who will be living in a country other than that in which they were born. Moreover, migration on the south-to-south axis is also growing, as people move from China and India to South America, Africa, and Asia. Refugee movements are also adding to a world migration that now appears to be happening in many different directions.[78]

In this regard, it will be painful and very difficult to achieve an immigration agreement that acknowledges the forces of globalization on human mobility and recognizes the de facto labor interdependence between Mexico and the United States and eventually among various countries. Such an agreement must acknowledge the existence of those already working in the United States—an amnesty of some kind to undocumented workers (yes, an amnesty program), even if disguised as something else—and the possibility of a guest worker program that will continue the supply of relatively inexpensive labor to U.S. businesses if they are to remain competitive in the twenty-first century. Compassion, and not just self-interest, also dictates the necessity of such an immigration accord, however painful it may be.

CHAPTER 4

Homeland Security and the Border

THE WAR ON TERROR COMES TO THE BORDER

I arrived in El Paso, Texas, on August 22, 2001, from Washington, DC. I had just finished my PhD at Georgetown University and I had been offered a position to teach at UTEP, where I stayed for 14 years before moving on to Rice University's Baker Institute to found the Mexico Center. At that time, I was looking forward to living on the U.S.-Mexico border, a land of a thousand aspirations but also a place of social and economic ills and very little democracy, as it is a land ruled mostly by federal bureaucrats. I was elated when I finally made it there. But my elation was not to last long. Three weeks after I arrived, with most of my boxes still unpacked, two planes crashed into the New York World Trade Center, a third into the Pentagon, and a fourth went down in Pennsylvania. The entire nation was aghast and in pain. The world came to a standstill as we all watched the harrowing images coming from New York and Washington, DC. We in El Paso saw the events unfold from afar. No one on the border would have thought that the border would be fundamentally changed after that attack. But it was.

In the early morning hours of September 11, 2001, the Border Patrol, U.S. Customs, and INS agents at the border POEs were conducting their work business as usual. I saw those agents that morning as I crossed the Cordova Bridge from Ciudad Juárez into El Paso. My nephew Guy was with me. I came up to the booth and asked the officer if he knew what had just happened. He nodded yes and waved me through hurriedly. They did not yet know the magnitude of what had just happened. But they were about to find out, and big changes were also about to come to the border.

In this chapter, I will examine what September 11 did to American culture in its broadest sense and to some extent to the Mexican and Canadian cultures as well, inasmuch as they share what at that time were two of the longest undefended borders in the world. I will look at the pre–September 11 history on the border to understand how previous border eras compare with the new security culture of the border. This analysis, as does the entire book, attempts to enlighten the nonborder resident so as to become aware of the impact of September 11 on the U.S.-Mexico border. At the end, I will assess whether the border is any more secure today than it was before the tragic events of September 11.

Examining these changes is important because every step to escalate "border security" has spillover effects into the country at large, and every move is ultimately the result of a decision made by elected officials and unelected bureaucrats without necessarily thinking about how they are affecting every border process and every border resident. Security became paramount, and such was the state of mind of border guards in the aftermath of September 11 that, in my view, they reacted in a way that tested rational processing of information by the mind. Emotions and paranoia were at their highest, and in many ways they still are. Their state of mind was still such that they engaged their imagination so that any risk, even remotely similar to a terrorist attack, was magnified and became real and imminent. The terrorist attacks led to confusion in Washington, certainly, but this was compounded in the border region, producing much economic deterioration, personal and family pain, and unnecessary criminalization of border residents. Everyone was affected by the decisions of politicians and bureaucrats who found it easy to focus their frustration on the U.S.-Mexico border, a place that ultimately had very little to do with anything that happened on September 11.

The psychological effects on policy makers and the material effects on border users are analyzed next because it is important to sort the decisions made out of rational choice from those made out of a state of mind that has to do more with the trauma of the attacks on New York and Washington, DC, than on any rational decision making. In the nation's capital, for example, the attacks led to a groupthink mentality. Subjective and emotional judgments prevailed everywhere and rationality and objectivity had no effect on policy makers—as it is still evident by the way Washington, DC, is still operating. Security swallowed everything—the way we viewed infrastructure, human mobility, trade, natural disasters and emergency management, and the borderline itself. This is understandable in that the emotional shock of that day was enormous, but they also became obsessed with a foreign ideology to the extent that they were willing to transform the American way of life in exchange for what is increasingly clear are modest gains in security. Many of the criticisms of the Department of Homeland Security today have to do with its being what some call a "bureaucratic monstrosity"—an agency that can barely function given its mandate, its size, and its budget.[1]

In the heat of the moment, it was hard for politicians, policy makers, and bureaucrats to understand why September 11 occurred and it was even harder for them to distinguish it from the ongoing and often acrimonious debates on the long-standing ills of the border. Time and time again, government actors linked the U.S.-Mexico border security issues with the terrorist attacks. The national debate as to why the United States had failed to prevent the terrorist attacks began when the second plane struck the North Tower in lower Manhattan. Watching the scenes on TV, many politicians and bureaucrats immediately began to assess what had happened. The paramount question was: what failed inside the U.S. government? This was a difficult question to answer, however straightforward it was. Within a few hours this difficult question was in the air. Politicians, media personalities, and talking heads all asked what had gone wrong. The answers varied, depending on whom you asked, but soon a remarkable but perhaps oversimplified consensus emerged. Nearly everyone zoomed in on immigration enforcement and lax border security. Later, intelligence failures would be added to the mix, but the border had already been dragged into the national security arena when many of us thought that it was a management issue. And yet for the border, undocumented migration, illegal drugs, security, and economic integration and trade became conflated with the war on terror.

The new war on terror produced a totalizing effect on the border. For too long after the terrorist attacks, there was a sense of vulnerability that could be assuaged only by protecting the U.S. periphery, viewing border users as enemies, and stiffening the penalties for even minor violations of a rule. All the language used to refer to the border indicated that many in Washington blamed lax border security for the terrorist attacks and wanted to bring programs and practices of the war on terror to the border. A group of American nationalists, for example, wrote on their web page:

For ... the ease with which the terrorists entered, and the bloodshed they have already perpetrated and may perpetrate in the future, the American people have to thank the open borders lobby—politicians who push for more immigration and fewer restrictions on entry, ideologues who insist that national borders and identities are obsolete, and Big Business, which demands a never ending flow of cheap labor, at the expense of American workers and the security of its own country.[2]

This linking of September 11 with the border, particularly the U.S.-Mexico border, precipitated a massive mobilization by the U.S. government to "protect" the nation's borders. September 11 and the U.S.-Mexico border would be inextricably linked for a very long time and remain so. Fifteen years after that ill-fated September 11, the border remains a harsh place, stagnating and struggling against a hostile national narrative and an ever more oppressive bureaucracy. Unfortunately, the linking of the war on terror to the border only complicated and obscured the region's problems and postponed the painful policy management decisions required to establish a workable border arrangement between Mexico and the United States. Only lately has the discourse on the border begun to shift, but only very slowly and mostly motivated by the frustrations of big business. Local residents still have very little to say about the inhabitability of their own space. The kind of authoritarianism exercised on border residents would hardly be tolerated by citizens elsewhere in the country.

The mobilization and reorganization to "protect America's borders" was believed in Washington to be able to produce a more secure border. But it has not. In fact, a central point of this book is to show the enormous failure of the border security regime, despite the enormity of resources thrown at "securing" the border. While it is true that undocumented migration is only now a fraction of what it was, other push and pull forces, more structural in nature, may be largely responsible for that. And the war on drugs has simply gone on, more virulently than before. And so far, it is hard to tell whether any terrorist attack has been averted, given that we have had none executed from this castigated border. The new border security regime was powerful enough, however, to inaugurate a new era in the Southwest: the "border security era."

THE BORDER AND THE IMMEDIATE AFTERMATH OF SEPTEMBER 11

This troubled reaction was not exclusive to Washington, DC, bureaucrats. The border bureaucrats got the message and were empowered by it. Within a few hours of that ill-fated morning's attacks, as flames ballooned from the windows of the Twin Towers in New York City and some of the walls of the Pentagon building lay in ruins, the first reaction of the street-level agents operating at the borderline in San Diego, Nogales, El Paso, Laredo, McAllen, Brownsville, and elsewhere in the Southwest was to shut down all crossings. All people, vehicles, and cargo were immediately brought to a halt. Many residents of Ciudad Juárez who were students or workers in El Paso at that time recall when officers came up the bridge and stopped the lines. All vehicles and pedestrians were prevented from crossing the bridge. Many of those on their daily routines were forced to return to the Mexican side. Those who had made it across to El Paso had to find a place to stay because they would not be allowed back on the bridges or feared they could not return to El Paso if they went into Mexico.

The effects of this irrational albeit understandable stoppage were immediate and devastating to the border—in the short run. Families were separated for days, unable to meet their loved ones across the border. Thousands of Mexican students could not attend classes at American schools and universities along the border. Shopping centers and malls all along the borderlands, from San Diego to Brownsville, showed a dramatic decrease in their daily business transactions as Mexicans could not easily come across the border to shop and do business. Tourism in Mexican and American cities along the border collapsed, leaving hundreds of hotel rooms and restaurant seats empty. Tourism revenue on U.S. border towns also suffered. And trade came to a standstill, costing companies hundreds of millions of dollars over just a few days.

Eventually, the border was reopened. But the world had fundamentally changed and, in many ways, the U.S.-Mexico border changed with it. Border crossers and borderland residents were some of the first in the nation to appreciate the changes produced by September 11 in the new security-conscious nation. Immediately, the treatment of crossers by border officers also changed. They were outright hostile and it remains so to this day. Everyone and everything crossing the border was and is suspect. Everywhere along the nearly 2,000-mile international line, the inspections of vehicles and people became very thorough and intense. The movement of trucks into the United States from manufacturing plants on the Mexican side became slow and cumbersome, taking many hours in inspection. Consequently, there was an enormous waste of fuel and human work hours. With the slowdown, pollution levels increased and productivity dropped as man-hours were wasted in lines and by trucks unable to meet their delivery deadlines. Just-in-time processes, which the maquiladora industry had been moving toward, came to a halt.

Those who were able to cross over the next few days found themselves under severe scrutiny and even questioning by border officials, sometimes with outright harassment and intimidation—something that has now become fully institutionalized. Slowly, all cross-border activity eventually resumed quasi-normal levels and even continued to grow but under a much stricter check system. The new system relied on fear as a deterrent to a large extent. Maria Rodríguez, who often came across to clean houses in El Paso and to shop and to visit her relatives, remembers walking over the crest of the Santa Fe Bridge and thinking "the border will never be the same again." Her waiting times as a pedestrian increased considerably and she remembers being afraid of being harassed by the border officials. They could easily take away her border-crossing card just on their own very subjective judgment that she could represent a threat to America. This kind of fear was all around—although everyone understood and empathized with the United States given what had happened. Perhaps the uncertainty of what would happen next justified the action of shutting the border and intensifying all checks. That was a natural short-term solution palatable to everyone, but in the long run it could contribute to building a fortress America that might not be healthy for anyone. Interestingly enough, shutting the border temporarily, the new intensive check system, the fresh border procedures, and the bureaucratic reorganization that was to come after September 11 would not affect cross-border interaction in the long run. The crunch was felt only in the few weeks following the attack. As we will see, all statistics show that even through late 2001, cross-border transactions resumed their usual pace. Now we are back up to "normal," but it is a new normal, a more oppressive normal. A poll commissioned by Univisión—the U.S. Spanish language television channel—shows that people have adjusted and about the same numbers on both sides say that things have gotten better on the border, about the same numbers say that things have gotten worse, and about the same numbers say that things are about the same—with U.S. side residents being slightly more pessimistic. Clearly, fifteen years after September 11, borderlanders have become accustomed to this new normal.[3] Perhaps they have forgotten how easy it was to cross the border in 2001.

BORDER WAIT TIMES

Perhaps no measure is more consistent with the living hell that the border has become than wait times. These went up immediately after September 11 and overall have not really come down. Border wait times have been studied by many scholars and policy makers. To border users, wait times are the daily painful reminder that the border is effectively closed. One can wait upwards of four hours to cross the border in places like El Paso and San Diego. One to two hours is the new normal in El Paso—but may reach up to four hours in Tijuana, for example. But cities on the American side are heavily dependent on an open border. Mexican students, shoppers, tourists, and workers fuel the economies of those cities. And they know that they have to constantly try to reduce wait times. The city of El Paso recently came up with a creative burden-sharing plan to reduce wait times. It simply raised the fees on vehicles and pedestrians in order to collect as much as $1.6 million a year more to hand over to CBP for overtime. The idea was that CBP would keep lanes open longer, open some earlier, and use some of that money to expedite the crossing. This has clearly not been the case. All that has happened is that local, mostly poorer residents have simply borne the burden of additional tolls but seen no return on investment. And even if wait times have been reduced by one minute for each crosser, that is hardly anything in lines that can take up to four hours.

DIAGNOSING THE FAILURES OF SEPTEMBER 11

After the few nightmarish days at the border, politicians and policy makers in Washington, DC, turned their attention to what had gone wrong. They began combing the bureaucracy for failures, but often their thoughts would go to the border. They settled on immigration failure, border-trade procedures, bureaucratic processes, and eventually on intelligence failure. Report after report reaffirmed these issues. These were the four great culprits, as Washington, DC, viewed them.

Immigration Failure

To many in Washington, DC, immigration procedures and immigration enforcement were evident culprits. The INS had spun out of control, they argued. It had failed to detect the terrorists who entered the United States on student visas because immigration enforcement had been thoroughly neglected. They said it had focused on visa adjudication and forgot immigration law enforcement altogether. INS bureaucrats were accused of having forgotten that they were also law enforcers, not merely employees pushing paper.[4] This conclusion was arrived at even though many argued that September 11 was not about immigration failure but about intelligence failure.[5]

From this conclusion, it was not very long until the powers that be in Washington, DC, conflated the border and immigration and determined that border openness was an element that contributed to failure in deterring the attacks. Border openness had reached unprecedented levels, according to many. This was absurd, of course, since the border had been slowly closing for decades and border control had accelerated since 1994, making it "more closed" than ever before in its history. They of course ignored those facts. Nevertheless, they alleged that people could come into the United States easily and stay as long as they wanted. There was no systematic tracking, for example, of those who overstayed their visas. (Two of the attackers had expired visas while in the United States.) Strangely enough, when pointing to the failure of the INS to stop the terrorists, all of whom entered the country legally, many would wander off in the direction of the debate on undocumented migration as a failure of law enforcement by both the INS and the Border Patrol. The 1990s were labeled a decade of wanton neglect in regard to border openness, with little distinction made between legal and illegal entries, between undocumented crossers and overstays, and on and on. In the same sentence, talking heads would mention overstayed visas, undocumented migration, legal migration, and open borders in an effort to blame the bureaucrats for failing to stop the terrorist attacks. This was of course inaccurate, given the unprecedented law enforcement along the border since Operation Hold the Line in 1994.

Trade too was dragged into the debate. The new ideology of North American integration, which emerged out of NAFTA in the 1990s, was blamed for the openness of the border. NAFTA and all this talk about North American integration, some argued, was the culprit because it had caused immigration authorities to lower their guard with a consequent lack of vigilance on the border. That too was inaccurate. In fact, in 1994, the same year NAFTA went into effect, the border became the object of enforcement operations designed to shut it down. The 1990s, as an "era of good feelings" about North American integration, but it was not an opening border. Nevertheless, the border would become the focus of the post-September 11 war on terror. Mexicans crossing the border were now viewed with heightened suspicion. Eventually, all crossers were viewed with suspicion. Even U.S. citizens residing on the Mexican side of the border were viewed as a threat, as unpatriotic. U.S. citizens who do not have a passport today, for example, are being subjected to harassment. CBP is even asking to impose fines on U.S. citizens who are not carrying their passports at the border.[6]

Moreover, U.S. immigration bureaucracies were also charged with a failure to share information with the State Department and other law enforcement agencies necessary to detect undesirables applying to enter the United States, or anyone overstaying his or her visa once inside the United States. This lack of information sharing by the INS with the State Department and with other law enforcement agencies was strongly held against the agency. The INS was held largely responsible for the ability of the September 11 terrorists to enter the United States, move about freely, and then carry out the activities they had in mind. The INS was blamed to the point of extinction. In effect, with the Homeland Security Act, the INS ceased to exist.[7]

Economic Integration, Trade, and Border Security

When it comes to the border, it is very hard to disentangle one issue from the other when it comes to finding culprits for September 11. Imperialistic bureaucracies have a further incentive to conflate all issues, in an effort to gain greater importance and control—and the budgets and privileges that come with it. The rhetoric on the openness of the border became furious. Border openness became the buzzword. Those searching for what had gone wrong went from faulting immigration law enforcement practices to focusing on the trade practices of the border. NAFTA had propelled trade between Mexico and the United States to unprecedented levels. Trade between Mexico and the United States increased from some \$80 billion in 1993 to \$250 billion in 2001.[8] It is now reaching unprecedented levels—over half a trillion dollars a year. Most trade crossed and still crosses the U.S.-Mexico border by land, in trucks, and in trains. With the substantial increase in cross-border trade, it became nearly impossible to inspect every truck. As already mentioned, anywhere between 4 and 5 million 18-wheeler trucks crossed the U.S.-Mexico border every year as of 2001.[9] There are now nearly 7 million. The capacity of the POEs to handle the volume of trucking that NAFTA produced was overwhelmed. Inspection was almost necessarily done randomly and only on a very small percentage of the trucks coming across. That is still the case—and no truck has ever been used to conduct a terrorist attack, by the way. But both the infrastructure and the number of inspectors were insufficient to do any more than random checks. When Congress passed NAFTA, they did not necessarily provide for the infrastructure to secure the volume of trade expected from the new agreement.[10]

After September 11, however, these "lax" trade inspection practices were blamed for the "porousness" of the border.[11] The media ran various random stories about how trucks were being used to smuggle undocumented workers and illegal drugs.[12] That was true, and it is still true, even with all the added inspections and technology and wait times. Moreover, some speculated that these same trucks and vehicles and even undocumented workers could cross a "dirty bomb" or a "briefcase bomb" into the United States.[13] These hypothetical border-jumping terrorists could conceal weapons of mass destruction or materials useful to terrorists once inside the United States. Fifteen years later, nothing like that has happened, but this possibility still sustains a burdensome bureaucratic apparatus and impedes smart border policies to manage the ongoing integration between the two countries at the borderline.

The rhetoric of the war on terror warped even the way border trade was viewed. Every truck driver was a potential terrorist and every truck became a potential terrorist weapon trying to penetrate into the United States and "harm America." The totalizing war on terror rhetoric had swallowed the debate on border trade as it had swallowed the immigration debate. From there, it was just a leap before politicians in Congress concluded that something had to be done about lax border-trade inspection practices. As with immigration, a series of new trade-related measures and programs were implemented to "secure the border" and prevent future terrorist attacks while "allowing the binational trade to flow freely." Interestingly, there was little talk about raising trade barriers or stopping the flow of trade, as with immigration. Immigrants are a vulnerable constituency, easy prey for politicians. Businessmen and large trading corporations are not. Thus the debate did not center on stopping trade. Trade in fact had to be allowed to flow. Congress was not about to hurt trade between Mexico and the United States because over $1 trillion of trade every two years touches many interests, which in turn touches many members of Congress. Thus Congress was unwilling to harm such powerful economic interests that ride on U.S.-Mexican trade. There were no rumblings against NAFTA, only against the lack of vigilance it had presumably produced along the border.

INCUMBENTS, CHALLENGERS, AND THE VOICELESS

The border security industrial complex—an iron triangle of politicians, bureaucrats, and the security industry—grew exponentially.[14] Everyone benefited. Politicians got the votes and the campaign funds. Bureaucrats got control, the gadgets, the salaries, and the prestige of their importance. And corporations got their profits from an ever-growing number of goods and services to "secure" the border. The members of this iron triangle came to be the border incumbents. Their priorities and interests constitute the stuff of border security. They strive to maintain the negative image of the border and they benefit from it. They resist change or any innovative way of managing the border and the binational relationship as it manifests itself at it. They have nearly all control of the border and its future.

The international business community is in many ways unhappy with the status quo. They want a seamless border. They want inspectors to do their job quickly and to move their goods on to where they are going. Any idle vehicle or driver at the crossing point is money wasted. They are, in many ways, challengers of the status quo. But there is nothing they can do, except negotiate at the margins—including registering vehicles and drivers in the expedited lanes, lobbying for certain permits and additional infrastructure, etc. They have had some success, but it is limited. The incumbents—law enforcement—would not allow a structural challenge to their power and control. They ultimately say who crosses and who does not, even if millions of dollars are lost and much pain and suffering is caused.

At the bottom of this hierarchy are border residents. They have no say in how the border is managed—on the costs imposed on their time and wealth, on how to serve their interests better; on the often abusive attitudes of border enforcement agents, on the restrictions on their right to free movement or due process, on how to plan for the future development of the region, on the impact of enforcement policies on their natural resources and their environment, and so on. Democracy is thin at the U.S.-Mexico border. Civil society is practically dead—especially crossborder civil society. And political participation is low. Workers cannot organize to weigh in on their future. And citizens seem to get away as quickly as they can, migrating to larger cities within Mexico or within the United

States. There is a sense of stagnation on the border. It has not grown economically; it has stabilized demographically; and opportunities are few and far between. It has gone from a frontier to a place where enforcement kills any possibilities for greater opportunity. It is nearly the antithesis of what it used to be, in spite of all the rhetoric about the dynamism of the border.

ARIZONA AND NEW MEXICO

Other analysts focused on border openness in Arizona and New Mexico as a fundamental problem that contributed to September 11, in spite of the fact that—again—the border had hardly anything to do with the terrorist attacks. Various quasi-military operations to seal the border around urban areas in the 1990s had succeeded in pushing undocumented workers to seek crossing points in those two states, particularly in Arizona, which saw its number of Border Patrol arrests soar. Around the time of September 11, Arizona alone still accounted for about half of the undocumented-migrant detentions on the border. This was perceived as a serious gap in border security, a gap through which terrorists could sneak into the country. That is no longer the case, but the anti-immigrant feelings stirred up in Arizona remain part of the political landscape.

The media contributed to this hysteria by covering stories that showed the presumed ability of terrorists and other undesirables to enter the country illegally by crossing the desert in Arizona. The *Arizona Daily Star*, for example, published an article stating that the American Border Patrol, a vigilante group, had conducted a "weapons of mass destruction smuggling test" successfully in the Arizona desert by sneaking a fake weapon of mass destruction and making it to a house in Sierra Vista without being caught.[15] Thus the backpacks of undocumented workers walking the Arizona desert were transmogrified into weapons of mass destruction and undocumented workers into potential terrorists ready to attack America. These speculations further conflated the problem of undocumented migration with the issue of national security with the attacks on New York and Washington, DC. They made no distinction between one or the other or the other. The state of the border was viewed as a national security threat. From there, the natural follow-up was a generalized discourse about "controlling" the border or "regaining control" of the border, as if the border had ever been under control in the past.

Of course, by 2007, the Arizona border crisis had reached its peak. The Secure Border Fence Act was passed that year and the construction of the border wall began in earnest. Groups of vigilantes came to the border from all over the state and harassed immigrants. The Border Patrol added resources and boots on the ground. Arizona itself became hostile to immigrants. And by 2010, the border in Arizona was already under control. The number of undocumented crossers is merely a trickle of what it used to be. Operational control of the border is nearly a reality. But this has not had an effect on the border management system. It has had an effect only on empowering border bureaucracies and pushing migrants to other places along the border, with the latest entry point being South Texas—although the overall numbers are only a fraction of what they used to be in any case.

DAMN THOSE BUREAUCRATS!

Eventually, analysts and politicians asking what had gone wrong focused on what they labeled outdated bureaucratic structures, the supposed backwardness of the technology used by U.S. officials on the border, and general bureaucratic inefficiency and incompetence, all of which translated into a "porous" border that represented a national security threat. The bureaucratic organizations of the U.S. government in charge of managing the border were blamed for contributing to a lawless, chaotic border that now threatened the very survival of the nation. All the agencies working on the border in 2001, from U.S. Customs to the Border Patrol to the DEA to the INS, were scrutinized and made part of the failure of September 11. The paranoia inside these bureaucratic organizations spread like wildfire because no one was certain about what was going to happen to them. As the hearings on the attacks of September 11 proceeded in Congress, these border agencies were accused of being insular in their missions and tasks. They were to blame for their inability to work together and the gradual collapse of communication among them. Eventually, the discourse became so intense that no agency was safe. They were all held responsible for the attacks. The result was that they all were reorganized into a single department in order to have them "work together." Whether they have achieved that level of coordinated efficiency by being placed under a single roof is something that has yet to be demonstrated. Early evidence shows that they have not.[16] There is in fact an increasing consensus that the Department of Homeland Security is simply too large to function well. It has created perverse incentives by establishing symbiotic relationships with the private security industry. It has enabled politicians to use security systematically for their own political and electoral gain. It has been given authority to waive all kinds of law and regulations that everyone else has to follow, at an increasing environmental cost to the borderlands. It has been accused of violating human and due process rights. Indeed, there may be no political will to hold that agency accountable, but the time is likely to come when it will face scrutiny. So far, however, it has successfully fended of most criticism.

The end result was that smart was confused with size. And good management was mistaken for absolute discretion and no accountability. And everyone went from a border user to a border sufferer.

INTELLIGENCE FAILURE AND THE BORDER

Unfortunately, though the terrorist attacks were later fully acknowledged by the *9/11 Commission Report* to be a consequence of intelligence failure, initially, a hard look at the intelligence structures took a backseat to immigration, trade, and border security legislation. And I use the world "legislation" deliberately. I use it instead of the word "reform" because there has been no reform in either the immigration or the trade or the anti-illegal-drug policy regimes that prevail on the U.S.-Mexico borderlands. The immigration system is still widely acknowledged to be a "broken system" and all reform attempts have failed since then. And the drug policy that was put in place decades ago at the federal level is still in place. It is the states that are beginning to challenge the federal prohibitionist regime, and only then in regard to marijuana. But in Congress, there has not been even superficial reform to any of these regimes that were put into place as a consequence of September 11. Trade, however, has been growing and is still a priority on the border. Immigration, both legal and illegal, continues and follows along the same principles as before—even if undocumented migration has diminished considerably. Illegal drugs are the grand failure. They are just as abundant as before and their price has decreased. The strategy to combat them is still a largely unilateral, supply-side strategy that has produced no results before or after September 11. If anything, the fundamental immigration, trade, and antidrug problems and policies remain essentially the same. We should also say that border management has not improved. The only thing that has changed is the structure of the bureaucracies that deal with these policy problems and the technology that has been deployed to help them.

Still, curiously enough, after information sharing ("intelligence failure") inside the U.S. government was identified as a serious problem that contributed to September 11, President George W. Bush himself was reputed to have resisted intelligence reform and was even unwilling to fire George Tenet, the director of central intelligence, for the intelligence failures related to the terrorist attacks. President Bush was also reputed to have resisted the creation of a director of national intelligence to coordinate all intelligence activities of the U.S. government. His legislative proposal focused instead on reorganizing the bureaucracies that dealt with immigration and trade on the border. The reorganization, however, was somewhat superficial, however massive it may have been. It had no substantial effect on the philosophy that underlay U.S. policy toward these fundamental issues. By 2006, it seemed that the creation of the Department of Homeland Security had, at best, created only a new layer of requirements for border crossers and a new layer of paperwork for the corresponding bureaucracies.

Eventually but somewhat reluctantly, the Bush administration and Congress would acknowledge intelligence failure as a major cause of September 11, and only then did President Bush add it to the mix of proposed legislation. Still, intelligence reform continued to be resisted in Washington, DC. The politician-favored suspects for failing to deter the terrorist attacks were: (1) immigration, (2) border openness (largely due to economic integration and trade), and (3) an ineffective bureaucratic organization. And both the president and Congress stuck to their guns. The creation of the Department of Homeland Security reflected their preoccupation with these three issues, not with intelligence failures. Sure, some members of Congress called for a serious restructuring of the intelligence system. These members of Congress felt vindicated by the *9/11 Commission Report*, which would agree that intelligence failure was a major cause of the attacks. In the end, however, the White House and Congress responded by passing intelligence legislation but not until 2005. For the first four years, their efforts went into legislating and implementing changes on immigration and trade practices. Illegal drugs seemed to have fallen out of the political agenda altogether. The DEA was not touched in the reorganization of border bureaucracies. Thus, through 2002, various acts of Congress focused on tightening border control and making changes to the immigration adjudication and enforcement and the trade control bureaucracies through the Homeland Security Act of 2002.

There is no doubt, however, that intelligence has gotten much better. Technology has advanced enough that communications can be better monitored and analyzed. Information can be obtained in real time. Law enforcement interconnectivity has also gotten better as databases are accessed quickly by border authorities. And so on. But this has only confirmed one important thing: the border has yet to be linked to any attempts to do harm to the United States. Most of the individuals "busted" are people who are trying to hedge the border for a better life—something that they should not be faulted for but encouraged to do. Moreover, the United States was given unprecedented access to Mexican intelligence during the Calderón administration (2006–12) and none of it showed any links to terrorism.

CONFLATING THE ISSUES

The matter of conflating the terrorist attacks with border issues deserves further attention because it has been very damaging to the border and a potential border agenda for the future. As late as March 2, 2005, Peter Gadiel, who testified in Congress, before the Subcommittee on Immigration, Border and Security, still sounded the same trumpet, declaring that:

We know there were intelligence failures leading up to 9/11. We know that com-placent government officials simply refused to believe that something like 9/11 could happen here. More than anything else, though, we know that our government failed to maintain control of our borders leading up to 9/11. Those 19 murderers counted on lax scrutiny of their visa applications and overwhelmed inspectors at our ports of entry. Once here, the terrorists counted on being able to hide in plain sight in the ocean of 10 million or more illegal aliens living in the United States. They benefited from the fact that enforcement of immigration laws inside the United States is virtually nonexistent and that Americans are so inured to this fact that no one—civilian or law officer—would notice them or interfere as they planned, rehearsed, financed, and then carried out their conspiracy to com-mit mass murder.[17]

This testimony before Congress shows the carelessness with which experts, politicians, talking heads, and others viewed September 11 through a single lens: border control. All issues were conflated: immigra-tion adjudication and enforcement, border security, trade and economic integration, border openness and control, etc. They were all "bad" and the bureaucrats that handled them "incompetent." In Gadiel's statement, there was hardly any attempt to carefully sort out the failures. Others were even more radical than Gadiel. There were even some attempts to relate al-Qaeda directly to the border! At a hearing before the Senate Select Committee on Intelligence on February 16, 2005, Adm. James Loy, deputy secretary of homeland security, testified that:

Entrenched human smuggling networks and corruption in areas beyond our bor-ders can be exploited by terrorist organizations. Recent information ... strongly suggests that al-Qaeda has considered using the Southwest Border to infiltrate the United States. Several al-Qaeda leaders believe operatives can pay their way into the country through Mexico and also believe illegal entry is more advanta-geous for operational security reasons. However, there is no conclusive evidence that indicates ... operatives have made successful penetrations ... via this method.[18]

Although 15 years later there is no evidence that the border poses a threat, this is the same kind of paranoia that prevails among radical anti-immigrant groups in the United States, and also in certain segments of the American public, today. The presidential campaign of 2016 demon-strates that the border can still be used by politicians to galvanize support during elections—whether in a state, such as Texas or Arizona, or in the presidential election. And it can still scare many Americans. It is under-standable that this image of the border spread quickly in the American public—there was much pain after September 11—and has remained there. It does not help that some candidates continue to use the border for political profit. A November 2005 Rasmussen Reports survey found that "sixty percent of Americans say they favor building a barrier along the border between the United States and Mexico." Only 26 percent were opposed to this approach.[19] Interesting, along the border, the opposite is true. According to the Univisión poll cited above, 77 percent of Mexican bor-der residents and 70 percent of American border residents do not consider building a wall important at all. Even so, after the border wall is nearly 700 miles and operational control of the border is much improved, there are those who still want to continue building the wall. If we do not address the root causes of undocumented migration through structural economic re-form and if we do not tackle the problem of illegal drugs through harm reduction strategies, the border will continue to be the focus of a misguided policy—in effect an easy target for the lazy politician.

There is a serious problem with this sort of mentality, however. The United States and Mexico are neighbors. Neither of them is going to go away. The relationship is only growing. Trade has in fact gone up. According to the U.S. Census Bureau, in 2016 Mexico is the second largest trading partner of the United States, with 14.8 percent of total trade—above China with 14.7 percent, and closing in on Canada with 15.3 per-cent of total trade.[20] Mexico's energy reform promises to integrate Mexico and the United States even further. And yet both countries relate to each other in a schizoid manner. Their border problems are very serious: human smuggling and trafficking, illegal drugs, the transit of Central and South American undocumented workers through Mexico, poverty, economic and human development issues, and the challenges of eco-nomic integration. But neither country has convinced the other that they require a new, joint border management system. Mexico and the United States must deal with these problems together. It is insufficient to build a wall along the border and pretend that the other side is nonexistent. A comprehensive, bilateral approach is required to deal with each of these issues under a single border regime that will benefit both countries. But this is not happening. There is almost no contact between the officials on one side and the other along the border—most substantive contacts are between Washington, DC, and Mexico City and far away from the border-lands. Each country operates under its own rules, with its own psycho-logical barriers to openness with each other. The sort of conflation of the issues that is present in the rhetoric cannot help either. Labeling the bor-der a dangerous place that must be sealed off is a recipe for a continuation of what has been happening on the border for the past 40 years. And 40 years of efforts to seal the border have only deepened the problem. This "close the border" mind-set has created better and more efficient illegal-drug criminal organizations, forced undocumented workers to rely on emerging human-smuggling networks, weakened cross-border social ties, and built a sense of separation that is detrimental to cross-border cooperation. Lumping all border issues together into a single, large crisis is counterproductive. A wall along the border is not just a wall; it impedes a serious look at the border and its dilemmas in order to find workable solutions for both Mexico and the United States.

REORGANIZING FOR BORDER SECURITY

With every border regime (frontier, customs, law enforcement, and now security) came the creation of new laws and new bureaucracies to "secure" the border, and the border came under much greater operational control with each stage. Clearly, the U.S. government's response to the border over many decades is explained by a logic of escalation. With every "border crisis," Congress has passed new legislation and has continually reorganized and increased the number of bureaucrats operating on the border. It has in effect done what Congress does best: thrown more resources at the problem, added new people, new rules, etc., but hardly ever tackled the problem structurally. There is no new border management system. There is only more of the same approach that has been in place for at least 100 years.

The advent of the security era of the U.S.-Mexican border, which resulted from the war on terror, could not be the exception to this historical trend. As a response to 9/11, Congress passed the Patriot Act, a law designed to enhance the authority of law enforcement agencies to fight terrorism.[21] In 2002, Congress moved on to reorganize the border bureaucracies. It passed the Homeland Security Act that year, which effectively established the Department of Homeland Security, pooling together 22 different agencies from various departments into a single unit with a workforce of some 180,000 bureaucrats and a budget of over $40 billion in FY2005.[22] The budget has only exploded since, to $65 billion in 2016. In regard to borders, Title IV of the Homeland Security Act explicitly created the Office of the Undersecretary for Border and Transportation Security, grouping all agencies responsible for border security under one individual.[23] A shrewd observer of border affairs could have predicted this response. Starting a few weeks after September 11, some of the most important security initiatives coming out of Congress and the White House were escalating the penalties against terrorists and those who could help them, increasing the budgets to secure the border, and reorganizing the bureaucrats that work on the region. These new laws and the bureaucratic reorganization they implied were supposed to make

U.S. borders more secure. By 2007, the Secure Fence Act was passed, waiving all kinds of federal laws required of all infrastructure projects, and further reinforcing the image of the border as a problem. The trends have only continued. There has been no letup on efforts to seal the border, even though other policies could and should be explored.

The border security initiative of the new department broke down into programs. The three most important of these programs were, first, C-TPAT, which began in November 2001. C-TPAT was designed to secure the supply chain—from the Mexican maquiladora plants to the transportation companies to the U.S. importers. All producers, importers, and carriers were required to register with CBP in order to receive preclearance before their merchandise and personnel got to the border. This would presumably expedite their crossing at the POE. New technology was introduced to scan the trucks in order to detect any specific loads that were not consistent with the declaration of the importer/exporter or the trucking company.

The second program was the National Targeting Center, which gathers statistics on all border crossers (people, vehicles, and transactions) for the purposes of detecting higher risk crossers and targeting inspections on those that have a higher probability of being associated with criminal or terrorist elements.[24] It integrates government, commercial, and law enforcement databases into an evolving, statistics-producing mechanism to make the latest criminal trends on the border available to law enforcement officers on the ground. The targets identified as higher risk are screened upon arrival at the POE, while the less risky crossers are only randomly checked. This was once again an example of the heavy reliance on technology to screen the considerable volume of traffic across the border.

A third was the US-VISIT Program (United States Visitor and Immigrant Status Indicator Technology Program), an entry and exit control system designed to enhance security and control all individuals crossing any border. It is a system initiated at airports and seaports and extended to land POEs on the U.S.-Mexico border. The system scans travel documents and takes fingerprints and pictures of the border crosser. The data are then run through databases to determine whether the individual is a presumed criminal or terrorist. This system also keeps track of all border-crossing information of any one individual over time. The U.S.-VISIT Program was eventually replaced by the Office of Biometric Identity Management. That office has deployed and upgraded infrastructure to collect biometric information on all individuals entering and eventually exiting the United States. This is the major entry but also exit control program that the U.S. government relies on, and it has slowly become interconnected with many other law enforcement databases. This effort required many more agents and gadgets and a very high investment by the U.S. government to control those who are entering *and* eventually exiting the country. Still, while it may be possible to control hundreds of millions of passengers and travelers who come in by air, land, and sea, it is still very hard to have a full on exit control. With the as of yet improvised implementation of land southbound inspections, this program is poised to grow, but it has become a nightmare and it now may take as long to exit the United States as it takes to enter it.

There were, of course, many other programs introduced to gain further "control" of the border. The time when American citizens could simply jump the border and return by simply declaring their citizenship was over. As of December 2007, anyone traveling across the border is required to carry a passport—and anyone not doing so will be subjected to harassment by authorities, with an additional threat to impose fines for noncompliance. In reality, this is a response to the unwillingness of the American public to support a national identification card. A national ID is unpalatable, but a passport can be required in its stead. With the kind of technology available today, all passports need is a sufficiently powerful chip to carry vast amounts of information on that person in the passport booklet. There are now numerous programs designed to control information, to track individuals on many criteria, and to maintain vast databases on all kinds of people around the world. The latest revelations of how the National Security Agency gathers and keeps information, as exposed by Edward Snowden, are evidence that technology has institutionalized the paranoia that September 11 created.

A NAGGING QUESTION

The efforts of the U.S. government to control the border, with all the programs that they bring, are not the real issue in any event. The U.S. government has the obligation to protect the American people. Programs also come and go. The U.S. government is entitled to invent programs and fund them. The vital questions that must be asked are: Are the policies and programs paying off? Are they making us safer but *also* protecting our economic prosperity and ensuring that our rights remain untouched? Is the game worth the candle? Are we now finally in control of the border without sacrificing much of what we enjoy? Is the war on terror on the border giving an acceptable return on investment? About 15 years after the disaster of September 11 and the U.S. efforts to wage a war on terror, we have had enough time and sufficient evidence exists to judge whether U.S. government got a reasonable bang for its buck and whether borderlanders themselves are better off with these policies as well.

Given the initial diagnosis and the eventual response of the U.S. government, it is probably accurate to say that no other geographical area of the country—perhaps with the exception of airports—underwent the intensive and extensive changes that the U.S.-Mexico border did. Speaking with some Canadian scholars in Victoria, Vancouver, Canada, in December 2005 and then visiting various points of that border over the years since, it became evident that they too worried about U.S. unilateral action on the Canadian border. And some things did change. But in the end, the U.S.-Canada border was not as deeply affected as the U.S.-Mexico border. Canadians were able to make some important concessions and give Americans unprecedented access to their own law enforcement, so that they could contain some of the harshest measures proposed for that border. Mexico was not in such a privileged position, partly because its own law enforcement is not trustworthy. Thus, in light of the bureaucratic restructuring in the areas of immigration, trade, and governmental organization on the border, it is reasonable to ask two important questions related to homeland security, specifically to border control. First, do the new practices and structures of homeland security place an undue burden on the border and its border residents? Second, do these burdens increase security while protecting prosperity?

Answering these two important questions is pivotal in order to understand what the border is today and what it may become tomorrow. The answer must be the result of a detailed before-and-after analysis of border practices and a careful cost-benefit analysis of the price paid by border residents and the added national security obtained in exchange for that price. The intuitive answers to these questions is that border residents bore the brunt of the U.S. government's response to September 11, perhaps more than any other area of the country, and that the added national security cannot be assessed in terms of terror because there has been no attempt at threatening the border infrastructure by terrorists. Instead, border residents have had to sacrifice their own local governance and democracy, and they and businesses pay the price for border enforcement. Immigration appears to obey its own logic, with the push and pull forces that affect it being phenomena away from the border itself. And there are no border-based successes on the war on drugs. Thus the picture is mixed, but there has been no true assessment of whether a change in border management strategies might actually pay off better for everyone—the nation and its security but also border users and their prosperity and rights. Let us see how each of the different areas targeted by homeland security reorganization has fared.

NEW IMMIGRATION PROCEDURES

The more important effect of September 11 on the border was the redefinition of immigration as a national security issue. Immigration has been a malleable issue in U.S. history. Its very location within the national bureaucratic framework illustrates how policy makers defined the issue of immigration over time, and what happened to the issue after September 11 definitely reflects a new way of thinking about it, even without fundamental immigration reform since the 1990s.

For a long time, immigration services were located in the U.S. Department of Commerce and Labor. This clearly framed the whole issue of immigration as one of labor and economic development. Migrants were seen as workers. They fueled the American economy and provided cheap labor to build this country. After the department was split into the U.S. Department of Labor and the U.S. Department of Commerce in 1913, immigration services continued to be located in the Labor Department, further indicating that immigration continued to be looked at through the labor needs of a fast-developing economy. Immigration quotas were largely assigned on the basis of the labor needs of American businesses across the country. Millions of people, mostly European, came to the United States to work. From time to time, there was some discomfort with open immigration and that was accompanied by deep anti-immigrant sentiments. These were particularly virulent around the turn of the twentieth century. But immigration continued to be looked at as a matter of economic development well into the twentieth century.

At the U.S.-Mexico border, many came across to work in farming and ranching, starting in the very early twentieth century. World War I increased the demand for Mexican labor and more Mexicans came across to work. The Mexican Revolution of 1910 also saw a new wave of Mexican middle-class people move to the border states, mostly fleeing the country's civil war. The demand for Mexican labor continued through the Roaring Twenties. But the Great Depression put an end to that flow, and in fact half a million Mexicans and Mexican Americans were rounded up and deported back to Mexico. At the border, Mexicans became the scapegoats for the economic ills of America. But during World War II, U.S. engagement in the war effort required again Mexican labor and many came back to work. The Bracero Program continued until the 1960s, under pressure from the very same farmers and ranchers who benefited enormously from Mexican cheap labor. And Mexicans continued to be cheap labor through the 1970s and 1980s.

But changes were lurking. Immigration services came to be perceived differently over time. The U.S. government began to shift its conception of the issue of immigration starting in the 1930s, probably as a consequence of the Great Depression. It finally was defined as a matter of law enforcement. This paradigmatic shift in the way immigration was viewed culminated in 1940 when the INS moved from the Department of Labor to the Department of Justice. Moreover, the Border Patrol, created in the mid-1920s and charged with preventing undocumented immigration, was also lodged in the Department of Justice.

September 11 would redefine the issue of immigration from a matter of law enforcement to a subject of national security—radicalizing the treatment of immigrants, mostly as criminals and potential terrorists, and increasing the penalties against undocumented migrants even further. The reaction to the attacks on New York and Washington led to the INS being broken up into two different branches, the Bureau of Citizenship and Immigration Services, in charge of immigration applications adjudication, and Immigration and Customs Enforcement, in charge of immigration enforcement. The idea was to ensure that immigration law enforcement would never be neglected again. In addition, both of these new agencies were placed under the Department of Homeland Security, effectively redefining the issue of immigration as a matter of national security. Immigration had gone from a purely economic issue to a matter of law enforcement and now to a concern of national security.

Several immigration-related programs were also changed. To a visa application there were new forms added to determine visa eligibility and new programs, like MANTIS, added to check on visa applicants in many different databases before approving travel to the United States. These forms and programs were to provide the consular officers with more information to conduct clearance and background checks in order to deny visas to those petitioners who might constitute a threat to the national security of the United States. On the other hand, B1/B2 visa holders, most of whom are residents of Mexican border towns, were now able to extend their stay beyond 72 hours. Foreign students were also affected. The Interim Exchange Authentication Program was implemented to ensure that students were who they claimed to be and that the government could keep track of those students wherever they went once inside the United States. This required foreign students to register with the government and notify it of any change of address within 10 days. It also required schools to "authenticate" the student by providing law enforcement with information regarding that student—a move fought by U.S. universities for privacy and bureaucratic reasons. Finally, the government stopped granting J-1 visas for agricultural workers, placing the farming sector of the economy in a bind across the southwestern border states and beyond. In addition, U.S. citizens could be required to carry passports, even if they are just crossing the Canadian or Mexican border for a few hours. A passport card was created for those who traveled across the border routinely and may not want to get a passport.

Additionally, all visa holders from Mexico traveling beyond the borderlands were required to have an additional entry card called I-94. In the past, this card was an entry permit, but there was no punitive effect if the individual overstayed the card and hardly anyone turned it in upon exit. However, the I-94 is increasingly an important mechanism to monitor exits and, although often granted for six months, all travelers are supposed to turn it in upon exit or they may be penalized by being denied entry at a future time, another way of ensuring that visa overstays are punished if they fail to declare their exit by turning in the I-94. All such control procedures for entries and exits are now becoming stricter.

CONSEQUENCES OF THE NEW IMMIGRATION PROCEDURES

The consequences of these changes were felt readily and heavily on the border. The J-1 visa stoppage left employers without workers on the U.S. side and laborers without jobs on the Mexican side. There were no consultations with Mexico on this matter, a fact that further cooled off the already chilly relationship between the two neighbors—the war on drugs under President Felipe Calderón between 2006 and 2012 would further complicate the relationship. Finally, the federal government attempted to deputize state and local police forces to perform immigration and customs enforcement, a move opposed by these entities as an unfunded mandate. Most cities and counties refused to participate on this over time, but important places, like suburbs in Dallas and towns in Pennsylvania and Arizona, fully participated in rounding up migrants and closing housing and other opportunities for them. A new hostile environment toward foreigners emerged, and although it subsided eventually, the 2016 presidential campaign may have kept it alive. The nonvisible consequences were even greater. There were fewer opportunities for border residents on either side of the border to interact with each other—what we have called "border intimacy" is being lost. Businesspeople and tourists saw their ability to interact across the border increasingly difficult because of the time it took the border inspectors to go through each vehicle and person. There is a new normal in terms of the length of the lines to cross the border and the arbitrary inspections that often subject people to suspicion with only a superficial look by the officer. In this regard, the most important impact is that the new immigration practices and the immigration procedures on the ground constitute today a further severance in the community ties between border towns, a shift bound to decrease the level of intimacy between twin-city populations. This severance of cross-border social interaction cannot be underestimated. It is more difficult now to interact across the border and increasing numbers of residents are choosing not to cross the border at all. This can only alienate both nations further, rather than build more bridges between them. The border has become indeed a difficult place to live in and navigate.

NEW TRADE PROCEDURES

The new security procedures in cross-border trade were presumably designed to prevent terrorists or anyone who would "wish America harm"[25] from entering the United States by utilizing the intense commercial links between Mexico, Canada, and the United States. Indeed, these commercial links are substantial and continue to grow. Canada and Mexico are now first and second trading partners of the United States.. Trade over the 1990s grew enormously, reaching totals in the hundreds of billions of dollars between the two borders. Trade during FY2015 on the Mexican and Canadian borders reached $1.2 trillion, more than trade with China, Brazil, India, Japan, Korea, Russia, and South Africa combined.[26] Much of this trade arrives by truck, with railcars in second place. According to the former CBP commissioner Robert Bonner in 2003, only about 10.3 percent of trucks and 9 percent of railcars were inspected intrusively or nonintrusively.[27] The numbers have not changed much since, although new technology has been introduced that can help sort out more quickly which trucks should go through a secondary scan and then, from there, which ones should go to a tertiary inspection. Unfortunately, this does not appear to have stopped the flood of drugs in any event. Laredo, Texas, has proven to be the busiest POE for trucks on the U.S.-Mexico border, with over 2.6 million trucks in 2014 alone.[28] Trade between the United States and Mexico reached $500 billion in 2011 and is now estimated to hover around $550 billion a year.

Unfortunately, NAFTA did not provide for serious infrastructure improvements necessary to accommodate the growth in trade. No substantive additional infrastructure has been added, with a few exceptions. The stress on infrastructure from the sheer volume of trade, e.g., almost 7 million trucks, has become evident. But the transportation infrastructure is of less concern here than the inspection infrastructure. Trade liberalization under NAFTA was particularly broad and has continued to expand for the last 23 years. Federal and local governments on both sides of the border placed some emphasis on improving capabilities and efficiencies in transportation across the border, but they neglected the serious investment required to ensure that drug traffickers, human smugglers, and even terrorists would not use the intense trade between the two countries as a conveyor belt for their contraband. Cooperation between the two countries on the ground remains bound by nationalistic rhetoric and suspicions of each other—witness the statements by Donald J. Trump regarding Mexico. Mutual trust is very low—mostly because American law enforcement eyes Mexican agencies with great suspicion. As it became clear in our chapter on illegal drugs, NAFTA has been quite a blessing for drug traffickers. They take full advantage of the inability of U.S. bureaucrats to inspect every truck in order to smuggle their cargo.

The new X-ray scanning machines that are used still may or may not detect illegal cargo, depending on how well hidden or camouflaged it may be. All in all, the capacity of CBP to make sure that contraband, both drugs and human, does not enter the country does not yet meet to the security needs of the United States. And it would be absurd to expect a resolution at the borderline in any event. Hence, Alan Bersin, the Assistant Secretary for International Affairs and Chief Diplomatic Officer for DHS, has proposed projecting the border outward and gathering information on national threats well before they reach the U.S. borders—a forward preventive strategy, so to speak. And he may be right, given that both undocumented migration and illegal drugs have a long reach that transcends the borderline and it would be absurd to tackle these problems only there. However, no substantive economic development program has been created for Central America to incentivize people to stay there—even though President Obama tried, and no real strategies for reducing drug consumption in the United States have been put in place beyond the grassroots efforts to change the laws on marijuana..

Nevertheless, after September 11 the U.S. government woke up to the fact that security on the border needed to be revamped. Steady improvements began on the POE lanes dedicated to handling the millions of trucks that cross the border. New technology was introduced to scan the trucks carrying cargo. New and more intense checks were conducted on the drivers of those trucks in the hope of preventing a terrorist from one day taking advantage of the border openness to conduct an attack on the United States. But over the years, I have developed serious doubts that we are tackling the problem in the right place. The forces of globalization may have more to do with undocumented migration and refugee flows, and drug consumption markets may be unresponsive to border-based strategies and may need new demand-side approaches rather than the traditional supply-side policies.

But going back to trade, there were specific adjustments to trade programs implemented such as the C-TPAT and the 24-Hour Rule on international textiles. There were also important efforts to process foods, particularly perishables, more quickly. Along the Canadian border, the Free and Secure Trade program was put into effect, a program that would later be extended to trucking on the Mexican border. But these are all efforts that face limits, given the sheer volume of cross-border flows. There is only so much one can squeeze in terms of efficiency gains if no structural change in border management occurs.

C-TPAT was designed to ensure that all the players of the supply chain (exporters, importers, and transporters) "know" and "trust" each other. The importer is obliged to develop and implement a plan to enhance security throughout the supply chain. When importers do not control the facilities, they are required to follow a series of recommendations by CBP to ensure that every responsible party along the supply chain complies with U.S. government rules. C-TPAT involves a series of rules pertaining to procedural and physical control of the product and designed to ensure that the personnel that work along the supply chain are properly trained so as to ensure the total security of the goods traded. The burden falls on the importer to comply with these rules and file the required C-TPAT documentation with CBP. Of course, this largely means that the U.S. government has shifted the costs of security to the cross-border businesses. They have to pay the price of "securing" the supply chain. In effect, the U.S. government has made it more expensive to operate across the border for everyone in the import/export business. The program began in 2001 and today almost 11,000 carriers are registered. Still, while it has helped, it has been insufficient to expedite the volume of traffic and, without a structural change in the way the two countries manage their trade-processing facilities, it is likely to be overwhelmed very soon. In other words, it seems to have alleviated risk but not fundamentally changed border management.

The 24-Hour Rule required carriers to file a cargo declaration 24 hours before the cargo is laden aboard the vessel at a foreign port. However, given that the 24-Hour Rule applied mostly to sea vessels abroad, it did not significantly impact the border, although it did impact some of the cargo moving from Mexico to the United States by vessel.

An additional trade security measure was the Container Security Initiative. This program was implemented to identify and target high-risk containers coming into the United States, to prescreen the containers identified as high-risk, to use high technology to scan these containers, and to replace old containers with smart or secure containers. Although this initiative affected the U.S.-Canadian border initially and not necessarily the U.S.-Mexican border, it has now expanded to global trade processing, along with C-TPAT. The 24-Hour Rule in both programs attempts to achieve a balance between security and trade. So far, quietly, it appears to be working, in spite of all the rhetoric about the border. Clearly, there were a whole new series of programs that also affected the U.S.-Canada border and did not initially arrive at the U.S.-Mexico border, including the Free and Secure Trade program, the Pre-Arrival Processing System, the National Customs Automation Program, as well as the Smart and Secure Trade Lanes Initiative. All of them have been slowly implemented on the U.S.-Mexico border. But they remain largely unilateral and do not truly amount to a joint border management strategy, which should be the ultimate goal in the twenty-first century.

THE CONSEQUENCES OF THE NEW TRADE SYSTEM

The Department of Homeland Security understood from early on that its solutions had to be designed to close the border, with the hope of detecting the undesirables that might want to exploit the openness of the border. There was no effort to create a truly U.S.-Mexico binational trade inspection regime where the Mexican government played a role to ensure that all trade was safe and secure. The U.S. government decided to work instead with the importers/exporters and the trucking companies to secure the supply chain. This indicates that there is still much distrust of Mexican authorities, and anyone visiting the border can quickly see that the channels of communication between U.S. customs authorities and Mexican *aduana* (customs) authorities are rather limited and the flows are increasingly confined to pre-secured channels. Konrad has described this system as a corridors and gateways border system. The border is essentially closed and "secure" corridors and gateways, or narrow bottle necks (POEs), are the only places where flows are allowed.[29]

The cost of the new measures, particularly C-TPAT and other antiterrorism programs, on the U.S.-Mexico border is bound to be considerable. Costs associated with compliance with the new measures include training and registering truck drivers, making the trucks and equipment comply with U.S. requirements, filing paperwork in advance for the cargo hauled by a given truck, etc., and all are borne by the manufacturing and the trucking industries on the border. Few protested these costs, however, because the U.S. government portrayed the measures as a must or the cargo would be subjected to intrusive inspections, which would mean outright delays upon arrival at the POE. Interestingly, these measures also symbolized that trade was now a matter of national security, not about economic prosperity, even if there is ample rhetoric around the idea that we must balance the two.

Some of the secure trade programs implemented after September 11 represent a transaction cost to the international supply chains located at border POEs. But no one knows how much the border really costs.[30] The new requirements decrease some of the profits by the companies, not just in what they pay in fees and for technology but also in vehicle and driver idle time at the bridges. Over time, however, these new programs seem to have made trade flows somewhat more efficient, though not perfectly efficient, by the use of technology and the use of lanes exclusive for trade trucks. Suppliers and importers initially scrambled to figure out all the rules of the new security measures and tried to integrate them into their costs. But nothing guarantees that the trucks are per se any more secure. Clearly, to this day drugs and sometimes humans are smuggled routinely in those same vehicles and trucks.

The new trade regime has increased the amount of time and resources spent complying with the new rules—time that is not always compensated in expedited processing at the POE. Sometimes, in fact, there are additional delays at the POEs because trucks and vehicles carrying cargo must comply with added security measures or deal with an agent's suspicions. Membership in C-TPAT requires clearly that those participating in the program be able to certify, to the satisfaction of the government agent, that their shipments come from the right suppliers and that the cargo is secure. Otherwise, they go to secondary and tertiary inspection. The added delays continue to cost maquiladoras and other businesses considerable resources.

C-TPAT is not cheap or easy. Those who wish to participate have to implement security policies and procedures as advised by the government, conduct periodic self-assessments to ensure that their supply chains have not been infiltrated, submit additional paperwork to CBP, train their employees and personnel in the new security procedures and policies, and guarantee that their cargo is not compromised. All these costs represent an added burden to those doing business along the border in twin plants. In addition to the costs directly related to the new security measures, there are lost production time, higher transportation costs, and lost business opportunities. I have yet to see a comprehensive study of the border as a transactional cost.

The inevitable consequence is that the border-trade regime is still largely run unilaterally by the United States; much of the cost for securing the supply chain has shifted to the business community; and the Mexican bureaucracy that sits largely idle on the border does not bear any burden in ensuring that trade going to the United States is safe and secure. The new patchwork of programs created by Homeland Security bears the burden of ensuring that the conveyor belt of the 7 million trucks crossing the border every year is not used by drug smugglers, human smugglers, and terrorists. Yet sometimes it still is.

THE VALUE ADDED OF THE NEW TRADE SYSTEM

The record on the new procedures regarding trade, particularly along the border, is mixed. Clearly, they have resulted in an increase in the security of the nation, broadly defined. Even if early on Stephen Flynn made it clear in his article in *Foreign Affairs* that there were still many patches to fill in, particularly at ports,[31] that is largely resolved. The border has hardened. But along the U.S.-Mexico border, the major effect has been the added burden and costs on importers and exporters even if cargo is more secure. Surely we all pay for this, given that merchandise that crosses the border is probably more expensive. This is in addition to the increased burden on the American taxpayer who has to foot the bill for the added personnel and technology along the nearly 2,100-mile border. However, when it comes to illegal drugs, the measures can hardly be called a success. Illegal drugs still "contaminate" the cargo of many of the vehicles that cross the border and go undetected. A Ciudad Juárez businessman complained to me at some point that they had no control over the trucks once they left the warehouse, and drug traffickers sometimes bribed the drivers to hide illegal drugs in the cargo. This, in fact, drew the attention of U.S. authorities, who demanded GPS systems in all trucks—an added cost to transporters—to track their path, time of travel, etc. The real problem here, therefore, remains only remotely a potential terrorist but more likely the "contamination" of the truck cargo by drug traffickers. Drug trafficking has not ceased in spite of the added inspection activities. Illegal drugs continue to represent a substantial business activity of the Mexican cartels, and trucking remains their main conveyor belt not only at the borderline but all along U.S. highways.

THE BURDEN ON BORDER RESIDENTS

Border residents bear the brunt of the new U.S. government measures on the southwestern border. As already mentioned, no area of the country was as affected as the U.S.-Mexico border after September 11. Even as New York City and other areas of the country recovered a sense of normalcy for the most part, the border continued to be affected and is still subjected to a series of security experiments.

In addition to the immediate effects felt by border residents in the days after September 11, there were other more permanent effects. The first is the increased militarization of the border, where fences, border patrols, aerostats, military personnel, intrusive evening lights, infrared technology, motion detectors, and other gadgets give the sense that the U.S.-Mexico border is a border at war, a border under siege. Instead of an increasingly integrated border, the Southwest has seen the worst type of separation compared to any other time in the history of U.S.-Mexican relations. And there is no letup in this process of militarization. Border agencies are largely unaccountable for what they do and refuse to subject themselves to surveillance of their work and procedures.

A second cost to border residents has to do with the added time and resources that it takes to do business on the border. It is increasingly more difficult to move across the international boundary to conduct daily activities, including academic, business, leisure, and family activities. The only people who take the border more casually today are the teenagers who live, for example, in El Paso, Texas, and wish to party across the border where the drinking age is 18, not 21. But that too is happening less frequently. And many in El Paso or San Diego now speak nostalgically about the time when they could cross just to have lunch and afterward could return quickly. The sense of community, at a cross-border level, is dying.

Some residents, for example, in El Paso, who benefited from the cheaper labor of Mexican maids, day laborers, and gardeners are now finding it increasingly difficult to find that labor. And of course, many border residents who cross to the U.S. side to work are under the increasing threat of being detected and excluded forever from participating in cross-border markets and general cross-border life.

Although the Dedicated Commuter Lanes between San Diego and Tijuana, and El Paso and Ciudad Juárez make it easier for American workers to cross to work in Mexico and come back and for Mexican students to cross to study in the United States, they are expensive and not available to everyone. To be fair, however, the Mexican government is the problem here—mostly. It demands US$400 a year for using the lanes, whereas the United States demands only $120 for a security clearance every five years. This is prohibitive for most border residents. In that sense, the greed of the Mexican government has few limits. Most residents who cannot afford the Dedicated Commuter Lanes have to suffer the exceedingly long lines in the regular lanes to come across, with the consequent pollution, man-hours lost, and resources up in smoke from the exhaust pipes of the tens of thousands of vehicles crossing the border every day through POEs.

With the increasingly exhaustive checks on pedestrians, there is also an increasing number of border residents that are prevented from going shopping or enjoying leisure activities on the other side of the border. Families are separated. Businesses on both sides of the border report that their commercial activity suffers from any slowdown at the bridges. Tourism is yet to reach the normal levels of the pre–September 11 period on the Mexican side. At this point, it is not likely to recover.

THE COSTS OF THE BORDER TO THE AMERICAN TAXPAYER

The actual costs to the government in full-time-equivalent personnel and in inspections budget have also increased considerably. The combined budgets of CBP and Immigration and Customs Enforcement are now $20 billion (FY2016). Several billion dollars are further spent on trade facilitation, technology upgrades, inspections, overtime, etc. CBP now has over 60,000 employees and does a relatively good job at the border. Operational control is certainly much better, but it does little to stop money laundering in the United States, weapons smuggling into Mexico, or seriously stopping drug smuggling into the United States. Some inter-agency cooperation issues remain as well. The CBP, for example, must work closely with the Food and Drug Administration and other agencies to synchronize their rules and procedures so that businesses and corpora-tions do not face delays or contradictory action upon their arrival at the border POE—although they have come a long way in that regard.

BACK TO NORMALCY?

The initial reaction to the terrorist attacks of September 11 affected the border quite deeply and continues to do so. And although the operational control of the border is much higher, there has been no deep reform to solve many of the border's problems. In other words, the border is still the border, with much less democracy and cross-border cooperation than there used to be. The opinion of local residents as to what exactly they would like to see happen is nonexistent. Sister cities along the border hardly ever cooperate on issues of urban planning, pollution, etc. In a recent visit to the State Department, I spoke about the democratic deficit at the border and I was told that stakeholders are often consulted—and I replied that corporate and political stakeholders are consulted but not regular citizens—borderlanders, whose lives are affected by what goes on. There was no reply to that. The security apparatus reigns supreme and would not allow that. And it is not clear that they have solved the problems of the border once and for all *just because* they have better con-trol of the border.

Take immigration, for example. Although there has been no consider-able reduction in the number of undocumented workers crossing the bor-der between POEs, no one really knows how many workers are still crossing the border without documents every year. Today, the apprehen-sions are around 479,000. The number of OTMs crossing the border with-out documents is still on the rise, making Central Americans now a greater number of undocumented crossers than Mexicans. The issue of immigration has undergone no real reform from Congress in order to deal with the demand for cheap labor in the United States, and U.S. authorities have done little to seriously investigate and tackle the push forces in Cen-tral America and other parts of the world. If anything, the security and economic conditions in Central America are deteriorating and are likely to push more people north, through Mexico and to the United States. In other words, what the war on terror has left is a reorganized immigra-tion bureaucracy, with no real reform or solution to the permanent prob-lem of undocumented or documented migration, with no real strategies to address the larger push and pull forces of migration, and with no real structural change in the kind and number of visas available to migrate or work legally on a temporary basis in the United States. The reorganization constitutes only a more sophisticated layer of requirements for border crossers and paperwork for the bureaucracies working on immigration issues. In that sense, the border is still the border.

Nearly the same thing can be said about illegal drugs. The U.S. drug war on the border has forced the cartels to consolidate their operations, to make their practices more efficient, to create new alliances, to shift their production here and there to access markets more quickly, and to take advantage of the economies of scale. Cartels have become flexible hierarchies, ready to respond to the contingencies of the drug war. And they generally succeed in doing so, as I have explained. It would appear that the border drug war waged by the United States has consolidated drug smuggling into large oligopolies that continue to send massive supplies of illegal drugs into the country. There are no strategic successes in the drug war, and the tactical successes of the drug war appear to have the ability to squeeze the small-time smugglers out and make it easier for the large, consolidated drug-smuggling organizations to operate. That the Sinaloa Cartel and another large cartel—the Jalisco Nueva Generación Cartel—emerged victorious from the war on drugs under Felipe Calderón in Mexico is just proof that the larger groups will probably survive and prosper. In the end, illegal drugs are just as abundant as ever. There is also evidence that their price is going down—especially heroin and confection drugs—and that the quality of the drugs is on an upward trend, both signs that on the issue of illegal drugs, the border is still the border.

But still, not everything is the same.

THE NIGHTMARES OF BORDER CROSSERS

Teresa Ibarra is a woman from a town in the southern part of the state of Chihuahua, across from El Paso and New Mexico. On a day before Christmas, she made her way to the border by bus. Her intention was to spend some time with her sister who lives in Albuquerque, New Mexico, and is married to an American citizen. Teresa holds a B1/B2 visa crossing card, just like the hundreds of thousands of other Mexicans do that allows them to cross the border into the United States to shop, visit relatives, etc. When Teresa got to the border inspection point, the agent treated her with great suspicion. He asked her a series of questions, which she did not refuse to answer, but her answers prompted only greater hostility by the border agent. Eventually, Teresa was taken to the "interrogation room" inside the POE building. She was questioned for nearly four hours on her status, activities, contacts, the reasons for her visit, etc. Her version of the story was checked and doubled-checked against the version of her sister and her sister's husband who were traveling with her. Teresa was eventually let go—there was nothing wrong with her record—but she felt humiliated, harassed, embarrassed, ill-treated, and her spirit was nearly broken.

Legal border crossers, like Teresa, are a diverse lot: American workers who commute into Mexico for managerial jobs in the manufacturing sector; Mexican students who study in schools and universities in the United States; American tourists who cross to shop, eat, or be entertained; Mexican shoppers who consume nearly $7 billion a year in retail goods on the U.S. side of the border; families crossing back and forth to visit their loved ones; investors, truckers, taxi drivers, maids, and gardeners.

Yet since the war on terror began, every one of these border crossers has had to undergo a closer scrutiny by border inspectors. Sadly, almost no one minds the closer scrutiny. And if they mind it, they have no choice. There is an understanding that after September 11, things are not the same and that closer inspection for the sake of national security is required. U.S. citizen border users tolerate it. Mexican border crossers readily acknowledge that there is not much they can do. What everyone minds is the harassing attitude of the CBP officials who increasingly make people feel unwelcome—even if their posted signs show CBP agents with a smile, claiming that they are there to serve and help. A quick interview with border crossers at various points of the border revealed that they are generally afraid of the arbitrariness with which an inspector often decides to pick on a given person. They also believe that agents pick on a border crosser based on "the way he dresses," or "the way he looks," or "the way he moves," and so on. Very often, border crossers are not given reasons for their detention and questioning. Anyone can be hauled to the back. They are kept in the dark. They are often kept for hours. They are accused of having this or that intention. In Teresa's words, "They make you feel like you are worth nothing, like you are a criminal." This has only gotten worse.

The story of Teresa is somewhat similar to the story of Megan, a UTEP student who is an American but lives in Ciudad Juárez and commutes to El Paso every day to go to school. She believes that the border inspectors exercise the most arbitrary reasons for questioning people and that the treatment they give border crossers today, particularly those on foot, is that of criminal suspects. Everyone, she says, is guilty until proven innocent. Our values have gone backwards. Such is the new, post–September 11 attitude along the border, to go with the new homeland security regime.

CONCLUSION

Fifteen years after September 11, we have seen unimaginable consequences on the U.S. border system. It is true that the border was already closing, albeit slowly. The aftermath of September 11, however, fell strongly on the U.S.-Mexico border. The initial burden on border residents was quite large: long lines on the bridges, more exhaustive inspections, a harsher treatment of legitimate border crossers, a drop in retail sales all along the border, obstructed commercial relations, and a deeper culture of suspicion overall. Add to this violations of human and due process rights, arbitrariness by border agents, and even deaths with no accountability by the Border Patrol. Scores of Mexicans for example have died at the hands of the Border Patrol or been killed by BP agents, sometimes shooting across the borderline.[32]

Elsewhere, I have demonstrated that much of the border is back to its normal levels of cross-border traffic, waiting lines, and shopping—even drugs and other contraband, including human smuggling, are back to normal. But this normal is not the pre–September 11 normal. It is a new normal, a tough normal—a normal imbued in a culture of suspicion and mistrust, in a lack of democracy and unaccountability, where everyone is suspect. Those that would close the border are here to stay. And the problems of the border continue unabated. The only move has been toward greater and greater enforcement of border laws..

Someone once said the definition of insanity is doing the same thing over and over again, but expecting different results. This may be true of the U.S. border security policy. The border security policy has been a largely unilateral approach by the United States. It has hardly engaged Mexico. It has hardly accounted for the globalization forces that come knocking on the U.S.-Mexico border—and that we ourselves promote through free trade and demands that others open their economies. Instead, the U.S. border policy has been one of escalation: more cops, more guns, more gadgets, more vehicles, more technology, more walls, and, unfortunately, more bureaucratic discretion, more abuses, etc. It is as if the U.S. government thought that the only route to go was to increase all of these, as if that were sufficient to stem the tide of labor moving toward the border by the millions. Congress is not about to change things. There is no political mood to take a hard look at the border and figure out a new way of managing it.

A new approach to security is needed, an approach that will be a North American approach, with a comprehensive solution that takes into consideration the tension between globalization and security. The ultimate goal should not be to close the border but to keep it open while keeping it secure. Until now, closing it has been the equivalent to securing it, clearly a mistake that swims against the tide of history and against the very policies that we elsewhere promote: openness, democracy, freedom, trade, and so forth.

CHAPTER 5

The Panopticon Border

THE PANOPTICON BORDER

Jeremy Bentham, an English philosopher born in 1748, is the author of a concept that best captures what is happening at the U.S.-Mexico border. Among his many works is the design of a panopticon penitentiary where the prison layout had rows of single cells arranged in tiers and running down long halls radiating from a central vestibule. It was designed much like the spokes of a wheel. Each cell, small and narrow, made for a single prisoner, had a tiny back window to the outside world. The front wall of the cell was all bars and looked into the narrow landings of the prison galleries. This layout, known as a panopticon, was labeled so because a single guard could watch an entire row of prisoners from a central position. In effect, he could see everything.[1]

Michel Foucault would later expand the concept of a panopticon prison in his work *Discipline and Punish: The Birth of the Prison*.[2] In *Discipline and Punish*, Foucault traces the history of the contemporary penal system. He sought to analyze the social and political context of the development and evolution of punishment and to examine how power relations among the various actors in a penal system affected punishment, its design and its implementation. Foucault correctly perceived that the powers of the state (government) had grown considerably and citizens were increasingly subjected to surveillance and punishment. He sensed that the reach of the state was becoming total. Government, he argued, was systematizing its grip on the lives of every individual, law-abiding and lawbreaker —a short step from controlling all lives in all spaces. Indeed, in Foucault's work, the new forms of punishment that the state planned were not necessarily created to rehabilitate but to exercise the power of the state to control individuals and then entire societies. The new modes of penalty were designed to deter those who would be lawbreakers, but over time they would reach the law abiding as well. In the end, the result of this process would be a slow but steady movement toward a society largely under surveillance and control by the state and punished—or rewarded—according to the designs of those who controlled the state.

Bentham's concept of a panopticon prison and Foucault's analysis of the surveillance and control powers of the state are particularly relevant to the border—sadly so. At the border, the U.S. government has undertaken the colossal task of increasing surveillance and control over land, individuals, processes, etc., by exercising the powers of a police state. The environment is truly oppressive and intimidating. In the borderlands, the U.S. government is waging a war to surveil and control everything. It is a totalizing power. It has fallen on law enforcement organizations, the primary agents of the U.S. government at the border, to wage this all-out "war on terror," which is ultimately choking the border and its vitality. Law enforcement agencies have continuously over the twentieth century, with a dramatic acceleration in the twenty-first century, escalated their efforts to create a system of total surveillance and complete control along the boundary line. George Orwell's *Nineteen Eighty-Four* is now child's play compared to what is going on at the U.S.-Mexico border. The final draft of the Department of Homeland Security's Strategic Plan outlines just that goal:

The protection of the Nation's borders—land, air, and sea—from the illegal entry of people, weapons, drugs, and other contraband while facilitating lawful travel and trade is vital to homeland security ... Over the past several years, DHS has deployed historic levels of personnel, technology, and resources to the Southwest border ... Through the collection, analysis, and proper sharing of information, the use of screening and identification verification techniques, the employment of advanced detection and other technologies, the use of "trusted traveler" or "trusted shipper" approaches, and cooperation with our international partners and the private sector, we can achieve security at our borders, [and] enforce the laws.[3]

The international boundary line between Mexico and the United States has turned into a virtual Maginot line, including, as we have seen, the stalemate between the "enemy" (particularly drug-trafficking organizations) and the United States. The real sufferers of all these wars are border residents.

Unfortunately, the strategy of surveillance and control along the borderline is a sure sign that the U.S. government is thus far not interested in a long-term, structural, and even democratic solution to the issues plaguing the border. It is a strategy of attrition; it is punitive; and it punishes the aspirations of borderlanders. Neither the White House nor Congress has provided the leadership to conceptualize and tackle the problems of the border from a broader perspective. Instead, the sheer force of the state, hammer-like, with all its resources, quasi-military operations, timetables, drills, and so on, has come down on the border to "regain control" of it. Any visitor to the border can see the new technologies being deployed there, including cameras, sensors, night goggles, X-ray machines, helicopters, Humvee-style vehicles, drones, etc. The increase in the number of Border Patrol agents, the watchful human eyes, is also quite evident—as are the increasing abuses of the border agents. All of these are at the disposal of the state to create the panopticon border of the twenty-first century, where everyone is under surveillance at all times, where everyone is tracked in every move, where everyone can be brought under the swift control of the government. Surveillance alone is supposed to deter any potential lawbreaking border crossers— even though it has hardly done so. On this new border, everyone is suspect of wanting to harm America. In this process, unfortunately, human rights take a backseat.

The ultimate goal of this panoptic strategy is to shut down the border and, myopically, define the world of the United States as an entity that ends at the border. In this view, there is little thought given to the forces that brew beyond the boundary line and eventually impact right up against it. On the border, the worst of the nightmares of George Orwell's *Nineteen Eight-Four*, with a ubiquitous Big Brother, are already a near reality.[4]

TECHNOLOGY AND THE PANOPTICON BORDER

What has facilitated the creation of a panopticon border is the progressive introduction of one important element to the border: surveillance and tracking high technology. Technology is in fact the absolutizing common denominator on the U.S.-Mexico border. This is a natural product of American faith in technology as a panacea for all ills. The U.S. government has continually sought to convert new technological improvements into increased capacity for surveillance activities at the border—and at home as well. It has provided the latest technological gadgets to those in charge of sealing the southwestern border, increasing operational control of the borderline. This trend toward the use of technology at the border had been gradual through the customs and law enforcement eras of the borderlands, but was accelerated after the terrorist attacks of September 11. Hardly anything today crosses the border that is not subjected to high-tech surveillance and inspection. The result has been the effective implementation of a panopticon border. Just a few examples will demonstrate how quickly this trend toward high-tech is developing on the border.

In October 2005, a group of students from a Texas university went to Monterrey, Mexico, to attend a parliamentary procedures workshop.

The same bus took them from San Antonio to Monterrey and back. On their return, when they arrived at the inspection point they were asked to get off the bus. The empty bus was taken to a driveway where a moving X-ray device (which looked like a small mobile home) with a long arm extending over the bus scanned the vehicle back and forth. These X-ray devices are now quite visible in nearly every POE along the border. They are also common in the yards where trucks cross and even some smaller vehicles arrive with import cargo. They are one of the key weapons with powerful new technology designed to detect illegal drugs and human cargo.

If these students wanted to go back to Monterrey just a couple of years later, each of them would have to carry a U.S. passport—or a passport card—equipped with the latest RFID. As per the Intelligence Reform and Terrorism Prevention Act of 2004, the United States requires all citizens to carry a passport upon reentry into the country as of January 1, 2008.[5] If someone comes back without a passport, border agents are likely to subject him or her to hours of scrutiny. No one's word is trusted at all. And no one is exempt from having to carry a passport that can be detected by the scanners even at a distance. By the time the individual reaches the inspection booth, in fact, his or her entire crossing history and annotations made by agents are already on the screen. The system captures who crossed, how many times, where, when, with whom, in what vehicle, etc. And the entire record is indelible. It is at any agent's fingertips at any time.

This of course makes it even harder for U.S. border residents to go across the border. The border is a very poor place. Many residents along the border counties are not even be able to afford a passport, and are cut off from their relatives in Mexico because they cannot afford the proper documents. Thus a secondary effect of this new rule is the dissolution of familial and social ties between border twin cities and their residents even more than they have already been dissolved over the last four decades.

Technology gives the U.S. government the ability to track people who use the border all the time and everywhere, because all new passports are required to be equipped with the RFID chip and any crossing is now recorded in the system. The chip could contain enormous amounts of data on an individual, and system data that would be easily accessible to any law enforcement official. Moreover, in an extreme case, these chips could even serve as homing devices. Privacy advocates, business travel groups, and some security experts opposed both the passport chip and the new passport requirements that the U.S. government wanted in place by the beginning of 2008 to no avail.[6] Now, any border user knows that all information is stored and readily available to the agent processing entry into the United States. No bit of data escapes the system today. An agent knows when you exited, came back, and left again, given that new exiting systems are increasingly being installed everywhere. At the same time, these cameras capture the pictures of the drivers upon exiting and at certain points within 100 miles of the borderline as they travel north. Thus the agents can see who you traveled with, what car you used, what time you passed that point, etc. Information is now absolute in the system—a system that is increasingly linked to many other law enforcement systems and databases around the country. Casual use of the border is over.

Driving along the border in Naco, Arizona, I saw a helicopter hovering along the steel wall that separates it from Naco, Sonora. The helicopter was hovering, looking for undocumented border crossers trying to make their way along the many walking paths weaving through the thorny bushes in the rugged desert. As of 2012, the Border Patrol employed more than four dozen helicopters, most of them deployed on the U.S.-Mexico border. It has now introduced UAVs and other equipment.[7] It is very common today to see helicopters scan the entire border at urban centers as well as rural areas. The UAVs or drones are much higher and smaller, and thus less visible, but they are there, gathering data all the time and communicating it to the well-equipped control centers. These UAVs are now gathering information from well within Mexico as well, presumably trying to detect the operations of drug cartels well before they reach the border. Phones are also being swept, inside and outside the United States, and certainly along the border on both sides, looking for information on all activity—criminal or not. It can become useful at any time.

There have been some doubts on the utility of UAVs as a method to improve border security. Such drones were initially tested at Fort Huachuca and Gila Bend in Arizona for use along the U.S.-Mexico border. [8] But these doubts have not mattered. The programs have only expanded since, with few or no real studies on their utility to deter illegal activity on the border. The Department of Homeland Security, through CBP, is bent on using drones as part of its equipment to conduct missions on the border. Hundreds of millions of dollars are budgeted to acquire this technology, along with more sensors and video technology for border surveillance. CBP would never allow itself to fall behind in technology. It has long been an imperial bureaucracy, and high-tech gadgets are part of the image they want to maintain—an image that is designed to be purposefully intimidating to border users. Deterrence by intimidation is a key component of CBP's strategy on the border.

While in Naco, looking up at the helicopter, which appeared to be looking down at my activities right up against the steel wall, I was struck by a row of tall posts with mounted cameras looking out in every direction. Such cameras have become an even more common sight along the border, particularly near urban centers but also in rural areas. Hundreds, perhaps thousands, of cameras now beam images of what is happening on the ground to a central location where they are scrutinized quickly. If any activity is detected by these cameras, it is immediately relayed to the Border Patrol agents in the field. More recently, driving along New Mexico's Highway 9, which hugs the border, somewhere between Sunland Park and Columbus, I turned south quickly and drove right up against the spikes that mark the border at that point. Within one minute, two border patrols were upon me. The eye of Big Brother proved effective. Of course, cameras have been a permanent feature of every POE for a very long time, but now they are being deployed extensively, everywhere, at and beyond the borderline, and are interconnected with operations centers. At a POE, one is under a surveilling camera 100 percent of the time. This trend is being extended to many other parts of the border, where powerful cameras can record what is happening five miles around. Many of these cameras have night-vision capabilities as well, so surveillance is now day and night.

Along the border today, it is also easy to run into high-intensity lights mounted on high towers and lampposts along every single urban and semiurban center. In rural areas, there are permanent electricity generators, burning fuel to produce electricity for those lights. High-intensity lights are portable; they can be easily hitched to a vehicle and moved to other areas, but more and more are being installed permanently. The idea behind these high-intensity lights is to produce sufficient illumination to deter undocumented border crossers from using certain passageways in the wilderness and to facilitate the job of the Border Patrol agents at night—although night vision is making this task increasingly easier. These lights facilitate the detection of any activity along the borderline. They add to the operational control of the border, further showing that all effects matter, material and psychological.

Driving along a ditch that runs parallel to the Rio Grande in West Texas, about 25 miles west of El Paso, I ran into a Border Patrol agent. He and I engaged in a very brief conversation—they do not usually talk to you anymore, but some may still engage you in conversation. I asked him about the sensors buried underground. The officer mentioned briefly that indeed the U.S. government was making increasing use of these underground sensors to detect any movement across the border. The sensors tend to be located in the more transited parts of the border, where undocumented crossers are known to journey, but are now being buried all along it. This information too is relayed to a central location and piped live to the Border Patrol agents in the field. Unfortunately, they can be triggered by wild animals as well and there are many false alarms. However, the wall is now preventing wildlife from crossing as well— perhaps damaging the ecosystems of the region.

Border Patrol vehicles are also increasingly intimidating. They now look like war zone vehicles. Any Border Patrol vehicle today, for example, is equipped with high-tech gadgets, including equipment to receive just-in-time information about what is going on around them from other sources. The border agents carry powerful weapons, including M16 rifles and other handguns. They also have infrared goggles, such as those that the U.S. military uses, to detect body heat, enabling them to locate human bodies hiding in the bushes, ditches, etc. Night-vision capability by the agents guarding the border makes it increasingly difficult for border crossers to enter undetected. The vehicles now isolate the detained completely in steel compartments and cages more appropriate for terrorists than economic migrants. The windows of some of them are covered with steel screens as well, giving them a militarized appearance. Agents have been accused of human rights abuses, but the Border Patrol refuses to review its operating procedures; so when a Border Patrol stops you, you had better comply with any minimal order or be subjected to physical force or worse. A friend of mine told me that Border Patrol agents sometimes talk of "tonks," referring to migrants, a reference to the sound their heads make when they are hit with the baton.

Closer to POEs, iris recognition technology—in addition to thumbprints—is now widely used at U.S. airports and is now increasingly extending to the border. When Mexican citizens request an I-94 permit to travel into the United States farther than 25 miles from the borderline, their iris print is taken and stored in the system. Iris technology is also used at American consulates, and there are plans to use it the Biometric Identity Management program to check everyone who exits the country in the future as well. Our own bodies are now being monitored and tracked—in a game of biopolitics that Foucault would easily recognize.

Statistical tools are also being used to track cross-border movement of people and vehicles. The statistical surveillance system implemented along the U.S.-Mexico border gathers patterns, as information is accumulated at every booth at every POE. If the system detects that a certain type of vehicle has been "busted" with drugs at several points along the border, a "memorandum" goes out urging agents to "watch out" for that type of vehicle because it might be likely that the drug traffickers are using such vehicles for their drug smuggling. If there is a spike in drug busts at a particular POE, inspection activity is ratcheted up because the spike indicates that that POE is being used more frequently. If a particular activity is associated with illegal activity, the statistics immediately alert everyone to the new pattern. And so forth. The statistical database accumulates information on a permanent basis, all the time, and relays it in real time to all agents working along the border. Moreover, a researcher at New Mexico State University, Stefan Schmidt, developed a mathematical model that will presumably predict where smugglers are likely to cross.[9] Models like these, many produced by the National Targeting Center, are increasingly being sought, even though they usually fail because they make the wrong assumptions about human behavior. Drug traffickers, for example, appear to always be ahead of the law enforcement game.

These are some of the multiple high-tech advances and devices being used today to gain control of the border. The overall result has been that the technology that the U.S. government uses on the border is increasingly more sophisticated and totalizing, aiding in the eventual complete operational control of the border. There is a much larger investment now in the use of high technology, turning the border into a veritable panopticon border where soon no one will be able to move without being seen or heard or noticed. Technology continues to change at a heady pace and will enable the U.S. government even more to acquire further operational capabilities on the border. There is indeed a race to close the border once and for all, and technology will probably accomplish this.

The Border Patrol and CBP, its parent agency, leverage technology to control ever more inches and yards of the borderline and gain information on individuals, vehicles, etc. They use biometrics, mobile surveillance systems, mobile video surveillance systems, vehicle and cargo inspection systems, night-vision devices, thermal handheld imaging devices, unattended ground sensors, personal radiation detectors, radiation isotope identification devices, Z backscatter X-ray vehicles, integrated fixed towers, UAVs, helicopters, over 10,000 SUVs, and even horses and dogs—not to mention ditches, walls, fences, and so on. All of these devices are interconnected through control centers, where information is received, processed, and acted on, in a matter of minutes. Clearly, Big Brother is here to stay—and it is called the Border Patrol. In a very clinical way, they call their punishment techniques "consequence delivery systems." Whoever thinks that the border is chaotic and out of control has clearly not been to the border.

MILITARIZATION OF THE BORDER

The use of technology to guard the border came accompanied by the increased use of quasi-military operations on the border. Timothy Dunn has successfully shown that low-intensity conflict precepts have been adopted by U.S. law enforcement agencies to conduct their operations along the border. In his study, he concludes that "overall, it seems clear that immigration and drug enforcement efforts in the U.S.-Mexico border region during the 1978–1992 period coincided to a significant extent with the precepts of the LIC [low-intensity conflict] doctrine."[10] As previously discussed, former congressman Silvestre Reyes's Operation Hold the Line in the El Paso area in 1994 took the militarization of the border even further. His efforts were an all-out assault on undocumented migration with an unprecedented strategy. Before Operation Hold the Line, some attempts had been made to use the military to guard the border and there had been renewed calls for the use of the National Guard to patrol the border. The military got involved in operations along the border, which they mostly took on as part of their training, as early as 1981–82. Still, it was Mr. Reyes who first implemented a massive border control operation with a distinct paramilitary feel to it. It was a blockade strategy taken right out of military manuals. In fact, the operation was originally titled Operation Blockade, but the name irked many groups inside the United States and upset the Mexican government. The name was then changed to Operation Hold the Line, which intended to choke the border and close it completely by positioning an agent every quarter of a mile, within sight distance of each other. This formation, stretching for about 25 miles along the Rio Grande, would make guarding the border a totalizing activity. Reyes also began to talk about interoperability among the various agencies working on the border. He personally briefed border agents on the newest trends and what was happening on the ground, and then personally debriefed them when they came off the field. In the absence of a national strategy, Reyes implemented an operation designed to use all the personnel and assets available to draft a blueprint of substantial deterrence on the border.[11]

Congressman Reyes's operation succeeded in sealing the border at El Paso. Arrests of undocumented workers dropped considerably in the sector. Of course, undocumented border crossers simply moved away from the urban areas into more rural and even more rugged, empty areas of the border, with many more deaths as a result. It was at this time that the number of undocumented-migrant deaths in the Arizona desert began to climb. Depending on the source, there have been between 2,100 and 6,000 undocumented migrant deaths in the Arizona desert since 1994. According to the Border Patrol, there were 1,954 casualties of the war on undocumented immigration between 1998 and 2004 alone, with anywhere between 300 and 500 dying every year since 2001. The real numbers we will never know. Most died of dehydration, hypothermia, heart attacks, and car accidents.[12] Doris Meissner, former chief of the then INS, acknowledged at that time that the multiplication of deaths on the southwestern border was an "unintended consequence" of the new aggressiveness of U.S. strategies on the border. If the United States managed to seal the urban centers, the rugged geography of the rest of the border, authorities said, would be the deterrent.[13] It has not been. In fact, while undocumented border crossings are down in the Sonoran desert (Arizona), the number of deaths is up.[14] The balloon effect was at work. Reyes's plan was succeeding, but only where he was operating, e.g., El Paso sector. The rest of the border, however, was ready to receive, and sometimes kill, the migrants who would not cease the pursuit of their "American dream."

Reyes's operation was so successful in El Paso in fact that it was imitated elsewhere, in California (Operation Gatekeeper), in Arizona (Operation Safeguard), and in the Lower Rio Grande Valley of Texas (Operation Rio Grande). In California, Border Patrol chief Gus de la Viña argued that such physical blockades did not fit the problems endemic to his San Diego sector. Instead, he argued for high steel walls to be built along the borderline. And he got them. The physical blockage of the border in the urban centers between California and Baja California now includes steel walls that a visitor can see running right into the sea. Such fences exist in other places along the borderline in Arizona as well. In Calexico-Mexicali, there are also water canals, dug like trenches and filled with water to serve as a deterrent to border crossers. Such canals are a common sight in various parts of Texas, along the Rio Grande.

It is hard to tell how much the militarization of the border has actually helped decrease the flow of undocumented migrants. Clearly, it has had an effect, but the 2008 financial crisis collapsed the lower-paid job markets in the United States, a major pull force for undocumented migrants. Since the U.S. job market has not yet fully recovered, we will not know that effect until we have a full recovery in the United States. What we do know is that Central Americans continue to come and they are still making it across, but in much lesser numbers than before. It is simply too risky, and the operational control of the border has made it easier to stop them. It has also raised the premium on migrants—about $10,000 per person as of 2016.

The training of the Border Patrol has also become more and more military-like. Although their job remains a law enforcement effort, it now has a distinct military feel to it. It could also be that many of them are former military and it is hard to turn them on to law enforcement that understands the importance of due process and human rights. In Arizona, they train with heavily armed Marines; in California, they get help from the National Guard in inspecting vehicles at POEs; in the Imperial Valley, they hunker down with soldiers using night-vision equipment to detect stealthy border crossers. Their vehicles used to be open vans and SUV-style vehicles. Today, they are trucks with steel cages welded on the platform that resemble military jeeps. Their weapons are also becoming more sophisticated, and military technology has been adapted for use on border operations. Driving along the Rio Grande riverbank in Fabens, Texas, I was stopped by a Border Patrol agent who wanted to check on my activity along the river. I was surprised at the number of gadgets at his disposal around his waist belt, besides his handgun. Within three minutes of his stopping me, several other Border Patrol vehicles were speeding toward us. Communication between patrols is now swift and support can be at hand within a couple of minutes. Somewhat upset at my use of their exclusive road along the Rio Grande, they escorted me out to the main highway in the town of Fabens and asked me not to use their road, newly improved by the military, again. Along the U.S.-Mexico border, there is a push to build a law enforcement military infrastructure in an effort to control the border.

These physical blockade strategies of the Border Patrol in El Paso during Operation Hold the Line have been imitated extensively along other sectors of the border since 1994. The logic of escalation at the border continues apace more than two decades later.

THE BORDER AS A SYMBOL OF A
STILL-RELUCTANT PARTNERSHIP

Mexico and the United States are not friends, even though it looks like they are. They may be friendly, but they are not friends. At least, they are not friends in the sense that Canada and the United States are friends. Mexico has never been a strategic partner of the United States in any of its alliances and it is not likely to be invited to be one anytime soon—in spite of the enormous trading relationship. And yet both countries understand that they are bound by destiny. Their geographical proximity makes them associates in a reluctant partnership. Both Washington and Mexico City like to stress the importance of their relationship in rhetoric, but there are really few real institutionalized mechanisms of cooperation between the two countries, and many such mechanisms come and go with personalities and executive administrations, even in the face of deepening economic integration under NAFTA. Under the George W. Bush administration, there were even fewer contacts between Washington and Mexico City than under the Bill Clinton administration, when there were periodic cabinet-level meetings between the two nations. And although the cabinet-level meetings resumed under President Obama—including the institution of a High Level Economic Dialogue—he clearly has not made Mexico a priority. In fact, Obama has deported more Mexicans than any other president—something that has never really pleased Mexican authorities, but there is little they can do about it. Americans often perceive Mexico as a source of trouble—drugs, immigration, and the potential of a terrorist attack staged from Mexico are always in the minds of Americans. Recent polls suggest that Americans still hold deeply negative views of Mexico and NAFTA.[15] Alternatively, Mexicans are preoccupied with the United States, but feel somewhere between abused and neglected by their neighbor. Across the border, Mexicans and Americans eye each other with deep suspicion to this day, well into the twenty-first century. Americans overestimate their generosity to Mexico, and

Mexicans view Americans as self-centered and demanding. Interestingly, there is a wide gap when it comes to the border, where the views of each other are much softer, as per the Univisión poll cited above and conducted in April 2016. The mutual distrust runs very deep. Mexico feels dominated by the United States; the United States seldom views the relationship as one of domination. It is possible to continue specifying the many divides between Mexico and the United States, but they have been plentifully explained elsewhere. Here, suffice it to say that they are engaged in a reluctant partnership.

More crucial to us here is that nowhere is this reluctance of both Mexico and the United States to be partners more manifest than on their borderlands. The millions of Americans who reside in the southwestern borderlands of the United States know the importance of Mexico. Mexico is an increasingly essential part of their lives. Their lives are closely intertwined with the lives of Mexicans living on the border and now well beyond. Through NAFTA, more than 6 million American jobs are now dedicated to exports to Mexico. The economic, social, and cultural ties are ever stronger but under threat of extinction by U.S. border policies—I am now convinced that to border agents the best border is one that no one ever crosses. And yet there is a veritable convergence at the borderlands as a symbol of the inevitable integration of North America. Most U.S. counties along the border, some 26 of them, are nearly solidly Mexican and Mexican American now. Spanish is a dominant language in the region. Family bloodlines cross the border millions of times, even with all the difficulties. Jobs on one side generate additional jobs on the other side. Put together, the economy of the border counties and border *municipios* would constitute a formidable manufacturing powerhouse.

The problem is not in the understanding of those who have to live on the border. They know and have known for a long time that they depend on each other. The problem is with those who live away from the border in the United States—and increasingly the U.S. political class that has made the border its whipping boy in electoral campaigns. The perceptions of nonborder residents are distorted by the media and the political rhetoric that is heard loud and clear in their living rooms. Their perceptions are heavily influenced by the media's attention to the negative news coming from the border and their neglect of the many positive things that happen on the borderlands. To a housewife in St. Louis, or a student in Portland, or a blue-collar worker in Sioux Falls, the border is a dangerous place. The media too are profiting from portraying the border as a dangerous place with shows like *The Bridge* and *The Border*. Few good stories about the border make it to the houses of typical Americans. To border residents, the border is home and they make the best of it, much as everyone else does in their community.

AGENT GONZÁLEZ AND THE PROBLEM
WITH THE PROBLEM

Peering through a hole in the steel wall that divides a small California border town from a tiny settlement on the Baja California side of the border, a Border Patrol agent sitting in his truck became aware that I was studying the borderline. Trained to be suspicious of every activity occurring anywhere near the wall, the agent sped toward me. Agent González (I read the name on his nametag) came out of the truck and walked toward me. He asked me what I was doing. I said I was studying the fence. I could read his face. He was not happy about it at all. He said that I should not be there because it was dangerous, because it was a liability for the federal government, because I should have gotten permission to be there, etc. He was behaving considerably more zealously than the Border Patrol agents I had encountered in New Mexico and Arizona. He ordered me to report to the nearest Border Patrol station and to ask for permission if I wanted to study the fence.

The barrage of questions that he shot at me prompted me to come up with some of my own. "Why is there no port of entry between these two towns?" I asked. "Is the settlement on the other side just a ranch? Or is it a full township? When people want to cross, where do they go?" He was visibly annoyed by my questions and said, pointing toward Mexico, "I don't know. That is Mexico on the other side. I don't know anything about it." He may have known about it or not. But he was annoyed. I left.

It dawned on me that the answer that Agent González gave me was quite revealing of the whole "problem of the border." Whatever he told me exactly, I heard something like this: "The other side is their problem. My problem begins here, with this fence. My job is not to view the problem of immigration comprehensively, but to view each person crossing the fence as a transgressor and anyone moving along it as a potential criminal. My job is not to know what is on the other side and how it relates to my job. My job is to prevent border jumpers from coming through. I do not care about what is on the other side. My care begins at this point and from here northward." Agent González epitomized the reality of the border. It is a dividing line. It separates. It determines our concerns, what we care about. It shapes our views of what it means. It limits our vision of the problem. It focuses the wars of the border on the dividing line. It prevents a global view of the matter. It gives meaning to our jobs and our careers. What the relationship between our "immigration problem" and what may motivate it on the other side of the borderline is, we do not care. On the other side of the fence, regardless of how strong the sun shines there too, there is only darkness. It is an abyss. It is the unknown. For a Border Patrol agent at the borderline, the other side of the fence might as well not exist. And perhaps he, the border-level bureaucrat, is not to blame. He is paid to guard the border. Period. His commands come from above. His orders are clear. The policy itself is someone else's matter. In some ways, it reflects the general attitude that underlies the policy of the U.S. toward Mexico.

Unfortunately, it is not any different for our politicians and the public than it is for Agent González in the field—and the presidential campaign of 2016 is further showing that nothing has really changed. Politicians in particular seem to be trapped in a myopic view of the border that forbids us from conceiving of it as a North American problem. This is worse than good fences making good neighbors. Good fences make the neighbor disappear until the neighbor's problem lands on "our" side of the fence. Then the solution becomes more guards, more walls, taller walls, more agents, more vehicles, more lighting and sensor systems, and more binoculars. Success is measured in terms of the number of arrests, jail time, deportations, etc., with little thought to whether the strategy overall is paying off. For decades, the United States has pumped hundreds of billions of dollars into fortifying the border, with little success in resolving the major causes behind the border troubles, in spite of the many tactical successes here and there.

As far as Agent González was concerned, there is a border war going on, and it has been raging for a long time. He is just a foot soldier in it. His job is to stop the invasion of human smugglers who lead more than 1 million undocumented workers, the enemy, across the borderline. He patrols the trenches. He watches the battle line. He detains the prisoners of the war on immigration. As far as the politicians are concerned, Agent González is a hero in action because the border is to be "protected," the "invasion" is to be stopped, "border security must be ensured," and so on. The strategy is a war of attrition, a continual grinding down of the border with more and more resources, even as drugs flow just as freely and human-smuggling rings prosper. Agent González's myopia extends from the borderlands to Washington, DC.

THE DEFINITION OF BORDER SECURITY

Agent González's perspective is important because it reveals that the two countries do not coincide on the definition of the border. In effect, Mexico's border is an open border. Americans can go into Mexico without a visa; they can travel at will inside Mexico and they can even reside in that country without much hassle—nearly 2 million Americans now live in Mexico, more than in any other country in the world and more than in the entire European Union. American citizens living and working in Mexico, from San Miguel to Chapala to Baja California and all along the border, can testify to the ease with which they can do so. Moreover, since

NAFTA went into effect, Mexico has become a nation open to trade and investment at unprecedented levels in its history—often to the detriment of certain Mexican economic sectors. Americans, however, benefit handsomely from this openness. In contrast, the U.S. border is a closed border, or more specifically, it is a border wide open to trade and investment but closed to labor. Labor is a fundamental component of any economy. Yet the United States has been very slow to acknowledge that Mexico has a comparative advantage in the labor that it can provide to a humming American economy. This discrepancy has been explored by Peter Laufer in *Wetback Nation: The Case for Opening the Mexican-American Border*.[16] Still, Mexicans are required to have a visa to enter the United States. They cannot easily obtain a permit either to work temporarily or to migrate to the United States. This creates an enormous pressure to move without a visa, overstay their visa, and even risk death at the border—although fewer are doing so now—and once in the United States, they chance living in the shadows of American society.

More important here is the fact that if Mexicans and Americans do not share a common definition of the border, it becomes obvious why they do not share a common definition of security. Not having a common definition of security means that there is no common definition of *border* security. That is a fact that impedes any serious cooperation between the two on "securing the border." Since September 11, it has become even more palpable that Mexico and the United States do not see eye to eye on the very definition of security. This disagreement weighs heavily on the border, although it has worked more to Mexico's disadvantage.

Thus it is important to examine the definition of security and what the security goals of each country are and how they rub at the border. There are two definitions of security. First, there is national security. Second, there is public security, also known as public safety in English, although it is difficult to translate into Spanish because "security" is used for both "security" and "safety." In any event, national security refers to the threats coming from outside and that jeopardize the nation as a whole—its people, its infrastructure, its economy, etc. Public safety refers to the safeguard of the citizens from each other, e.g., criminal activity by citizens on other citizens or their property. The U.S. definition of security focuses on the concept of national security, external threats.

There is also evidence that in the United States, national security and public safety are increasingly becoming conflated conceptually—at least in the law enforcement community. Since September 11, the two concepts have merged and citizens and aliens are often seen as threatening national security in both senses. A passenger on a domestic flight who might be perceived as behaving erratically may be shot to death by the Air Marshals because he or she poses a "national security threat," which in such a case is nearly indistinguishable from a crime. In fact, the Patriot

Act seems to conflate the two types of security definitions—a considerable departure from the past. The February 2005 conviction of Lynne F. Stewart, a lawyer, for "smuggling messages out of jail from a terrorist client," is an example that U.S. citizens can be seen as a threat to national security.[17] The detention of U.S. citizens, such as José Padilla, without due process by the Justice Department under the George W. Bush administration was another example that the distinction between national security and public security is increasingly blurred. Under Obama too this confusion has remained, and American citizens have been killed without due process because they are a national security threat, where otherwise they could be held as criminals and granted their constitutional rights. Thus the new concept of "security" in the United States is primarily one of "national security," but combines some elements of public safety. Undocumented migrants too have been considered more and more a "national security" threat, whereas they are simply individuals who broke immigration laws and have crime rates much lower than natives. Elevating them to the level of a "national security" threat, however, justified additional measures that skip constitutional entanglements such as due process rights—already an ominous sign in what is supposed to be a liberal democracy. The fundamental assumption, however, is that if a public safety threat can be found in a domestic context, the threat should be first considered from a national security perspective; in effect, it should be asked first if the very survival and way of life of the United States is at stake. Rarely is this the case, but the survival and well-being of the nation are primordial in this narrower understanding of security and give law enforcement a good excuse to continue to chip away at any citizen rights over time and to become more secretive and less accountable. There must in the future be a debate in the United States on the issues of security once again, but there is no political will to do so now.

Mexico views these two terms quite separately and quite distinct from one another, although the Calderón administration began a process of conflating them. National security in the traditional sense, however, is not Mexico's main concern. Foreign threats to Mexican sovereignty are not a reality that Mexicans consider important today, even if they did in the past. If there is any threat to Mexican sovereignty, most Mexicans, in fact, believe that it would come from the United States. Public safety, however, is a big concern in Mexico, although it appears to be part of a major problem with the rule of law and a broken system of administration of justice:

Inadequate public security presently ranks near the top of Mexico's political agenda and has become central in shaping U.S.-Mexico relations. There is much debate about the meaning of "public security" ... The debate concerns the boundaries of the concept and whether and how to include such issues as income inequality, poverty, education, popular culture, morality, and the like.[18]

The threat of organized crime, for example, is a serious worry to the Mexican government. They are increasingly concerned about drug cartels and the effects that they have on the country's economy and society. Between 2006 and 2012, President Calderón perceived them to be the major threat to Mexico's public safety and he even elevated the threat to one of national security because he saw drug cartels and organized crime in general as a threat to the very survival of Mexico's political institutions. The onslaught that would follow that assumption would result in the death of 125,000 Mexicans and the disappearance of another 25,000. It also cost the PAN party the elections in 2012. President Peña decided that the political liability of continuing the war on drugs would be so great that he let up on fighting organized crime and, consequently, it has returned to victimize large segments of Mexican society. Mexico's own conflation of the issue in the last few years has resulted in an ineffective government, unable to provide for its own definition of national security or its own definition of public safety.

Mexicans worry also about the safety of Mexican undocumented workers traveling to the United States and their human rights once inside the United States. On the one hand, several Mexicans have been shot to death by Border Patrol agents, even across the line, as in the case of Sergio Hernández Guereca in 2010.[19] On the other hand, Mexico has even declared that poverty and environmental degradation are in and of themselves threats to the security of the country. Mexico understands security to be a much broader concept than a terrorist threat coming from abroad and has been trying to bring the United States into that discussion. That is not likely to happen. And in any event, this is an agenda that can go nowhere as long as the two countries do not see eye to eye on how these issues affect their relationship and their shared border, and how to tackle them together.

Nevertheless, there are points of connection where the two countries could conceivably cooperate to make the border safer. If public safety, say in regard to organized crime, specifically drug trafficking, is a preoccupation of both nations, then there can be an overlap in their definitions of security, and this constitutes an opportunity for cooperation. That such connections exist with minimal mechanisms of cooperation is a glaring example of how the political will of both governments has failed to produce sustained, effective collaboration on one of the most serious problems of the border and beyond. I do not personally consider the Mérida Initiative, begun in 2007 by President Bush and President Calderón, a successful initiative, given that, although it has managed to capture many cartel capos, it has failed to help Mexican administration of justice institutions truly advance. In fact, it could be said that today, Mexico's rule-of-law issues are just getting worse, rather than better. Thus, and unfortunately, the U.S. government does not trust the Mexican government and the Mexican government is still highly suspicious of U.S. intentions—more so under the Peña administration than the Calderón administration. U.S. antidrug bureaucrats, for example, can cite many examples of intelligence sharing where the information has been compromised by a corrupt Mexican official leaking it to criminal organizations— although there are also instances of spectacular collaborations, such as the operation against Arturo Beltrán Leyva in December 2009. This operation was accomplished with U.S. actionable intelligence by the Mexican marines. Similarly, Joaquín "El Chapo" Guzmán was captured in Mazatlán, Sinaloa in February 2014, in part thanks to American electronic surveillance of his telecommunications. More recently, Mexican military chased Sinaloa Cartel members across the border into the Arizona desert, with permission from the United States, and captured almost two dozen members of that criminal organization. Still, Mexico suffers from a historical paranoia regarding U.S. violations of its sovereignty in the past and the United States suffers from deep-seated suspicions of Mexico's true ability to collaborate in joint operations. This mutual discomfort does not allow the two countries to work together fully in fighting drug trafficking at the border from the same perspective of mutual benefit. Each tackles the problem differently and separately, which enables the drug-trafficking organizations to operate between the cracks.

The blurring of the distinction of the definitions of national security and public safety in the United States, and increasingly in Mexico, affects not only the ability to discern what to do and how far to go, but also the border in yet another way. If the border and its ailments are not viewed as a matter of public safety but rather are defined as a matter of national security, then increased militarization of the border, undue surveillance, excessive punitive measures, and even human rights abuses are all justified. Unfortunately, such militarization is no longer seen as an anomaly but rather as normal, a natural response to the presumed threats that the border represents. All such threats on the border have now been welded into a single department, Homeland Security, and given unprecedented historical coherence and permanent justification. The border is not a zone amenable to joint management. It is two zones that represent a problem to each other. That is bound to make things far worse, rather than better for everyone. Moreover, because it is the survival or welfare of the country that is at stake, a unilateral response is perceived as appropriate by the United States. Such an approach, however, irks Mexico considerably because that definition of security has a lot to do with the threats the United States faces but not the threats that Mexico faces.

Thus instead of focusing on the points of connection and seeking a new border management system where the two countries can work together, the two governments go their separate ways, and the border lacks a coherent, binational approach to ensure that it is a safe and prosperous place for the many millions of Mexican and American citizens that live and work and study in the borderlands. Paradoxically, we find that criminals and other undesirables find a wedge of safe haven in the gray area where joint solutions do not exist. Instead of closing the gaps where they operate with joint policies, we broaden them with unilateral policies.

THE CONSTRUCTION OF BORDER SECURITY

That Mexico and the United States cannot agree on a common definition of security is testimony to the fact that security on the U.S.-Mexico border is a socially constructed concept and, worse yet, as we have demonstrated, that it is the security bureaucracies that are in the driver's seat. They decide what the threat is; they lobby the politicians to adopt their definition of the threat; they ask for the budgets and the gadgets; and they get them—only to go back the next year and repeat the cycle. Politicians, policy makers, and the media choose to portray the three great issues of the borderlands—drugs, immigration, and homeland security—as threats to the nation as a whole, and the information that they feed to the public is largely shaped by the bureaucracies that benefit from the "border chaos." The way issues are perceived is not a trivial matter, because changing the discourse around them may help find broader, more successful solutions. For example, undocumented immigration from Mexico to the United States is an economic phenomenon spurred by the economic asymmetries between the two. If Mexico cannot generate enough jobs to absorb its unemployed and underemployed, those people will tend to flow to the United States in search of work—although it is true that economic conditions in the United States are not good, diminishing a major pull force, and important demographic changes in Mexico have also reduced the pressure on migration north. Still, as long as Mexico's wages are significantly lower than those in the United States, labor will go where higher wages can be had. Labor demand in the United States will also make it possible for an undocumented worker to imagine himself or herself working in the United States. It has been sufficiently shown that undocumented immigration has a lot to do with the networks that already exist between certain communities in Mexico and specific U.S. metropolitan areas, but these ties are certainly weakening among Mexicans, even as they are strengthening among Central Americans. Those already in the United States inform those at home that there is a job to be had. They are further encouraged to make the trek to the border and beyond because they also know that once they reach a U.S. metropolitan area, they will not be caught. Finally, as already indicated, increasingly more higher-income and more educated Mexicans are choosing to migrate to the United States, largely motivated by the lack of public safety, a deficient justice system, difficult economic conditions, and terribly bad public goods and services in exchange for higher and higher taxes.[20]

Yet officials and the media in the United States have chosen to view undocumented migration not as an economic issue but as a security issue. They seldom talk about the economic forces that constitute the push and pull forces for migrants. And there has been no progress in fixing the immigration system to accommodate a more labor-oriented definition of migration and restore the circular migration that existed prior to the current system. In effect, the U.S. law enforcement community has chosen to "construct" its own definition of security by referring to migrants as a national security threat and using language that includes the words "invasion," "war," "threat," "crisis," "disorder," "chaos," "frontlines," etc. Security concepts arise "out of discursive practices within states."[21] Since September 11, this kind of rhetoric has only increased exponentially, and 15 years later, it continues unabated. And language matters in the construction of an environment and the creation of solutions to a given problem. Whereas under the Clinton administration the concern was with "managing the border," today the concern is with "controlling the border."[22] Whereas immigration was then a law enforcement issue, it is labeled a national security issue today. Each of these labels implies different solutions, even if there is remarkable continuity between them. Political discourse is being captured by a new rhetoric that necessarily leads to quasi-militarized techniques of responding to border issues. In a previous section, we have also explored how there is a strong tendency to conflate the issues by labeling every one of them a matter of national security.

UNHELPFUL RHETORIC

Although one would like to think that the American public has all the information it needs at its disposal to make appropriate judgments about the border, the views of the majority are largely shaped by the media and those who would be news makers, more specifically politicians. How the media frame the issues and the rhetoric that politicians use in their border narratives heavily affects the perceptions of the border among Americans. This was obvious through 2005 and it is certainly obvious in the 2016 presidential race. Donald Trump has raked in delegates for the Republican convention partly by promising to build a "beautiful wall" along the U.S.-Mexico border—one that Mexico would pay for!

On August 17, 2005, a *New York Times* headline read "Citing Border Violence, Two States Declare a Crisis." On August 20, 2005, referring to the same border states, Arizona and New Mexico, a headline read "United States of Emergency." On August 23, 2005, a headline in the same paper read "For One Family, Front Row Seats to Border Crisis." On August 24, 2005, also in the *New York Times*, was the headline

"Homeland Security Chief, with Nod to Public Discontent, Tells of Plan to Stabilize the Border." On December 3, 2005, a *Baltimore Sun* editorial called to "Regain Control of Our Borders." On December 4, 2005, in the same paper, a headline read "Rival Drug Gangs Turn the Streets of Nuevo Laredo into War Zone." Similar headlines could be found across the country in large papers, such as the *Washington Post*, the *Los Angeles Times*, the *Dallas Morning News*, and the *Houston Chronicle*. The broadcast media have employed the same kind of rhetoric. Some national anchors and TV show hosts have chosen to talk about the border as a lawless, chaotic place where violence and illegality reign. Fox News has contributed to this kind of rhetoric perhaps more than any other network. In all, the rhetoric keeps growing more alarming. All these stories portray the border as being under siege by all kinds of criminal organizations. In addition to the many articles in the print media and the hundreds of reports on the border in the broadcast media, several books have come out as well detailing what is happening at the border as a disaster, as a national security threat, etc.[23] This sense of urgency is found nearly everywhere in the national debate regarding the border.

Politicians too entered the fray, mostly to profit from it, as politicians are wont to do. John Kerry himself, well before he ran for president in 1996, wrote a book, *The New War: The Web of Crime that Threatens America's Security*, in which he said that a new war had to be waged against criminal organizations that flouted the border, continuously smuggling both drugs and human beings.[24] For Kerry, the border was seen as practically governed by criminal organizations. Patrick Buchanan, when he ran for president in 1996, advocated the construction of a border wall that would be patrolled by the military.[25] The idea was eventually dismissed as too controversial. But, in 2005, Representative Duncan Hunter of California, who chaired the House Armed Services Committee, insisted on his presumed necessity of building two parallel steel and wire fences with a lighted strip from the Gulf of Mexico to the Pacific Coast.[26] Mexico's Foreign Ministry immediately released a communiqué arguing against the construction of this wall. But border walls have been going up nevertheless and are now nearing a hundred miles total along the border between El Paso and San Diego. Others have been quite vocal, like Congressman Tom Tancredo (R-CO), who on December 12, 2005, said that 51 terrorists had been arrested crossing the border illegally. Congressman Tancredo never really defined what the definition of a terrorist crossing the border illegally is.[27] Citations by politicians regarding the lack of control along the border can be found by the thousands. By 2007, all these politicians had their dream come true. The Secure Fence Act was passed that year, and now we have at least 700 miles of walls/fences along the border. In 2016, Republican presidential candidate Donald J. Trump has promised to build a "beautiful wall," meaning that he intends to wall out the entire 2,000-mile border and then make Mexico pay for that wall, confiscating migrants' remittances if necessary.[28]

Of course, they forget that the border has never really been under control. It has always been out of the total control of the U.S. government. Moreover, those who would speak of border control hide the fact that as the current border strategies of the United States to control the border have escalated, the same problems have only gotten worse and the consequences more deadly. But the political class seems to have forgotten how to deal with public policy issues creatively.

Although the reality is that most Americans would like to see the border secured, the majority also supports resolving the situation of the undocumented-resident population in the United States in favor of a green card for those who have already been here a long time, have worked and paid taxes, and have no criminal record. That would actually make most of the 11 million undocumented residents come out of the shadows and be fully integrated into mainstream America. Interestingly, that makes sense, given that the undocumented-resident population has actually been stable and has perhaps even declined for the last 10 years.[29]

The words used to describe the border have continued to escalate the tone of the debate regarding the border throughout 2016. This flurry of alarming notes has been repeated hundreds of times over the years. During his administration, President George W. Bush sounded like a man trying to find a workable solution for immigration, but many in Washington, DC, in the president's own party, would likely be unhappy with a solution that would grant undocumented workers amnesty. They continued to focus the problem of immigration on the border, among many other ills. Many politicians responded to the president's message in a manner equally unhelpful in the search for creative, long-term, binational solutions to a common border. The same politicians and policy makers that contributed heavily to the "securitization" of the border by using language that resembles the media's and that of certain vigilante groups that patrol the border from time to time rejected the idea of any kind of amnesty for undocumented workers. President Obama has deported millions of undocumented workers too, trying to push for immigration reform while being tough on migrants so as not to open a political front for Republicans. Even so, they did not concede and most bills have met the same fate, death on arrival.

It is lamentable that the media and politicians often feed off the same cycle of news and create a border crisis by the images and representation of border problems. Obviously, the issues of the border are serious. They need to be dealt with seriously. But the rhetoric of those who do not reside on the border is very often unhelpful in finding good solutions to these problems.

STILL TALKING PAST EACH OTHER AT THE BORDER

Leaving aside the fact that there is no agreement on the definition of security between Mexico and the United States, the political leaders, those who could actually fix the border, seem to be talking past each other—when they talk to each other at all. Although some assessments say that the U.S.-Mexico relationship is advancing and security cooperation is overall better today than ever, there are two fundamental items missing from the relationship. First, there is little political will in either country to take a serious look at the border and to figure out how to solve common problems together. Second, there is little vision among the leaders of both sides in regard to the future of the border. It is remarkable how much continuity there is in this. The consequence is that, if the relationship is altogether on hold, at the border there is nearly a total abandonment. Indeed, a striking feature of the border is that sometimes bureaucrats look each other in the eye from across the fences but seldom do they talk to each other at all. There is very little contact on the ground among officials of agencies whose mission is to guard the border on either side.

A sign that the two nations are talking past each other is the fact that Mexico tried to reach out to the United States early in the Fox administration by creating a "border czar" position within the Mexican government. And although the position did not come with real resources and jurisdictional power, one of the important elements of its undoing was the fact that the titular holder of that post in the Mexican government, Ernesto Ruffo Appel, could not find a counterpart in the U.S. government to talk to. In general, there is very little dialogue between the two nations to solve their common problems. And NAFTA has not produced any other intergovernmental institutions that could help take a serious look at the border with an eye to finding common solutions. I know there are important people trying to push the border agenda, not the least of which is Alan Bersin, a longtime student and friend of the border, but these heroes are often swimming against the tide of current history, even if the long-term vision of the border is on their side.

A NEW APPROACH FOR THE FUTURE

The 1990s were an odd time for the border. It would seem almost as if the border suffered from the schizophrenia of both Washington, DC, and Mexico City. The 1990s saw some of the strongest movement to "militarize" the border on the part of the U.S. government. Yet NAFTA brought about all sorts of speculations about North American integration and the birth of a North American community. There was enormous optimism around in the air. Finally, it was thought, Mexico and the United States would break decades of mutual suspicion and begin a long-term process of integration. This was manifest in the visit that President George W. Bush paid to President Vicente Fox at his ranch in the state of Guanajuato. September 11, however, brought about the "securitization" of the border, with "security" being defined in very narrow and conventional terms as a threat to the survival and welfare of the country. The catastrophic events made the U.S. government retreat from its orientation toward North American integration. Yet the integration, at least the economic integration, of North America continues apace, a fact that both the Mexican and the U.S. governments have failed to understand. There is clearly also a cultural convergence in the Southwest, where Mexicans and Mexican Americans are beginning to constitute important majorities in border states and many counties. Yet the two governments have failed to build any credible institutions that can effectively systematize the future of the relationship and the future of the border. Border issues are resolved one at a time, with great difficulty, often too late and sometimes not at all. Both countries generally react to border troubles, and recriminations about each other's behavior along the boundary line are plentiful. A narrow definition of security by the United States and a perceived lack of cooperation from Mexico around U.S. concerns is slowing the process of cross-border cooperation even further.

It is therefore unfortunate that the war on terror has come to the border, because the economic opportunities and market forces, as well as the cultural convergence at work in the borderlands, could help push forward toward a binational agreement on how to deal with the border. The political will and the political vision of leaders in Washington, DC, and Mexico City, however, lag well behind. Everyone, it seems, is thinking very small. A new approach to North American security is needed, one that will ensure the periphery well beyond the border. Over the last 10 years, not much has changed either. In fact, as I explained, the bureaucratic interests vested in profiting from the border wars are more entrenched than ever, now further aided by technology and a poisonous rhetoric that does not let up.

NAFTA AND THE BORDER

On January 1, 1994, NAFTA went into effect. At that time, and in spite of the Zapatista rebellion in southern Mexico and a peso devaluation, with a corresponding financial crisis at the end of the year, there was enormous optimism about the integration of North America. Finally, Mexico and the United States, along with Canada, had recognized their common destiny—at a minimum, their geographical ties—and come together to formalize their economic integration. There was considerable talk about the North American continent, comparing it with the European Union.

And NAFTA has been very successful. Since it went into effect, it has propelled trade among the three countries to unprecedented levels. Financial flows among the three countries multiplied, and travel among the three also grew dramatically. The opportunities for interaction among Mexicans, Canadians, and Americans burgeoned. North America was becoming an integrated region. Most trade barriers between the three countries were eliminated.

But NAFTA was not altogether good. And its effects along the border can be easily intuited. First, there was very little in the NAFTA negotiations that dealt with the possibility that in some sectors in Mexico, the gap between the haves and the have-nots would actually grow, compelling many of the have-nots to leave their home in search of a better life in the United States. The development gap between Mexico and the United States has widened and the United States never made provisions for the possibility of increased migration. The number of undocumented workers after NAFTA went into effect grew from 3 to 12 million in the United States—although, again, only 6.7 million of those are Mexicans. Curiously enough, NAFTA also did not plan for the increase in traffic between Mexico and the United States. Trade grew 12 to 13 times over, but the infrastructure for receiving and inspecting the increased trade along the border lagged well behind. The inability to inspect every truck, for example, meant that they would eventually serve as a conveyor belt for illegal drugs, as we explored in Chapter 3.

There is a theory known as functionalism. It is a favorite of those who study the European Union—with all its current trials and tribulations. They claim that if two distrusting partners begin cooperating on a small issue, they might just build the trust to cooperate on a slightly more important issue, and so forth. By the time they realize it, they have built lots of trust and solid mechanisms of cooperation. If these mechanisms are then institutionalized, soon they will have strong links with each other and their partnership will not easily be destroyed. The favorite example of functionalists is Germany and France, which, after warring each other unceasingly, managed to serve as the two engines of the European Union by moving from a single issue (coal and steel) to forming a solid confederation today. In North America, NAFTA, as broad as it is, has not produced any new mechanisms for cooperation on other issues, and certainly none for cooperation on the problems that plague the U.S.-Mexico border. NAFTA did not address the creation of credible institutions to coordinate border policy. And it certainly never addressed the issue of security. Even if it was not meant to do so, it has now spilled over into any areas other than trade and investment flows. September 11 only drove a deeper wedge between Mexico and the United States. Hardly anyone stopped to consider that the border is where NAFTA would have some of its most negative effects: an overburdened infrastructure, the more efficient flow of drugs, and the congregation of undocumented migrants pushed by the development gap between the two countries and pulled by the opportunities for employment in the United States. NAFTA addressed none of these "security" problems. In other words, NAFTA has been a blessing for the economies of the two countries, but it has been a curse to the border. The social and economic dislocations in Mexico have turned to security problems on the border for the United States. There was an evident lack of foresight among the drafters of NAFTA.

THE NORTH AMERICAN SOLUTION

On March 23, 2005, President George W. Bush, President Vicente Fox, and Prime Minister Paul Martin met. The background was West Texas. In that meeting, they announced the Security and Prosperity Partnership of North America. This initiative was based on the idea that security and economic integration go hand in hand. The reality before and after, however, has been that no progress has been made in setting up any kind of bilateral or trilateral institutional mechanisms to deal with security for North America, much less with border security. In fact the Security and Prosperity Partnership is yet one more stillborn initiative. There was a list of good wishes, but no real mechanism to follow through, no individuals appointed to oversee its implementation, no office to go with that, and no money behind it.

President George W. Bush's concept of security, a unilateral definition with a unilateral solution largely based on force, was laid to waste in Iraq and became a controversial legacy for Bush himself. The concept of border security that he outlined on November 29, 2005, in Tucson and El Paso is no different. It meant more of the same. Obama at least has not been openly optimistic. His policies have been a crude realism, harsh on immigrants and tough on the border, even though he occasionally says otherwise. Thus the responsibility of both politicians and policy makers is to begin to look to a new era and create a new approach to the border. I want to suggest that this approach must be a North American one. In addressing immigration, it is probably convenient to address the development gap between Mexico and the United States. In addressing drug trafficking, it is probably important to find ways to build reliable cross-border mechanisms of cooperation to disintegrate the powerful criminal drug cartels that continue to operate in the vacuum of a lack of intergovernmental cooperation between the two countries—the most important of these being the Sinaloa Cartel, particularly after the Calderón administration pulverized two of the others. In addressing the potential of terrorists infiltrating the border, it is probably important to address an integrated travel system in the whole of North America where clearance checks are coordinated and standardized among all three. Doing so would take enormous pressure off the border law enforcement community and, above all, the burden of suspicion that all border residents must live with day to day. The problems of the border are more a symptom of larger forces than a cause of those problems. They must be looked at as such.

Even important initiatives like the "smart border" approach, essentially more technology underlain by strong networks of prechecks and preclearances, are not enough. The problems of North America must be addressed together, just as the problems of the border must be addressed comprehensively. Forty years of a single-track solution on the border have only made the border worse, costing hundreds of billions of dollars and now thousands of lives. Ignoring the forces of globalization in North America has been costly and deadly. And it is clear that the border is not more secure now than before. As Chapters 2, 3, and 4 have shown, the drug trade continues to flourish with organizations better equipped to handle new law enforcement efforts; undocumented workers continue to flow just as much as before; and the possibility of a terrorist coming through the border was low in the first place but may still happen, reason enough to cooperate across North America.

Everything points to a North America solution. But there are two elements lacking in the American leadership: political vision and political will. That vision was actually beginning to flicker early in the Bush and Fox administrations but has not continued under the Obama administration, while the Calderón administration was mired in a massive drug war in Mexico that impeded a longer-term vision and the Peña administration is simply not interested in anything like it. In Guanajuato, Mexico, both presidents endorsed a North American vision in February 2001. However, September 11, like a flash of light on an open pupil, shut down all possibility of a broader vision. President Bush's reaction was first to retreat the concept of North America back to within the borders of the United States and then to fall into the unilateral temptation of finding a U.S.-based solution to national security threats. Iraq and the failure that followed only retrenched this approach; and there is little stomach today to think beyond our own borders.

Clearly, September 11 killed any hopes for a North American community that includes Canada, the United States, and Mexico forging a future together. The idea of a North American community was the late Robert Pastor's, eloquently presented in his book *The North American Idea*.[30] The North American solution Pastor proposed called for a council or a commission similar to the European Commission to begin to identify and define common North American problems. This commission should be trilateral and both prepare the common agenda for executives and legislative bodies and give these issues continuity after the people occupying those posts are long gone. Its studies, conclusions, and recommendations should facilitate further integration and cross-border cooperation on economic, social, diplomatic, and law enforcement efforts. It should also seek to standardize policy across North America—in the longer term, that is. Such a commission would embody a forward-looking approach to border problems. This is quite different from being stuck in the same reactive approach, always lagging behind the problems of the border or the problems of the continent, for that matter. Clearly, the time for a North American community has not yet come.

The biannual meetings of cabinet members that took place under the Clinton administration, and have continued in a much quieter and less effective form as the High Level Economic Dialogue inaugurated by President Obama and Peña, should be restored to power and made more visible and forward looking. Top-level officials should convey to their underlings the importance of dealing with the issues from top to bottom, in a comprehensive way. Members of Congress should give the interparliamentary group a more institutional character, with permanent membership, and organization behind it. The purpose of the group should be to gather the feedback from the commission and introduce it in the legislative agenda of each country. The most painful change will have to occur in the United States, which is largely used to wielding power that enables it to act unilaterally or multilaterally. Canada and Mexico are already quite conscious of the importance of their relationship with the United States and may be better prepared psychologically to make the leap into a trilateral framework than is the United States. It is also very likely that Canada and the United States will have to take some responsibility for closing the development gap between them and Mexico. People from Mexico cross the border because they are aware of the wage levels that can be had in the United States and because of what that money represents to their families back home. At the bottom, it is that simple. A slate of policies and sufficient aid designed to close that gap should do the job. Mexico has promoted free-market ideas and adopted market capitalism, but has gotten few political concessions from its neighbors in return. The window may close in 2018, if a more nationalistic presidential candidate finally galvanizes the frustration of Mexicans and is elected to office, only to put more distance between the two and sever U.S. interests from the Mexican agenda.

DEFINING A NORTH AMERICAN COMMUNITY

The vision of a North American community can emerge from the top to the bottom or from the bottom to the top. It is not likely after September 11 that the creation of a North American community will come from the bottom, even though it is at the grass roots, particularly along the border, that most interaction occurs and where integration is most visible. It is also at the grassroots level, though, that several loud groups are organizing and lobbying the media, the public, and the politicians to "close the border." It is no longer a matter of opening or closing the border. It is now a vital matter of building it and managing it for the benefit of all, especially its 15 million residents.

Instead, the initiative to create a North American community that might take some of the pressure off the border will have to be based on political leadership. Astute political leadership might be able to accomplish it given that over the past 20 years there has been a convergence of values in North America. Although some argue that the values of Latin Americans are fundamentally different from the values of Anglo-America, more and more Mexicans hold the same values of personal freedom and democracy that Americans do. There is also a convergence on public policy, particularly with Mexico's turn to the right by opening its economy to market forces and inserting it in the process of globalization. Political leadership can shift the discourse on the border to the need for creating a larger trilateral community to propel an integrated economy to eliminate border problems. A guest worker program would probably go a long way toward that.

THE NORTH AMERICAN SECURITY BUBBLE

For a long time, Canada and the United States have defined a continental perimeter for the purposes of defense that ended at the U.S.-Mexico border. NORAD was largely in charge of this continental defense within that perimeter. During the attacks of September 11, it was a Canadian in Cheyenne Mountain who was in charge at the moment of the attack. The U.S. Department of Defense did not replace him. They trusted a Canadian to be able to respond appropriately in defense of North America in case of an attack. This trust was built over time between the two countries, but also out of the determination that there was a North American perimeter that could be capsulated and defended as a unit.

No such links exist between Mexico and the United States, in spite of the increasing economic integration, cultural convergence, particularly in the Southwest, and increasing military interaction. Law enforcement continues to be the major problem. But still, law enforcement and military coordination could help both countries go a long way in building that trust required for the solution of common problems, particularly on human mobility and public safety. All three countries, for example, could redefine their security perimeter as a North American, three-country perimeter. It would certainly allow Mexico to commit to certain standards on human rights and justice system improvements with the incentive that it would gain a seat at the North American table. It would allow Mexico to legislate its own rule of law from outside, as it legislated its transition from outside to a market economy by signing on to NAFTA. Immigration and customs in all three countries could work together to stave off terrorist threats and to ensure that cross-border interaction among all three is safe. Then, their attention could turn to Central America, the immediate backyard of a consolidated North America.

BUREAUCRATIC POLITICS AT THE BORDER

In the early 1970s, Graham T. Allison published his book *Essence of Decision: The Cuban Missile Crisis*. In it, he argued that bureaucracies build stakes in what they do. Various studies after that have tested his theory and concluded that there is a lot of powerful evidence to show that bureaucrats tend to build stakes around what they do because enhancing the budgets and the prestige of what they do redounds in various perquisites and privileges for themselves. In other words, bureaucrats have a stake in preserving and enhancing the organizations they work for and portraying their mission as indispensable. Consequently, they develop a stake in exaggerating the threat they face because then they can make the argument that their organization needs even more moral and financial support. Now, put together Allison's theory of bureaucratic politics with the idea that institutions are harder to dismantle or destroy than they are to create, and it becomes clear that creating enormous law enforcement bureaucracies to "secure" the border is equivalent to generating a momentum around the law enforcement approach to the border. Undoing this approach, given that most of the investment in gaining control of the border is going to law enforcement, will be even harder in the future. The momentum of thousands of bureaucrats conceiving their mission as shutting the border and receiving nearly $13 billion for it will be very hard to undo. This is important to point out because it may in the future preclude the possibility of reversing that trend toward a North American solution to the U.S.-Mexico border problems.

THE BORDER REINSTATED

The U.S.-Mexico border is a region in permanent transition. It has had periods of stability, but the historical trend has been toward closing it. The twentieth century saw a dramatic escalation of law enforcement efforts and, in the 1980s and 1990s, an appeal to the military to "defend the border." The early twenty-first century has accelerated that trend. In fact, border policy in the United States has been quite linear: increased

efforts to seal the border, but very little thought to the unintended consequences. NAFTA has created a new conveyor belt for drugs; sealing urban
centers from undocumented migration has increased the number of
deaths in Arizona; the use of better technology to detect drugs has given
the large cartels a comparative advantage; and so on. U.S. policy on the
border has a lot of symbolic content useful to politicians and bureaucrats
who want to portray an image of control. But the border has never been
under control. In fact, the law enforcement escalation has coincided with
a rise of both powerful drug cartels and now powerful smuggling organizations. Yet the persistent failures of the U.S. government's border policies do not seem to face anyone in Washington, DC. Underlying this,
there is a denial that the United States' and Mexico's economies are
increasingly interdependent and are likely to become even more so in
the future. Mexico and Canada are the two natural economic partners of
America, given their proximity and the comparative advantages that they
hold vis-à-vis the United States. This is not to say that politicians do not
get together, as President Obama and President Peña did in Guadalajara,
Mexico, and proclaim all the goodness of integration. But interaction is
not integration. Trading has winners and losers, and we have made no
provision for the losers. People coming and going does not guarantee
respect. And so on. We have confused activity with integration. We are
far from it.

This observation points to a paradox. The fortification of the U.S.-
Mexico border has come on the heels of an unprecedented economic,
cultural, and political convergence. As Mexico has embraced the liberalization paradigm promoted aggressively by the United States, North
America is practically a border-free economy—except for certain sectors
such as the energy sector in Mexico, which remain largely closed, and of
course, except for labor, a main reason for the immigration disaster on
the border. Sooner or later, NAFTA will have to be renegotiated in order
to further integrate the North American economies, simply because it
pays off. Labor will have to be part of that agreement, if there is to be a solution to the undocumented-immigration issue.

North America is also increasingly alike in its values. The growth of
Hispanics in the United States has spurred a surge in the cultural influen-
ces that Mexico exerts in the American society. The Hispanic media, for
example, is today the fastest-growing media sector in the United States.
According to a Pew Hispanic Center report, half of the Hispanic population prefers to speak Spanish and 28 percent are bilingual.[31] Other forms
of cultural convergence are very obvious throughout the Southwest and
increasingly beyond.

There is also an increased political convergence in North America.
Although Canada and the United States have shared their democratic values for a long time, Mexico is fast moving in their direction. Under the

Vicente Fox and Felipe Calderón administrations in Mexico, the country became more democratic. Mexicans enjoyed unprecedented levels of freedom, even if public security remained a very serious concern. The media became freer than ever, though problems remained given killings of some journalists. But more and more Mexicans say today that a democratic government is better than any other form of government. Only 13 percent would trade democracy for a prosperous economy.[32] To be sure, nothing is assured. We have seen no effort from the Peña administration to reinforce the gains made in freedom and democracy in the last two decades. There has in fact been a renewed repression in the freedom of expression and some important setbacks on the democratic front. Violations of human rights are up as well. Corruption is also worse than ever. And there has been no progress on the rule of law. The Peña administration appears not to be interested in moving forward on those fronts. If the United States does not have a plan to ensure that Mexico is ready to be part of North America, the process will be much more difficult and it will ultimately result in a colder relationship, one that will affect the border even more deeply.

But globalization will push in the opposite direction. It is interesting, then, that as borders are lowered by these globalizing trends, politicians and bureaucrats roll in the U.S. police apparatus along the U.S.-Mexico borderlands. Hence the paradox: the economic, cultural, and political convergence of North America is denied in U.S. policy by an unprecedented effort to police the border. There is little understanding of how these two great waves clash against each other on the borderlands, producing the kinds of undesirable border trends that are so widely talked about. It is at this juncture that the state should not retreat from tackling the larger problems of North American integration, because they hold the key to the great pressures of the border, much as they do in Ceuta and Melilla between Africa and Spain or between Poland and the far eastern Europe.

And there is something even more ominous about the cultural convergence along the U.S.-Mexico borderlands. As the face of America changes, its future can be seen emerging right along the Southwest. Although growth in the Latino population is slowing down, the presence of Mexicans in the United States is a phenomenon that will last for decades.

THE BORDER AS THE FUTURE OF NORTH AMERICA

There is a vital reason why the border requires a new look, and it has to do with the future of America. For the observant eye, driving down the Texas border counties, this becomes all too obvious. Any visitor to West Texas and the South Texas Rio Grande Valley should be struck by the nearly solid nature of their Hispanic population in those counties. In effect, cities like Brownsville, Laredo, Eagle Pass, Del Rio, and El Paso are now any-where between 80 and 95 percent Mexican American and Mexican. The same trends hold state by state. Texas is now 38 percent Hispanic, New Mexico is 43 percent, Arizona is 30 percent, and California is 35 per-cent. Nevada and Colorado now have large Hispanic populations as well.[33] Hispanics are projected to total about 103 million Americans in the year 2050, or roughly 25 percent of the population of the country.

Yet Hispanics tend to have some of the lowest socioeconomic indicators in the country. As the country becomes more Hispanic, this does not bode well for the border states—or for the nation as a whole. Hispanic median income is well below the rest of the nation, at $32,997. The poverty rate among Hispanics is 22 percent, compared to 12 percent for the nation as a whole. Only 52 percent of Hispanics have a high school education, revealing that a high percentage do not reach that education level. Only 11 percent of Hispanics aged 25 and over have college degrees. The border already sees many of these symptoms, particularly in the Texas borderlands. If the 43 counties of Texas that constitute the border-lands were a separate state, they would rank 1st in poverty rate (23%), 1st in percentage of schoolchildren in poverty (38%), 1st in unemploy-ment rate (8%), 1st in percentage of adult population without a high school diploma, 1st in birthrate, 3rd in death rate due to diabetes, 51st in per capita income, 49th in households with telephones, and 51st in annual average wage in construction.[34] In all, these statistics show that the border is a largely impoverished area, with many infrastructure and socioeco-nomic deficiencies and enormous income inequality. It resembles Mexico much more than it resembles the United States.

These trends are detrimental to the country as a whole because Hispanics are likely to constitute the most important minority in the nation today and may be a quarter of the population in the next decades. Their low averages will certainly drag all national averages down if they do not catch up with the population as a whole. This will place the United States in a comparative disadvantage vis-à-vis other countries. If the bor-der can serve as a crystal ball to the future of the country, the numbers do not bode well for anyone. Only a well-devised, binational plan to tackle the issues of the border can help both sides catch up much faster to the rest of the United States, a fact that in and of itself would ease a lot of the pressures that collide on the border and make it look like a third world nation, rather than the thriving area that it is, caught between the lack of political will and the dearth of political vision of the leaders of both countries.

Nevertheless, the border is young. And it should resent the old estab-lished centers of power in Washington, DC, and Mexico City in any event. Both areas are largely centers of neglect. Border residents have felt the neglect from Washington. They also feel a common bond with Mexico in their history and their geography. There is also an acknowledgment that there is a high degree of economic interdependence. Multiple studies by the Federal Reserve Bank, El Paso Branch, show time and again that there is already a high degree of economic interdependence between border cities. The Mexican maquiladora industry has spurred a good deal of economic growth in U.S. border counties.

...BUT NO END IN SIGHT

Unfortunately, as the three border wars grind on, in a quasi-mechanical, monotonous, and increasingly dehumanizing routine, there is little hope that the U.S. government, its growing border bureaucracy, or the American public will arrive at a permanent, long-term solution to these border wars. If anything, the idea of sealing the border enjoys enormous support, in spite of the fact that occasionally someone may acknowledge that thus far the same approach has not worked at all. But the country has gone conservative. Everyone is ready to be "tough on crime" and "tough on terror" and "tough on migrants," a stand that translates into unwavering support for current U.S. policies of escalation in policing the border. Few would even speak of a longer-term solution to border issues, much less of a North American solution. The political cost of this kind of rhetoric could be too high.

Similarly, agencies working on the border have developed their own interests in maintaining current policy. If a whole new approach to the border were adopted, they would be out of a job. Bureaucracies become addicted to the dollars, the jobs, and the careers that are made in these border wars. More technology, more buildings, more equipment, and larger budgets mean greater prestige and lifelong careers for many agents on the border. That is how they make their living. Why would they advocate a different approach? In fact, nearly every bureaucrat, appointed or civil service, who testifies in Congress argues for more resources. And everyone is unwilling to publicly acknowledge the futility of the border battle.

Most Americans are oblivious to the costs of these border wars. Most Americans do not live on the border. But millions of them benefit from the undocumented labor they hire to trim their lawns, clip their bushes, clean their houses, prepare their meals, and raise their children. Americans are addicted to the availability of cheap labor and cheap goods and services, the prices of which are kept low in many places by the labor of those who live in the shadows, always afraid of being caught, deported, and separated from their families. Moreover, millions of Americans are addicted to illegal drugs, drawing many to the business of drugs with deadly consequences for many, not just along the border. Cocaine, heroin, marijuana, and methamphetamine addicts represent a huge market whose horrifying effects are lived day to day at the border, though most consumers live away from the border. They have no incentive to reach into their consciences and consider the motivations of the drug lords and dealers or the cost of the drug war on the American taxpayer. They are not in the trenches of the border; they cannot see; they cannot care.

There is therefore a huge coalition of politicians, bureaucrats, and the American public that have a stake in keeping the borders open, even if the rhetoric is fiery when it comes to the "insecurity" of the border. But consensus will not be easy. The Democrats are largely unable to bring to fruition their preferences in Congress, so it will all depend on what the Republicans want to do. And the Republicans are almost unified in their approach—to shut down the border. The next president will need to be a magician to find a solution that is acceptable to Republicans.

CONCLUSION

Winston Churchill said that Americans could always be trusted to do the right thing, after they have tried everything else. There is no doubt that the American public is, at heart, a generous public. There is little doubt that most Americans are by and large good people. But when it comes to the border, almost all reason is lost. September 11 spurred just such loss of reasonableness by Congress, politicians, and a large segment of the general public. The border is viewed as a chaotic, violent, and law-less land, whereas it actually is a place of great human struggles and epic lives—and the American side is definitely a very peaceful and law-abiding place! Although there is crime, violence, drug trafficking, human tragedy, and dire poverty along the border, the borderlands are also a place of wealth production, rich family interactions, and daily interaction among people from both Mexico and the United States.

To not acknowledge that the destinies of the two nations are tied is to be blind. To not understand that the prosperity of both countries is increas-ingly dependent on one another is absurd. To not recognize that the secu-rity of the United States depends on the actions, the needs, and the future of its neighbors is incongruous with current trends. Nowhere is this more clearly outlined than in the border counties of the United States and the border municipalities of Mexico. Drugs flow north; human smugglers carry people north; and undocumented workers flow north. Guns flow south; and financial capital and direct investments flow south. But goods and services—they flow both ways. Millions of Mexican citizens live in the United States. Almost 2 million Americans live in Mexico. Over $1 trillion in goods and services are exchanged every two years in bina-tional trade between Mexico and the United States. If all these figures do not imply the necessity of a North American security and prosperity regime where everyone participates in building a safer North America (including Canada, of course), then there is no argument to be made but one for isolation and crude nationalism.

The mutual interdependence of the two countries dictates a new vision of security and partnership, within a more democratic border—one that takes into account the wishes and desires of its residents. It also exposes the weaknesses of the current security regime: unilateral, enforcement based, with a logic of escalation, and ultimately against history. It is clear that the problem of security at the border needs to be viewed as being a much larger problem so that solutions can also be larger and the North American security regime stronger. Canada and Mexico are indispensable partners in this North American perimeter. And the United States already trusts Canada with its own security, given the close cooperation that exists between these two countries. It is time now to bring Mexico into that circle of trust, perhaps with a plan that will slowly integrate Mexico further into North America. A safer, stronger, and democratic Mexico is good for the United States and for American security. To postpone pushing Mexico in that direction is simply to postpone the inevitable and to make it even more painful to have to acknowledge this mutual interdependence in the future.

Notes

CHAPTER 1

1. Danna Harman, "Mexican Drug Cartels' Wars Move Closer to the U.S. Border," *USA Today*, http://www.usatoday.com/news/world/2005-08-17-mexican-cartels_x.htm (accessed October 30, 2005).

2. Paul Strand, "Border Invasion: Stemming the Illegal Flood," CBN News.com, http://www.cbn.com/cbnnews/news/050414a.asp (accessed November 23, 2005).

3. Edwin Mora, "Napolitano: Terrorists Enter U.S. from Mexico 'from Time to Time,'" CNS News.com, July 30, 2012, http://cnsnews.com/news/article/napolitano-terrorists-enter-us-mexico-time-time (accessed September 1, 2015).

4. Jon E. Dougherty, "Lawmaker: Terror War Spilling across Border: Concern Rising Following Arrest of al-Qaeda Suspect in Mexico," *WorldNetDaily*, http://www.wnd.com/news/article.asp?ARTICLE_ID=47401 (accessed November 27, 2005).

5. Thomas Hobbes, "The Leviathan," Project Gutenberg, http://www.gutenberg.org/files/3207/3207-h/3207-h.htm (accessed June 30, 2016).

6. Rep. Sue Myrick, "Hezbollah Car Bombs on Our Border," *Washington Times*, September 1, 2010. See http://www.washingtontimes.com/news/2010/sep/1/hezbollah-car-bombs-on-our-border/ (accessed June 30, 2016).

7. Numbers can be calculated from the U.S. Census Bureau as well as the Mexican National Institute for Statistics and Geographic Information (INEGI). See www.census.gov and www.inegi.gob.mx.

8. Scott Rogerson, in *Weekly Alibi* of Albuquerque, New Mexico; as cited in Robert T. Moran, *Uniting North American Business: NAFTA Best Practices*, 2nd ed. (Boston: Butterworth Heineman, 2002), 146.

9. The 1853 Gadsden Purchase Treaty, http://www.yale.edu/lawweb/avalon/diplomacy/mexico/mx1853.htm (accessed December 10, 2005).

10. Tony Payan, "How a Forgotten Border Dispute Tormented U.S.-Mexico Relations for 100 Years," *Americas Quarterly* (Winter 2016). See http://www.americasquarterly.org/content/how-forgotten-border-dispute-tormented-us-mexico-relations-100-years.

11. The total numbers can be calculated by adding the populations of U.S. counties and Mexican *municipios* at U.S. Census Bureau and the Mexican National Institute for Economics, Geography and Information.

12. Michael Dear and Andrew Burridge, "Cultural Integration and Hybridization at the United States-Mexico Borderlands," *Cahiers de Géographie du Québec* 49, no. 138 (December 2005): 301–18.

13. Juan Mora-Torres, *The Making of the Mexican Border* (Austin: University of Texas Press, 2000), 6.

14. The Contract Labor Law of February 26, 1885; the Contract Labor Law of February 23, 1887; the Payson Act of March 3, 1887; and the act of October 19, 1888. See http://people.sunyulster.edu/voughth/immlaws1875_1918.htm (accessed on June 29, 2016).

15. Yoku Shaw-Taylor, *Immigration, Assimilation and Border Security* (Lanham: Scarecrow Press, 2012), 125.

16. George T. Kurian, ed., *A Historical Guide to the U.S. Government* (New York: Oxford University Press, 1998). See also http://www.archives.gov/research_room/genealogy/immigrant_arrivals/mexican_border_crossings.html#special (accessed February 1, 2005).

17. George T. Díaz, *Border Contraband: A History of Smuggling across the Rio Grande* (Austin: University of Texas Press, 2015).

18. Bruce Bagley, *Drug Trafficking and Organized Crime in the Americas: Major Trends in the Twenty-First Century* (Washington, DC: Woodrow Wilson Center, 2012). See https://www.wilsoncenter.org/sites/default/files/BB%20Final.pdf.

19. Peter Andreas, *Border Games: Policing the U.S.-Mexico Divide* (Ithaca: Cornell University Press, 2009).

20. Tony Payan and Amanda Vasquez, "The Costs of Homeland Security," in Emmanuel Brunet-Jailly, ed., *Borderlands: Comparing Border Security in North America and Europe* (Ottawa, ON: University of Ottawa Press, 2007).

21. *The 9/11 Commission Report*, 2004. See http://avalon.law.yale.edu/sept11/911Report.pdf.

22. American Civil Liberties Union, "Complaint and Request for Investigation of Coercion, Abuse of Power, and Excessive Force by Customs and Border Protection at Ports of Entry along the U.S.-Mexico Border," 2016. See https://www.aclu-nm.org/wp-content/uploads/2016/05/RCBR-2016-POE-Admin-Complaint-Recommendations-FINAL-VERSION.pdf?556820 (accessed July 1, 2016).

23. Christophe Sohn, "Modelling Cross-Border Integration: The Role of Borders as a Resource," *Geopolitics* 19, no. 3 (August 2014): 587–608.

24. "US Border a 'Safety Valve' for Latin Poor," *Providence Journal* (Rhode Island), May 11, 2005, http://www.commondreams.org/views05/0511-26.htm (accessed November 27, 2005).

25. "President Discusses Border Security and Immigration Reform in Arizona," http://www.whitehouse.gov/news/releases/2005/11/20051128-7.html (accessed November 29, 2005).

26. "Bush Vows to Harden Border Policy." In his speech, he focuses on crime, danger, and high costs linked with illegal crossings. Available at http://www.chron.com/disp/story.mpl/metropolitan/3489624.html.

27. "Governor Schwarzenegger Delivers a Speech on Closing Borders," http://www.foxnews.com/story/0,2933,153988,00.html (accessed November 28, 2005).

28. Jurisdiction Boundary Marking Act, available at http://www.constitution.org/pol/us/jbma.htm (accessed November 29, 2005).

29. "President Discusses War on Terror at National Endowment for Democracy," available at http://www.whitehouse.gov/news/releases/2005/10/20051006-3.html (accessed November 29, 2005).

30. Michael Hedges, "Bush Budget Scraps 9,790 Border Patrol Agents: President Uses Law's Escape Clause to Drop Funding for New Homeland Security Force," *San Francisco Chronicle*, February 9, 2005, 8-A.

31. "President Bush Signs Homeland Security Act," available at http://www.whitehouse.gov/news/releases/2002/11/20021125-6.html (accessed November 29, 2005).

32. Timothy J. Dunn, *The Militarization of the U.S.-Mexico Border 1978–1992: Low-Intensity Conflict Comes Home* (Austin: University of Texas at Austin Press, 1996).

33. Andreas, *Border Games*.

34. Secure Border Initiative, Customs and Border Protection, http://www.cbp.gov/xp/cgov/newsroom/fact_sheets/secure_border_initiative/secure_border.xml (accessed December 5, 2005).

35. Customs and Border Protection, *Secure Border Initiative*, http://foiarr.cbp.gov/streamingWord.asp?i=297 (accessed June 29, 2016).

36. A Secure Europe in a Better World, "Europe Deals with Its Borders," https://www.consilium.europa.eu/uedocs/cmsUpload/78367.pdf (accessed June 29, 2016).

37. *Frontline*, "Thirty Years of America's Drug War," http://www.pbs.org/wgbh/pages/frontline/shows/drugs/cron/ (accessed December 9, 2005).

38. "Illegal Immigration and Enforcement Along the U.S.-Mexico Border: An Overview," http://www.dallasfed.org/research/efr/2001/efr0101a.pdf (accessed December 9, 2005).

CHAPTER 2

1. See "Pot-Laden Truck Creates Armed Standoff," *El Paso Times*, November 19, 2005.

2. See "Former EP Border Agent Sentenced for Letting Drug Couriers Pass," *El Paso Times*, September 23, 2005.

3. See Michael Marizco, "Smugglers Getting Sneakier," *Arizona Daily Star*, December 26, 2004.

4. See "Portrait of a Mexican Drug Lord," CBS News, Mexico City, October 24, 2003, http://www.cbsnews.com/stories/2003/10/24/world/main579960.shtml (accessed October 10, 2005).

5. Elliot Spagat, "Half-Mile Drug Tunnel and a Massive Bust: Ton of Coke, 7 Tons Pot Seized," Associated Press, April 21, 2016, http://www.thecannabist.co/2016/04/21/half-mile-tunnel-found-on-us-mexico-border-cocaine-seized/52500/.

6. U.S. Government Accountability Office, *Lack of Progress on Achieving National Goals*, December 2, 2015, http://www.gao.gov/assets/680/673929.pdf.

7. Quoteauthors, http://www.quoteauthors.com/charles-caleb-colton-quotes/ (accessed June 28, 2016).

8. U.S. National Institute on Drug Abuse, *Drug Facts: Nationwide Trends*, June 2015, https://www.drugabuse.gov/publications/drugfacts/nationwide-trends (accessed June 28, 2016).

9. Mark Thornton, *The Economics of Prohibition* (Salt Lake City: University of Utah Press, 1991).

10. Adam Smith, *The Wealth of Nations* (Great Britain: Capstone, 2010).

11. "Survey: Illegal Drugs: Stumbling in the Dark," *The Economist*, July 28, 2001.

12. Gordon H. Hanson, "What Has Happened to Wages in Mexico since NAFTA? Implications for Hemispheric Trade," February 2003, https://gps.ucsd.edu/_files/faculty/hanson/hanson_publication_it_NAFTA.pdf (accessed June 28, 2016).

13. "Mexico," http://data.worldbank.org/country/mexico.

14. David J. Pyle analyzed various theories examining the economics of crime and establishing a strong, but not absolute relationship between crime and unemployment and low incomes in *The Economics of Crime and Law Enforcement* (New York: St. Martin's Press, 1983).

15. Rodrigo Negrete Prieto and Gerardo Leyva Parra, "Los NiNis En México: Una Aproximación Crítica a Su Medición," *Revista Internacional de Estadística y Geografía* 4, no. 1 (January–April 2013), http://www.inegi.org.mx/RDE/RDE_08/RDE_08_Art6.html.

16. U.S. Department of Labor, Bureau of Transportation Statistics, http://www.bts.gov/programs/international/border_crossing_entry_data/us_mexico/pdf/entire.pdf (accessed June 21, 2005).

17. "Siete Presidentes, Pocos Resultados: 40 Años De Expansión Del Crimen Organizado," NarcoData, Winter 2015, http://narcodata.animalpolitico.com/7-presidentes-pocos-resultados-40-anos-de-expansion-del-crimen-organizado/ (accessed June 29, 2016).

18. James Windle and Graham Farrell, "Popping the Balloon Effect: Assessing Drug Law Enforcement in Terms of Displacement, Diffusion, and the Containment Hypothesis," *Substance Use and Misuse* 47, nos. 8–9 (June 7, 2012): 868–76.

19. See Peter Braunstein and Michael William Doyle, *Imagine Nation: The American Counterculture of the 1960s and '70s* (New York: Routledge, 2002). See also *Pulse Check: Drug Markets and Chronic Users in 25 of America's Largest Cities* (Washington, DC: Executive Office of the President, Office of National Drug Control Policy, January 2004). The current issue of the publication and previous

Pulse Check issues can be found at http://www.whitehousedrugpolicy.gov/ drugfact/pulsecheck.html (accessed September 28, 2005).

20. Several books that analyze the relationship between an illegal product and the consumer market for it—essentially black-market economics—are: Lawrence J. Kaplan and Dennis Kessler, eds., *An Economic Analysis of Crime* (Springfield: Thomas, 1976); Annelise Graebner Anderson, *The Business of Organized Crime: A Cosa Nostra Family* (Stanford: Hoover Institution Press, 1979); David J. Pyle, *The Economics of Crime and Law Enforcement* (New York: St. Martin's Press, 1983); André Bossard, *Transnational Crime and Criminal Law* (Chicago: University of Illinois at Chicago, 1990); Susan Pozo, ed., *Exploring the Underground Economy* (Kalamazoo, MI: W. E. Upjohn Institute for Employment Research, 1996); and R. T. Naylor, *Wages of Crime: Black Markets, Illegal Finance, and the Underworld Economy* (Ithaca: Cornell University Press, 2002).

21. For a recounting of these efforts in the Caribbean, see Charles M. Fuss, *Sea of Grass: The Maritime Drug War, 1970–1990* (Annapolis: Naval Institute Press, 1996).

22. See various chapters in Bruce M. Bagley and William O. Walker III, eds., *Drug Trafficking in the Americas* (Miami, FL: University of Miami North-South Center, 1994).

23. This story is told at length and quite eloquently by one of the greatest chroniclers of the Mexican illegal-drug business, Jesús Blancornelas, in his book *El Cártel: Los Arellano Félix: La Mafia Más Poderosa en la Historia de América Latina* (México: Plaza Janés, 2002), 46–52.

24. Juan Diego Saldaña and Tony Payan. "The Evolution of Cartels in Mexico: 1980–2015," Rice University's Baker Institute Mexico Center, http://baker institute.org/research/evolution-cartels-mexico-1980-2015/.

25. Drug Policy Alliance. "The Federal Drug Control Budget: New Rhetoric, Same Failed Drug War," February 2015, http://www.drugpolicy.org/sites/ default/files/DPA_Fact_sheet_Drug_War_Budget_Feb2015.pdf.

26. This game of escalation and the logic behind it is explained in Peter Andreas's *Border Games: Policing the U.S.-Mexico Divide* (Ithaca: Cornell University Press, 2001), 3–14.

27. *The Price and Purity of Illicit Drugs: 1981 to 2007* (Washington, DC: Institute for Defense Analysis, October 2008), https://www.whitehouse.gov/sites/ default/files/ondcp/policy-and-research/bullet_1.pdf (accessed June 28, 2016).

28. Governing the States and Localities, *State Marijuana Laws Map*, May 2016, http://www.governing.com/gov-data/state-marijuana-laws-map-medical -recreational.html (accessed June 28, 2016).

29. America Y. Guevara, "Propaganda in Mexico's Drug War," *Journal of Strategic Security* 6, no. 5 (Fall 2013): 131–51.

30. Interview with a former member of the Juárez Cartel, who wished to remain anonymous. Interview conducted in Ciudad Juárez, Chihuahua, on August 3, 2005.

31. Hear the story of drug smuggling through the Tohono O'odham Reservation on National Public Radio's website at http://www.npr.org/templates/ story/story.php?storyId=1125387 (accessed November 20, 2005).

32. Interview with a federal court employee in El Paso, Texas, who wished to remain anonymous. Interview conducted on August 18, 2005.

33. Melissa Del Bosque and Patrick Michels, "Homeland Insecurity," *Texas Observer*, January 2016, https://www.texasobserver.org/homeland-security -corruption-border-patrol/ (accessed June 28, 2016).

34. John Burnett, "Corruption at the Gates: Series Explores Lure of Money, Prestige among U.S. Border Agents," National Public Radio, September 12–13, 2002. Entire report at http://www.npr.org/programs/atc/features/2002/sept/ border_corruption/ (accessed October 2, 2005).

35. Bureau of Justice Statistics, *National Transportation Statistics 2005* (Washington, DC: Department of Transportation, 2005). Tables at http://www.bts.gov/ publications/national_transportation_statistics/2005 (accessed October 5, 2005).

36. "Securing the Global Supply Chain," Customs and Border Protection, Washington DC, November 2004, http://www.cbp.gov/border-security/ports -entry/cargo-security/c-tpat-customs-trade-partnership-against-terrorism (accessed July 2, 2016).

37. "C-TPAT: Customs-Trade Partnership against Terrorism," U.S. Customs and Border Protection, http://www.cbp.gov/border-security/ports-entry/cargo -security/c-tpat-customs-trade-partnership-against-terrorism (accessed July 2, 2016).

38. Interview in San Antonio, Texas, with "James," a trucking company operator who asked to remain anonymous. Interview conducted on August 5, 2005.

39. Ibid.

40. Dudley Althaus and John Otis, "Is Mexico Going to Be the Next Colombia?" *Houston Chronicle*, June 17, 2005, http://www.chron.com/news/ nation-world/article/Is-Mexico-going-to-be-the-next-Colombia-1483400.php (accessed June 28, 2016).

41. Sarah Morgenthau, "Interim Report of the CBP Integrity Advisory Panel," *CBP IAP Interim Report*, June 29, 2015, https://www.dhs.gov/sites/default/files/ publications/DHS-HSAC-CBP-IAP-Interim-Report.pdf (accessed July 2, 2016).

42. See http://www.cbp.gov/linkhandler/cgov/careers/customs_careers/ border_careers/border_patrol_factsheet.ctt/careers_bpa_fact.doc (accessed September 7, 2005).

43. Andrew Becker, "Crossing the Line: Corruption at the Border," The Center for Investigative Reporting, http://bordercorruption.apps.cironline.org.

44. Interview with a member of the Juárez Cartel in Ciudad Juárez, Chihuahua. Interview conducted on August 4, 2005.

45. Rubén Ruiz, "Ejecutan a Tres Ex Policías," *El Imparcial*, June 7, 2005.

46. Tony Payan, Kathleen Staudt, and Z. Anthony Kruszewski, *A War That Can't Be Won: Binational Perspectives on the War on Drugs* (Tucson: University of Arizona Press, 2014).

47. "Mexico Travel Warning," U.S. Passports & International Travel, January 19, 2016, https://travel.state.gov/content/passports/en/alertswarnings/ mexico-travel-warning.html (accessed 2016).

48. Carlos Antonio Flores Pérez, "Political Protection and the Origins of the Gulf Cartel," *Crime, Law and Social Change* 61, no. 5 (June 2014): 517–39.

49. Interview with a member of the Juárez Cartel in Ciudad Juárez, Chihuahua. Interview conducted on August 4, 2005.

50. Blancornelas, *El Cártel*, 46–52.

51. Joaquín Villalobos, "Doce Mitos de la Guerra Contra el Narco," *Nexos*, January 1, 2010, http://www.nexos.com.mx/?p=13461 (accessed July 2, 2016).

52. See Ambassador Antonio O. Garza's press release at the U.S. Embassy in Mexico City's website, http://mexico.usembassy.gov/mexico/ep050610violence.html (accessed October 30, 2005).

53. Interview with a U.S. federal court employee in El Paso, Texas, August 18, 2005.

CHAPTER 3

1. Customs and Border Protection, *CBP Border Security Report FY2015*, December 2015, https://www.dhs.gov/sites/default/files/publications/CBP%20FY15%20Border%20Security%20Report_12-21_0.pdf (accessed June 29, 2016).

2. Jie Zong and Jeanne Batalova, "Asian Immigrants in the United States," *Migration Policy Institute*, January 6, 2016, http://www.migrationpolicy.org/article/asian-immigrants-united-states (accessed June 29, 2016).

3. Tony Payan and Erika de la Garza, eds., *Undecided Nation: Political Gridlock and the Immigration Crisis* (United Kingdom: Springer, 2014).

4. Roxanne Doty, *The Law into Their Own Hands: Immigration and the Politics of Exceptionalism* (Tucson: University of Arizona Press, 2009).

5. Missing Migrants Project, *Migrant Fatalities Worldwide*, http://missing migrants.iom.int/latest-global-figures (accessed June 29, 2016).

6. Francisco E. Balderrama and Raymond Rodríguez, *Decade of Betrayal: Mexican Repatriation in the 1930s* (Albuquerque: University of New Mexico Press, 2006).

7. Francisco E. Balderrama and Raymond Rodríguez, *Decade of Betrayal: Mexican Repatriation in the 1930s* (Albuquerque: University of New Mexico Press, 2006).

8. Ronald L. Mize and Alicia C. S. Swords, *Consuming Mexican Labor: From the Bracero Program to NAFTA* (Toronto: University of Toronto Press, 2010).

9. *El Paso Herald Post*, April 28, 1956.

10. Adam Goodman and Verónica Zapata Rivera, "Mexico: Bracero Guestworkers, Unpaid," *Upside Down World*, October 17, 2013, http://upside downworld.org/main/mexico-archives-79/4513-mexico-bracero-guestworkers -unpaid (accessed June 30, 2016).

11. Garrett M. Graff, "The Green Monster: How the Border Patrol Became America's Most Out-of-Control Law Enforcement Agency," *Politico Magazine*, November/December 2014, http://www.politico.com/magazine/story/2014/10/border-patrol-the-green-monster-112220 (accessed June 30, 2016).

12. Brandon Judd, "Testimony of Brandon Judd on Behalf of the National Border Patrol Council," November 18, 2013, https://oversight.house.gov/wp-content/uploads/2013/11/Judd1.pdf.

13. "City Crime Rankings 2013," http://os.cqpress.com/citycrime/2012/CityCrime2013_CityCrimeRankingsFactSheet.pdf.

14. Alex Nowrasteh, "Unaccompanied Minors Crossing the Border—the Facts," Cato Institute, June 17, 2014, http://www.cato.org/blog/unaccompanied-minors-crossing-border-facts (accessed July 2, 2016).

15. Daniel E. Martínez, Guillermo Cantor, and Walter A. Ewing, "No Action Taken: Lack of CBP Accountability in Responding to Complaints of Abuse," American Immigration Council, May 2014, http://www.americanimmigration council.org/sites/default/files/No%20Action%20Taken_Final.pdf (accessed July 1, 2016).

16. Anna González-Barrera, "More Mexicans Leaving than Coming to the U.S.," Pew Research Centers Hispanic Trends Project RSS, November 19, 2015, http://www.pewhispanic.org/2015/11/19/more-mexicans-leaving-than-coming-to-the-u-s/ (accessed July 1, 2016).

17. See "American Immigration: An Overview," U.S. English Foundation, http://www.us-english.org/foundation/research/amimmigr/Chapter3.PDF (accessed November 20, 2005).

18. U.S. Customs and Border Protection, *2012–2016 Border Patrol Strategy Strategic Plan: The Mission to Protect America*, https://www.cbp.gov/sites/default/files/documents/bp_strategic_plan.pdf (accessed June 30, 2016).

19. Lutheran Immigration and Refugee Service, *At the Crossroads for Unaccompanied Migrant Children: Policy, Practice & Protection*, July 2015, http://lirs.org/wp-content/uploads/2015/07/LIRS_RoundtableReport_WEB.pdf (accessed June 30, 2016).

20. Washington Office for Latin America, *Increased Enforcement at Mexico's Southern Border*, November 2015, http://www.wola.org/files/WOLA_Increased_Enforcement_at_Mexico's_Southern_Border_Nov2015.pdf (accessed June 30, 2016). See also Elijah Stevens, "Mexico's Southern Border Plan Fuels Violence," InSight Crime: Investigation and Analysis of Organized Crime, November 10, 2015, http://www.insightcrime.org/news-briefs/mexico-southern-border-plan-fuels-violence (accessed June 30, 2016).

21. Ted Robbins, "Illegal Immigrant Deaths Burden Border Towns," National Public Radio, October 6, 2005, http://www.npr.org/templates/story/story.php?storyId=4948382 (accessed November 19, 2005).

22. Tara Brian and Frank Laczko, *Fatal Journeys: Tracking Lives Lost during Migration* (Geneva: International Organization for Migration, 2014), http://www.iom.int/files/live/sites/iom/files/pbn/docs/Fatal-Journeys-Tracking-Lives-Lost-during-Migration-2014.pdf (accessed July 2, 2016).

23. Maureen Meyer and Adam Isacson, "On the Front Lines: Border Security, Migration, and Humanitarian Concerns in South Texas," Advocacy for Human Rights in the Americas, February 27, 2015, http://www.wola.org/publications/south_texas_report (accessed July 2, 2016).

24. John Carlos Frey, "Graves of Shame: New Evidence Indicates Wrongdoing in the Handling of Migrant Remains in Brooks County," July 6, 2015, http://www.texasobserver.org/illegal-mass-graves-of-migrant-remains-found-in-south-texas/ (accessed July 2, 2016).

25. Anna Brown and Mark Hugo López, "Mapping the Latino Population by State, County and City," Pew Research Center, August 29, 2013, http://www

.pewhispanic.org/2013/08/29/mapping-the-latino-population-by-state-county -and-city/ (accessed June 30, 2016).

26. Peter M. Ward, *Colonias and Public Policy in Texas and Mexico: Urbanization by Stealth* (Austin: University of Texas Press, 1999).

27. Adrian X. Esparza and Angela J. Donelson, *Colonias in Arizona and New Mexico: Border Poverty and Community Development Solutions* (Tucson: University of Arizona Press, 2008).

28. Pew Research Center, *Most Mexicans See Better Life in U.S.: One in Three Would Migrate*, September 23, 2009, http://www.pewglobal.org/2009/09/23/ most-mexicans-see-better-life-in-us-one-in-three-would-migrate/ (accessed June 30, 2016).

29. An excellent collection of essays that defines and explores push forces is *Border Crossings: Mexican and Mexican American Workers*, Jason Mason Hart, ed. (Wilmington, DE: SR Books, 1998).

30. This is a perennial argument in regard to U.S. documented and undocumented immigration. For interesting arguments on this, see John McAuley, "Immigrants Keep U.S. Economy Supple," *Minnesota Star Tribune*, September 4, 2002.

31. Doty, *The Law into Their Own Hands*.

32. Aaron Terrazas, "Mexican Immigrants in the United States," Migration Policy Institute, February 22, 2010, http://www.migrationpolicy.org/article/ mexican-immigrants-united-states-0 (accessed June 30, 2016). Also, "Survey of Recent Immigrants at the U.S. Consulate in Ciudad Juárez," conducted by Brenda Thomas and Tony Payan, 2003–4.

33. Daniel Chiquiar and Alejandra Saucedo, "Mexican Migration to the United States: Underlying Economic Factors and Possible Scenarios for Future Flows," Migration Policy Institute, April 2013, http://www.migrationpolicy.org/ research/mexican-migration-united-states-underlying-economic-factors-and -possible-scenarios-future (accessed June 30, 2016).

34. Bureau of Transportation Statistics, Border Crossing/Entry Data, http:// transborder.bts.gov/programs/international/transborder/TBDR_BC/TBDR _BC_Index.html (accessed June 30, 2016).

35. Elizabeth Salamanca Pacheco, "New Migration Patterns: High-Skilled Entrepreneurial Migration from Mexico to the United States," México Center, November 2015, http://bakerinstitute.org/media/files/files/25c21136/MC-pub -EntrepreneurialMigration-111715.pdf (accessed June 30, 2016).

36. Heather Horn, "Birth Right Citizenship Wasn't Born in America," *The Atlantic*, September 1, 2015, http://www.theatlantic.com/international/archive/ 2015/09/birthright-citizenship-donald-trump-england/403159/ (accessed June 30, 2016).

37. Matt Sheehan, "Born in the USA: Why Chinese 'Birth Tourism' Is Booming in California," *Huffington Post*, May 14, 2015, http://www.huffingtonpost.com/ 2015/05/01/china-us-birth-tourism_n_7187180.html (accessed July 2, 2016).

38. Ralph Blumenthal, "Smuggling Trial in Texas Focuses on Trucker's Role," *New York Times*, March 13, 2005.

39. Jeffrey S. Passel and D'Vera Cohn, "Homeland Security Produces First Estimate of Foreign Visitors to U.S. Who Overstay Deadline to Leave," Pew

Research Center, February 3, 2016, http://www.pewresearch.org/fact-tank/2016/
02/03/homeland-security-produces-first-estimate-of-foreign-visitors-to-u-s-who
-overstay-deadline-to-leave/ (accessed June 30, 2016).

40. It is important at this point to make a stop and clarify that of the 12 million
or so undocumented workers residing in the United States as of 2012, only 6.7 million were of Mexican origin. While the majority, there are undocumented workers
from many other countries in Central and South America, Asia, Africa and even
Canada. Homeland Security Office of Immigration Statistics, "Estimates of Unauthorized Immigrant Population Residing in the United States: January 2012,"
March 2013, http://immigration.procon.org/sourcefiles/illegal-immigration
-population-2012.pdf (accessed June 30, 2016).

41. Tony Payan and Erika De La Garza, eds., *Undecided Nation: Political Gridlock
and the Immigration Crisis* (Gewerbestrasse, Switzerland: Springer International,
2014).

42. Saskia Sassen, *Expulsions: Brutality and Complexity in the Global Economy*
(Cambridge: Harvard University Press, 2014).

43. "War on Undocumented Immigrants Threatens to Swell U.S. Prison Population," *Huffington Post*, August 23, 2013, http://www.huffingtonpost.com/2013/
08/23/undocumented-immigrants-prison_n_3792187.html (accessed June 30,
2016).

44. "BOP Statistics: Inmate Offenses," Federal Bureau of Prisons, January 30,
2016, https://www.bop.gov/about/statistics/statistics_inmate_offenses.jsp
(accessed June 30, 2016).

45. *U.S. Sentencing Commission Preliminary Quarterly Data Report*, U.S.
Sentencing Commission, 2014.

46. Congressional Budget Office, *The Impact of Unauthorized Migrants on the
Budgets of State and Local Governments*, December 2007, https://www.cbo.gov/
sites/default/files/110th-congress-2007-2008/reports/12-6-immigration.pdf
(accessed July 1, 2016).

47. "Immigration," Gallup, http://www.gallup.com/poll/1660/immigration.
aspx (accessed July 1. 2016).

48. James Lyall, Jane Yakowitz Bambauer, and Derek E. Bambauer, *Record of
Abuse: Lawlessness and Impunity in Border Patrol's Interior Enforcement Operations*,
American Civil Liberties Union, October 2015, http://www.acluaz.org/sites/
default/files/documents/Record_of_Abuse_101515_0.pdf (accessed July 1, 2016).

49. Lindsay Eriksson and Melinda Taylor, "The Environmental Impacts of the
Border Wall Between Texas and Mexico, Austin: University of Texas Law
School, https://law.utexas.edu/humanrights/borderwall/analysis/briefing-The
-Environmental-Impacts-of-the-Border-Wall.pdf (accessed July 1, 2016).

50. "Mexico's Gangs Use 'Narco-Tunnels' to Smuggle Migrants," InSight
Crime, September 7, 2011, http://www.insightcrime.org/news-analysis/mexicos
-gangs-use-narco-tunnels-to-smuggle-migrants (accessed July 1, 2016).

51. Ana González Barrera and Jens Manuel Krogstad, Pew Research Center,
"U.S. Deportations of Immigrants Reach Record High in 2013," October 2,
2014, http://www.pewresearch.org/fact-tank/2014/10/02/u-s-deportations-of
-immigrants-reach-record-high-in-2013/ (accessed July 1, 2016).

52. Even the most modest numbers can be staggering. If 300,000 migrants pay to make it to the United States every year and each pays $2,500 (and many pay as much as $10,000), the total amounts to $750 million. This is not counting those who do not make it but pay anyway or those who pay more than once or those who pay more.

53. Pia M. Orrenius, "Illegal Immigration and Enforcement along the Southwest Border," Federal Reserve Bank of Dallas (June 2001), *New York Times*, March 13, 2005, http://www.dallasfed.org/research/border/tbe_orrenius.html (accessed September 15, 2005).

54. Muzzafar Chishti and Faye Hipsman, "Unaccompanied Minors Crisis Has Receded from Headlines but Major Issues Remain," Migration Policy Institute, September 24, 2014, http://www.migrationpolicy.org/article/unaccompanied -minors-crisis-has-receded-headlines-major-issues-remain (accessed July 1, 2016).

55. Catherine E. Shoichet, "The Last Flight and First Steps: 'Historic' Surge of Cubans Crossing into U.S.," CNN, June 1, 2016, http://www.cnn.com/2016/05/ 31/us/border-cuban-migrants-el-paso/ (accessed July 1, 2016).

56. Department of Homeland Security, Office of the Inspector General, "Detention and Removal of Illegal Aliens," April 2006, https://www.oig.dhs.gov/assets/ Mgmt/OIG_06-33_Apr06.pdf (Accessed July 1, 2016).

57. Kristel Mucino, "Mexico's Migration Crackdown Creates Spike in Apprehensions, Dangerous Shifts in Migrant Routes," Washington Office for Latin America, November 9, 2015, http://www.wola.org/news/mexicos_migration _crackdown_creates_spike_in_apprehensions_dangerous_shifts_in_migrant _routes (accessed March 15, 2016).

58. Robert Lee Maril, *Patrolling Chaos: The U.S. Border Patrol in Deep South Texas* (Lubbock: Texas Tech University, 2004).

59. For one such example, see Claire Sterling, *Crime without Frontiers: The Worldwide Expansion of Organized Crime and the Pax Mafiosa* (Sacramento: Time Warner Paperbacks, 1995).

60. See http://www.fairus.org (accessed July 1, 2016).

61. The advocates of such an increase ignored the considerable problems in finding and recruiting qualified people and then hiring and training these potential new hires. See U.S. Government Accountability Office, *Border Patrol Hiring: Despite Recent Initiatives, Fiscal Year 1999 Hiring Goal Was Not Met* (Washington, DC: U.S. Government Accountability Office, December 1999). Recruiting and training law enforcement agents at such neck-breaking speed is also complicated because it is hard to vet out bad candidates quickly, train them well, and then hold them accountable. Fast growth in any agency is usually associated with often catastrophic mistakes.

62. "Budget-in-Brief Fiscal Year 2016," U.S. Department of Homeland Security, https://www.dhs.gov/sites/default/files/publications/FY_2016_DHS_Budget _in_Brief.pdf (accessed July 1, 2016).

63. Eduardo Porter, "Illegal Immigrants Are Bolstering Social Security with Billions," *New York Times*, April 5, 2005. See also Roy Germano, "Unauthorized Immigrants Paid $100 Billion into Social Security over Last Decade," Vice News, August 4, 2014, https://news.vice.com/article/unauthorized-immigrants-paid -100-billion-into-social-security-over-last-decade (accessed July 1, 2016).

64. Lisa C. Gee, Matthew Gardner, and Meg Wiehe, "Undocumented Immigrants' State and Local Tax Contributions," Institute for Taxation and Economic Policy, February 2016, http://www.itep.org/pdf/immigration2016.pdf (accessed July 1, 2016).

65. "Tax Administration: IRS Needs to Consider Options for Revising Regulations to Increase the Accuracy of Social Security Numbers on Wage Statements," U.S. Government Accountability Office, GAO-04-712, August 2004. See also "Social Security: Better Coordination among Federal Agencies Could Reduce Unidentified Earnings Reports," U.S. Government Accountability Office, GAO-05-154, February 2005.

66. Tony Payan, *Cops, Soldiers, and Diplomats: Agency Behavior in the War on Drugs* (Lanham: Lexington Books, 2007).

67. "Stryker Training," *The Monitor*, March 3, 2005, 30–31.

68. Jesse Katz, "A Good Shepherd's Death by Military," *Los Angeles Times*, June 21, 1997, http://articles.latimes.com/1997-06-21/news/mn-5538_1_military-missions (accessed July 1, 2016).

69. Paul J. Weber, "Texas Approves $800 Million for Border Security," *PBS NewsHour*, June 16, 2015, http://www.pbs.org/newshour/rundown/texas-approves-800-million-border-security/ (accessed July 1, 2016).

70. Cynthia Green, "Federal Grand Jury Investigating Wal-Mart's Use of Undocumented Migrants," http://www.laborresearch.org/story.php?id=332 (accessed September 18, 2005).

71. "Employer Sanctions," Federation for American Immigration Reform, 2016, http://www.fairus.org/issue/employer-sanctions (accessed July 1, 2016).

72. Phillip Bump, "Where America's Undocumented Immigrants Work," *Washington Post*, March 27, 2015, https://www.washingtonpost.com/news/the-fix/wp/2015/03/27/where-americas-undocumented-immigrants-work/ (accessed July 1, 2016). More recently, the Pew Research Center found similar results: Jeffrey S. Passel and D'Vera Cohn, "Chapter 2: Industries of Unauthorized Immigrant Workers," March 26, 2015, http://www.pewhispanic.org/2015/03/26/chapter-2-industries-of-unauthorized-immigrant-workers/ (accessed July 1, 2016).

73. Text of the lawsuit found at http://www.vdare.com/misc/tyson_complaint.htm (accessed September 18, 2005).

74. Doty, *The Law into Their Own Hands*.

75. Ralph Blumenthal, "Citing Violence, 2 Border States Declare a Crisis," *New York Times*, August 17, 2005, http://www.nytimes.com/2005/08/17/us/citing-violence-2-border-states-declare-a-crisis.html?_r=0 (accessed July 1, 2016).

76. Department of Justice, "Justice Department Reaches Settlement in Civil Rights Lawsuit against Maricopa County, Arizona, and Maricopa County Sheriff," July 17, 2015, https://www.justice.gov/opa/pr/justice-department-reaches-settlement-civil-rights-lawsuit-against-maricopa-county-arizona (accessed July 1, 2016).

77. Adam Liptak and Michael D. Shear, "Supreme Court Tie Blocks Obama Immigration Plan," June 23, 2016, http://www.nytimes.com/2016/06/24/us/supreme-court-immigration-obama-dapa.html (accessed July 1, 2016).

78. "International Migration at All-Time High," World Bank, December 18, 2015, http://www.worldbank.org/en/news/press-release/2015/12/18/international-migrants-and-remittances-continue-to-grow-as-people-search-for-better-opportunities-new-report-finds (accessed July 1, 2016).

CHAPTER 4

1. Chris Edwards, "Make America Safer: Shut Down the Department of Homeland Security," Cato Institute, October 27, 2014, http://www.cato.org/publications/commentary/make-america-safer-shut-down-department-homeland-security (accessed July 1, 2016).

2. Sam Francis, "J'accuse: The Open Borders Lobby Are to Blame for Terrorism," *Vdare*, September 20, 2001, http://www.vdare.com/francis/open_borders.htm (accessed July 1, 2016).

3. Univisión, "Mexico-U.S. Border Survey." Document shared with author by Univisión personnel in June 2016.

4. See U.S. Government Accountability Office report, "Immigration Enforcement: DHS Has Incorporated Immigration Enforcement Objectives and Is Addressing Future Planning Requirements," GAO-05-66, October 2004.

5. Margaret D. Stock and Benjamin Johnson, "The Lessons of 9/11: A Failure of Intelligence, Not Immigration Law," *Immigration Policy Focus* 2, no. 3 (December 2003).

6. Lorena Figueroa, "Citizens with No Passport at Border Face Fines," *El Paso Times*, April 22, 2016, http://www.elpasotimes.com/story/news/2016/04/22/citizens-no-passport-border-face-fines/83405410/ (accessed July 1, 2016).

7. See press release of the U.S. Department of Justice, "Department of Justice Announces INS Restructuring Plan Splitting Service and Enforcement Functions," November 14, 2004, http://www.usdoj.gov. See also Doris Meissner, "Two Jobs for One INS," *Washington Post*, March 18, 2002, A29; Cheryl Thompson, "INS Tightens Rules for Visitors," *Washington Post*, April 9, 2002, A1; Cheryl Thompson, "INS Role for the Police Considered," *Washington Post*, April 4, 2002, A15; Dana Milbank, "Bush Poised to Back New Border Agency," *Washington Post*, March 19, 2002, A1; and Dana Milbank and Cheryl Thompson, "House Panel Agrees on Plan to Split INS," *Washington Post*, March 22, 2002, A8.

8. U.S. Census Bureau, Foreign Trade Division, Data Dissemination Branch, Washington, DC, http://www.census.gov/foreign-trade/balance/c2010.html#2001 and http://www.census.gov/foreign-trade/balance/c2010.html#199 (accessed November 5, 2005).

9. See Bureau of Transportation Statistics at http://www.bts.gov/publications/transportation_statistics_annual_report/2001/html/chapter_07_table_01_219.html (accessed November 5, 2005).

10. See "Construcción de una Communidad de América del Norte," The Council on Foreign Relations, http://www.cfr.org/content/publications/attachments/NorthAmerica_TF_final_esp.pdf (accessed July 1, 2016).

11. Congressional Research Service Report, "Border Security: Inspections, Practices, Policies, Issues," May 26, 2004.

12. U.S. Info State, U.S. Department of State, http://usinfo.state.gov/eap/east _asia_pacific/chinese_human_smuggling/smuggling_in_the_press/crime.html (accessed November 4, 2005).

13. Terence Jeffrey, "A Case of Selective Enforcement," *Town Hall*, November 4, 2005, http://townhall.com/columnists/terryjeffrey/2003/07/02/a_case_of _selective_enforcement (accessed July 1, 2016).

14. To understand this complicated relationship—the iron triangle—see Dan Briody, *The Iron Triangle: Inside the Secret World of the Carlyle Group* (Hoboken: Wiley and Sons, 2003).

15. Ignacio Ibarra, "Border Group Claims WMD Test," *Arizona Daily Star*, July 22, 2004.

16. "Testimony by Secretary Michael Chertoff Before the House Homeland Security Committee," April 13, 2005, http://www.dhs.gov/dhspublic/display? theme=45&content;=4460 (accessed December 1, 2005).

17. Testimony of Peter Gadiel, U.S. House of Representatives, Judiciary Committee, http://judiciary.house.gov/OversightTestimony.aspx?ID=289 (accessed November 5, 2005).

18. U.S. Department of Homeland Security, "Testimony by Deputy Secretary of Homeland Security Admiral James Loy Before the Senate Select Committee on Intelligence," http://www.iwar.org.uk/homesec/resources/natsec2005/loy.htm (accessed November 5, 2005).

19. See http://www.rasmussenreports.com/2005/Immigration% 20November %207.htm (accessed November 15, 2005).

20. U.S. Census Bureau, "Top Trading Partners 2016," https://www.census .gov/foreign-trade/statistics/highlights/toppartners.html (accessed July 1, 2016).

21. Patriot Act, http://www.epic.org/privacy/terrorism/hr3162.html (accessed July 1, 2016).

22. *Homeland Security: Overview of Homeland Security Management Challenges* (Washington, DC: U.S. Government Accountability Office, April 20, 2005), 2–4. See also the Homeland Security Budget Sheet for FY 2005, http://www.dhs.gov/ dhspublic/interapp/press_release/press_release_0541.xml (accessed October 19, 2005).

23. Homeland Security Act, Title IV, http://www.dhs.gov/dhspublic/ interweb/assetlibrary/hr_5005_enr.pdf (accessed October 20, 2005).

24. U.S. Customs and Border Protection National Targeting Center, *Identifying Risks Early* (Video), https://www.cbp.gov/newsroom/video-gallery/2014/02/ identifying-risks-early (accessed July 1, 2016).

25. See U.S. Department of Homeland Security, http://www.dhs.gov/ dhspublic/ (accessed November 21, 2005).

26. Brookings Institution, Chart: U.S. Trade with Canada and Mexico Equals BRICS + Japan + Korea Trade, http://www.brookings.edu/blogs/brookings -now/posts/2013/11/chart-us-trade-canada-mexico-brics-japan-korea (accessed March 24, 2016).

27. See remarks from former CPB commissioner Robert Bonner at http:// permanent.access.gpo.gov/websites/www.cbp.gov/xp/cgov/newsroom/

commissioner/speeches_statements/archives/2003/sept092003_2.xml.htm (accessed November 30, 2005).

28. Bureau of Transportation Statistics, http://transborder.bts.gov/programs/international/transborder/TBDR_BC/TBDR_BCQ.html (accessed July 1, 2016).

29. Victor Konrad, "Toward a Theory of Borders in Motion," *Journal of Borderlands Studies* 30, no. 1 (March 2015): 1–17.

30. Elaine Schwartz, "Transaction Costs: Delays at the San Diego-Tijuana Border," *EconLife*, May 31, 2013, http://econlife.com/2013/05/transaction-costs-delays-at-the-san-diego-tijuana-border/ (accessed July 1, 2016).

31. Stephen Flynn, "The Neglected Home Front," *Foreign Affairs*, 83, no. 5 (September/October 2004): 20–33.

32. Mark Binelli, "10 Shots across the Border," *The New York Times Magazine*, March 6, 2016.

CHAPTER 5

1. Jeremy Bentham, "Panopticon," in Miran Božovič, ed. and trans., *The Panopticon Writings* (London: Verso, 1995), 29–95.

2. Michel Foucault, *Discipline and Punish: The Birth of the Prison* (New York: Vintage Books, 1995).

3. "Strategic Plan FY 2012–2016," U.S. Department of Homeland Security, February 2012, https://www.dhs.gov/sites/default/files/publications/DHS%20Strategic%20Plan.pdf: 7 (accessed March 24, 2016).

4. See George Orwell's *Nineteen Eighty-Four*, Part 1, http://orwell.ru/library/novels/1984/english/en_p_1 (accessed December 5, 2005).

5. See "New Requirements for Travelers between the United States and the Western Hemisphere," http://travel.state.gov/travel/cbpmc/cbpmc_2223.html (accessed December 5, 2005).

6. Ryan Singel, "Passport Chip Criticism Grows," *Wired News*, http://www.wired.com/news/privacy/0,1848,67066,00.html?tw=wn_story_related (accessed November 1, 2005).

7. U.S. Customs and Border Protection, *2012–2016 Border Patrol Strategic Plan: The Mission: To Protect America*, https://www.cbp.gov/sites/default/files/documents/bp_strategic_plan.pdf (accessed March 24, 2016).

8. Michael Peck, "DHS's Border Drones Prove Ineffective," *Federal Times*, January 13, 2015, http://www.federaltimes.com/story/government/dhs/programs/2015/01/07/dhs-border-drone-cbp/21385613/ (accessed March 24, 2016).

9. Louie Gilot, "Researcher Says Math Can Protect Border," *El Paso Times*, December 12, 2005, A-1.

10. Timothy Dunn, *The Militarization of the U.S.-Mexico Border 1978–1992: Low-Intensity Conflict Doctrine Comes Home* (Austin: University of Texas at Austin Press, 1996), 149.

11. Ellwyn R. Stoddard, *U.S.-Mexico Borderlands Issues: The Bi-national Boundary, Immigration, and Economic Policies*, Vol. 1 of the *Borderlands Trilogy* (El Paso: The Promontory, 2001), 42–45.

12. "Migrant Deaths in Southern Arizona," *New York Times*, May 21, 2013, http://www.nytimes.com/interactive/2013/05/21/us/migrant-deaths-in -southern-arizona.html?_r=0 (accessed July 1, 2016).

13. Marc Cooper, "On the Border of Hypocrisy: The Unintended Consequences of Getting Tough on Illegal Immigration," *LA Weekly*, December 5–11, 2003.

14. Nigel Duara, "Why Border Crossings Are Down but Deaths Are Up in Brutal Arizona Desert," *Los Angeles Times*, October 27, 2015, http://www.latimes .com/nation/la-na-ff-immigrant-border-deaths-20151021-story.html (accessed July 1, 2016).

15. "New Poll Shows Americans Continue to Have Deeply Negative Views of Mexico, Are Divided over NAFTA," *PRNewswire*, June 28, 2016, http://www .prnewswire.com/news-releases/new-poll-shows-americans-continue-to-have -deeply-negative-views-of-mexico-are-divided-over-nafta-300290940.html (accessed July 1, 2016).

16. Peter Laufer, *Wetback Nation: The Case for Opening the Mexican-American Border* (Chicago: Ivan R. Dee, 2004).

17. William Glaberson, "Verdict in Stewart Case: Impact," *New York Times*, February 11, 2005.

18. John Bailey and Jorge Chabat, *Transnational Crime and Public Security: Challenges to Mexico and the United States* (La Jolla: University of California, 2002), 1.

19. Tony Payan, "Border Killing as a Symbol of Failed Policy," CNN, June 11, 2010, http://www.cnn.com/2010/OPINION/06/10/payan.border.shooting/ (accessed July 1, 2016).

20. Elizabeth Salamanca Pacheco, "New Migration Patterns: High-Skilled Entrepreneurial Migration from Mexico to the United States," Mexico Center at Rice University's Baker Institute, November 2015, http://bakerinstitute.org/ media/files/files/25c21136/MC-pub-EntrepreneurialMigration-111715.pdf (accessed July 1, 2016).

21. "On Security," in Ronnie D. Lipschutz, ed., *On Security* (New York: Columbia University Press, 1995), 9.

22. Allan Bersin, "Statement Before the U.S. House Committee on the Judiciary, Subcommittee on Immigration and Claims Hearing on Border Security and Deterring Illegal Entry into the United States," 105th Congress, First Session, 1997, House Report 105–32, 16.

23. An example of this kind of literature is Jon E. Dougherty's *Illegals: The Imminent Threat Posed by Our Unsecured U.S.-Mexico Border* (Nashville: WND Books, 2004). Other examples sounding the same kind of alarm about the border are: Frosty Wooldrige's *Immigration's Unarmed Invasion: Deadly Consequences* (United States: AuthorHouse, 2004); Jon E. Dougherty, *Illegals: The Imminent Threat Posted by Our Unsecured U.S.-Mexico Border* (Nashville: HarperCollins Christian, 2009); Darrell Ankarlo, *Illegals: The Unacceptable Cost of America's Failure to Control Its Borders* (Nashville: HarperCollins Christian, 2010); and Sylvia Longmire, *Cartel: The Coming Invasion of Mexico's Drug Wars* (New York: St. Martin's Press, 2011); among many others.

24. John Kerry, *The New War: The Web of Crime That Threatens America's Security* (New York: Simon & Schuster, 1997), 149.

25. Katherine McIntire Peters, "Up against the Wall," October 1, 1996, GovExec.com, http://www.govexec.com/magazine/1996/10/up-against-the -wall/427/ (accessed July 1, 2016).

26. See Bill O'Reilly's November 9, 2005, interview with Congressman Duncan Hunter at http://www.foxnews.com/story/0,2933,175030,00.html (accessed November 20, 2005).

27. See Congressman Tom Tancredo's press release link at http://tancredo .house.gov/press/pressers/1212Tancredo51TerroristSuspectsCrossedBorder Illegally.htm (accessed December 13, 2005).

28. Donald J. Trump, "Immigration Reform That Will Make America Great Again," https://www.donaldjtrump.com/positions/immigration-reform (accessed July 1, 2016).

29. "Unauthorized Immigrant Population Trends for States, Birth Countries and Regions," Pew Hispanic Center, December 11, 2014, http://www.pew hispanic.org/2014/12/11/unauthorized-trends/ (accessed July 1, 2016).

30. Robert A. Pastor, *The North American Idea: A Vision of a Continental Future* (Oxford: Oxford University Press, 2011).

31. Pew Hispanic Center, "Latino Choices in News Media Are Shaping Their Views of Their Communities, the Nation and the World," press release, http:// www.pewtrusts.org/en/about/news-room/press-releases/2004/04/19/latinos -choices-in-news-media-are-shaping-their-views-of-their-communities-the -nation-and-the-world (accessed December 2, 2005).

32. "Democracy's Ten Year Rut," *The Economist*, October 27, 2005.

33. The numbers are estimates from the U.S. Census Bureau, http://www .census.gov/popest/estimates.php (accessed November 13, 2005).

34. The source of this and other numbers regarding Texas can be found at Texas Comptroller of Public Accounts, http://www.window.state.tx.us .specialrept/specialrept/snapshot (accessed November 29, 2005).

Bibliography

ARTICLES

"AIC/Zogby Mexican Opinion Poll: Report." Americans for Immigration Control, June 11, 2002. http://www.immigrationcontrol.com/AIC_Zogby_Mexican _Poll.htm (accessed September 10, 2005).

Althaus, Dudley, and John Otis. "Is Mexico Going to Be the Next Colombia?" *Houston Chronicle*, June 17, 2005. http://www.chron.com/news/nation-world/ article/Is-Mexico-going-to-be-the-next-Colombia-1483400.php (accessed June 28, 2016).

"American Immigration: An Overview." U.S. English, November 20, 2005. http://www.us-english.org/foundation/research/amimmigr/Chapter3.PDF (accessed December 7, 2005).

"At the Crossroads for Unaccompanied Migrant Children: Policy, Practice & Protection." Lutheran Immigration and Refugee Service, July 2015. http://lirs .org/wp-content/uploads/2015/07/LIRS_RoundtableReport_WEB.pdf (accessed June 30, 2016).

"Attorney General Wants More Border Patrol Helicopters." *Aviation Today*, January 1, 2002. http://www.aviationtoday.com/cgi/rw/show_mag.cgi? pub=rw&mon=0102&file=0102civup.htm (accessed December 9, 2005).

Bachelet, Pablo. "Tucson a Hub for Mexicans' Drug Trade." *Arizona Daily Star*, August 1, 2005.

Bagley, Bruce M. *Drug Trafficking and Organized Crime in the Americas: Major Trends in the Twenty-First Century*. Washington, DC: Woodrow Wilson Center, August 2012. https://www.wilsoncenter.org/sites/default/files/BB%20Final .pdf (accessed July 1, 2016).

Becker, Andrew. "Crossing the Line: Corruption at the Border." Center for Investigative Reporting. http://bordercorruption.apps.cironline.org (accessed July 2, 2016).

Binelli, Mark. "10 Shots across the Border." *The New York Times Magazine*, March 6, 2016.

Blumenthal, Ralph. "Citing Violence, 2 Border States Declare a Crisis." *New York Times*, August 17, 2005. http://www.nytimes.com/2005/08/17/us/citing -violence-2-border-states-declare-a-crisis.html?_r=0 (accessed July 1, 2016).

Blumenthal, Ralph. "Smuggling Trial in Texas Focuses on Trucker's Role." *New York Times*, March 13, 2005.

Brian, Tara, and Franck Laczko. *Fatal Journeys: Tracking Lives Lost during Migration* (Geneva: International Organization for Migration, 2014). http://www.iom.int/ files/live/sites/iom/files/pbn/docs/Fatal-Journeys-Tracking-Lives-Lost -during-Migration-2014.pdf (accessed July 2, 2016).

Brown, Anna, and Mark Hugo López. "Mapping the Latino Population by State, County and City." Pew Research Center, August 29, 2013. http://www .pewhispanic.org/2013/08/29/mapping-the-latino-population-by-state -county-and-city/ (accessed June 30, 2016).

Bump, Phillip. "Where America's Undocumented Immigrants Work." *Washington Post*, March 27, 2015. https://www.washingtonpost.com/news/the-fix/wp/ 2015/03/27/where-americas-undocumented-immigrants-work/ (accessed July 1, 2016).

Burnett, John. "Corruption at the Gates: Series Explores Lure of Money, Prestige among U.S. Border Agents." National Public Radio, September 12, 2002. http://www.npr.org/programs/atc/features/2002/sept/border_corruption (accessed October 2, 2005).

Chiquiar, Daniel, and Alejandra Saucedo. "Mexican Migration to the United States: Underlying Economic Factors and Possible Scenarios for Future Flows." Migration Policy Institute, April 2013. http://www.migrationpolicy.org/ research/mexican-migration-united-states-underlying-economic-factors-and -possible-scenarios-future (accessed June 30, 2016).

Clark, Rebecca L., and Scott A. Anderson. "Illegal Aliens in Federal, State, and Local Criminal Justice Systems." The Urban Institute, June 30, 2000. http:// www.urban.org/url.cfm?ID=410366 (accessed October 15, 2005).

"Complaint and Request for Investigation of Coercion, Abuse of Power, and Excessive Force by Customs and Border Protection at Ports of Entry along the U.S.-Mexico Border." American Civil Liberties Union, 2016. https://www .aclu-nm.org/wp-content/uploads/2016/05/RCBR-2016-POE-Admin-Complaint -Recommendations-FINAL-VERSION.pdf?556820 (accessed July 1, 2016).

"Construcción de una Comunidad de América del Norte." The Council on Foreign Relations, November 25, 2005. http://www.cfr.org/content/publications/ attachments/NorthAmerica_TF_final_esp.pdf (accessed December 1, 2005).

Cooper, Marc. "On the Border of Hypocrisy: The Unintended Consequences of Getting Tough on Illegal Immigration." *The L.A. Weekly*, December 5–11, 2003.

Council on Foreign Relations. "Construcción de una Communidad de América del Norte," http://www.cfr.org/content/publications/attachments/NorthAmerica _TF_final_esp.pdf (accessed July 1, 2016).

Dear, Michael, and Andrew Burridge. "Cultural Integration and Hybridization at the U.S.-Mexico Borderlands." *Cahiers de Géographie du Québec* 49, no. 138 (December 2005): 3011–18.

Del Bosque, Melissa, and Patrick Michels. "Homeland Insecurity." *Texas Observer*, January 2016. https://www.texasobserver.org/homeland-security-corruption -border-patrol/ (accessed June 28, 2016).

"Democracy's Ten Year Rut." *The Economist*, October 27, 2005.

Dougherty, Jon E. "Lawmaker: Concern Rising Following Arrest of al-Qaeda Suspect in Mexico." *WorldNet Daily*, November 25, 2005. http://www.wnd.com/ news/article.asp?ARTICLE_ID=47401 (accessed November 7, 2005).

Duara, Nigel. "Why Border Crossings Are Down but Deaths Are Up in Brutal Arizona Desert." *Los Angeles Times*, October 27, 2015. http://www.latimes .com/nation/la-na-ff-immigrant-border-deaths-20151021-story.html (accessed July 1, 2016).

Edwards, Chris. "Make America Safer: Shut Down the Department of Homeland Security." Cato Institute, October 27, 2014. http://www.cato.org/publications/ commentary/make-america-safer-shut-down-department-homeland-security (accessed July 1, 2016).

Eriksson, Linda, and Melinda Taylor. "The Environmental Impacts of the Border Wall between Texas and Mexico." Austin: University of Texas Law School. https://law.utexas.edu/humanrights/borderwall/analysis/briefing-The -Environmental-Impacts-of-the-Border-Wall.pdf (accessed July 1, 2016).

"Federal Drug Control Budget: New Rhetoric, Same Failed Drug War." Drug Policy Alliance, February 2015. http://www.drugpolicy.org/sites/default/ files/DPA_Fact_sheet_Drug_War_Budget_Feb2015.pdf (accessed July 1, 2016).

Figueroa, Lorena. "Citizens with No Passport at Border Face Fines." *El Paso Times*, April 22, 2016. http://www.elpasotimes.com/story/news/2016/04/22/ citizens-no-passport-border-face-fines/83405410/ (accessed July 1, 2016).

Flores Pérez, Carlos Antonio. "Political Protection and the Origins of the Gulf Cartel." *Crime, Law and Social Change* 61, no. 5 (June 2014): 517–39.

Flynn, Stephen. "The Neglected Home Front." *Foreign Affairs* 83, no. 5 (September/October 2004): 20–33.

"Former EP Border Agent Sentenced for Letting Drug Couriers Pass." *El Paso Times*, November 23, 2005.

Francis, Sam. "J'accuse: The Open Borders Lobby Are to Blame for Terrorism." *Vdare*, September 20, 2001. http://www.vdare.com/francis/open_borders.htm (accessed July 1, 2016).

Frey, John Carlos. "Graves of Shame: New Evidence Indicates Wrongdoing in the Handling of Migrant Remains in Brooks County." *Texas Observer*, July 6, 2015. http://www.texasobserver.org/illegal-mass-graves-of-migrant-remains -found-in-south-texas/ (accessed July 2, 2016).

Gee, Lisa C., Matthew Gardner, and Meg Wiehe. "Undocumented Immigrants' State and Local Tax Contributions." Institute for Taxation and Economic Policy, February 2016. http://www.itep.org/pdf/immigration2016.pdf (accessed July 1, 2016).

Germano, Roy. "Unauthorized Immigrants Paid $100 Billion into Social Security over Last Decade." Vice News, August 4, 2014. https://news.vice.com/ article/unauthorized-immigrants-paid-100-billion-into-social-security-over -last-decade (accessed July 1, 2016).

Gilot, Louie. "Researcher Says Math Can Protect Border." *El Paso Times*, December 12, 2005.

Glaberson, William. "Verdict in Stewart Case: Impact." *New York Times*, February 11, 2005.

González-Barrera, Anna. "More Mexicans Leaving than Coming to the U.S." Pew Research Centers Hispanic Trends Project RSS, November 19, 2015. http:// www.pewhispanic.org/2015/11/19/more-mexicans-leaving-than-coming-to -the-u-s/ (accessed July 1, 2016).

Goodman, Adam, and Verónica Zapata Rivera. "Mexico: Bracero Guestworkers, Unpaid." *Upside Down World*, October 17, 2013. http://upsidedownworld.org/ main/mexico-archives-79/4513-mexico-bracero-guestworkers-unpaid (accessed June 30, 2016).

Graff, Garrett M. "The Green Monster: How the Border Patrol Became America's Most Out-of-Control Law Enforcement Agency." *Politico Magazine*, November/December 2014. http://www.politico.com/magazine/story/2014/10/ border-patrol-the-green-monster-112220 (accessed June 30, 2016).

Green, Cynthia. "Federal Grand Jury Investigating Wal-Mart's Use of Undocumented Migrants." The Labor Research Association, September 18, 2005. http:// www.laborresearch.org/story.php?id=332 (accessed December 13, 2005).

Guevara, America Y. "Propaganda in Mexico's Drug War." *Journal of Strategic Security* 6, no. 5 (2013): 131–51.

Hanson, Gordon H. "What Has Happened to Wages in Mexico since NAFTA? Implications for Hemispheric Trade." https://gps.ucsd.edu/ _files/faculty/hanson/hanson_publication_it_NAFTA.pdf (accessed June 28, 2016).

Harman, Danna. "Mexican Drug Cartels: Wars Move Closer to the U.S. Border." *USA Today*, August 17, 2005. http://www.usatoday.com/news/world/2005 -08-17-mexican-cartels_x.htm (accessed October 30, 2005).

Hedges, Michael. "Bush Budget Scraps 9,790 Border Patrol Agents: President Uses Law's Escape Clause to Drop Funding for New Homeland Security." *San Francisco Chronicle*, February 9, 2005.

Horn, Heather. "Birth Right Citizenship Wasn't Born in America." *The Atlantic*, September 1, 2015. http://www.theatlantic.com/international/archive/2015/ 09/birthright-citizenship-donald-trump-england/403159/ (accessed June 30, 2016).

Ibarra, Ignacio. "Border Group Claims WMD Test." *Arizona Daily Star*, July 22, 2004.

"Illegal Immigrants Are Bolstering Social Security with Billions." *New York Times*, April 5, 2005.

"Illegal Immigration." *Migration News*, October 2005. https://migration.ucdavis. edu/mn/more_entireissue.php?idate=2005_10 (accessed December 1, 2005).

Jeffrey, Terence. "A Case of Selective Enforcement." *Town Hall*, November 4, 2005. http://www.townhall.com/opinion/columns/terencejeffrey/2003/07/02/ 170036.html (accessed November 16, 2005).

Katz, Jesse. "A Good Shepherd's Death by Military." *Los Angeles Times*, June 21, 1997. http://articles.latimes.com/1997-06-21/news/mn-5538_1_military -missions (accessed July 1, 2016).

Konrad, Victor. "Toward a Theory of Borders in Motion." *Journal of Borderlands Studies* 30, no. 1 (March 2015): 1–17.

Liptak, Adam, and Michael D. Shear. "Supreme Court Tie Blocks Obama Immigration Plan," June 23, 2016. http://www.nytimes.com/2016/06/24/us/supreme-court-immigration-obama-dapa.html (accessed July 1, 2016).

Lutheran Immigration and Refugee Service. *At the Crossroads for Unaccompanied Migrant Children: Policy, Practice & Protection*, July 2015. http://lirs.org/wp-content/uploads/2015/07/LIRS_RoundtableReport_WEB.pdf (accessed June 30, 2016).

Lyall, James, Jane Yakowitz Bambauer, and Derek E. Bambauer. "Record of Abuse: Lawlessness and Impunity in Border Patrol's Interior Enforcement Operations." American Civil Liberties Union, October 2015. http://www.acluaz.org/sites/default/files/documents/Record_of_Abuse_101515_0.pdf (accessed July 1, 2016).

Marizco, Michael. "Smugglers Getting Sneakier." *Arizona Daily Star*, December 26, 2004.

Martínez, Daniel E., Guillermo Cantor, and Walter A. Ewing. "No Action Taken: Lack of CBP Accountability in Responding to Complaints of Abuse." American Immigration Council, May 2014, http://www.americanimmigrationcouncil.org/sites/default/files/No%20Action%20Taken_Final.pdf (accessed July 1, 2016).

McAuley, John. "Immigrants Keep U.S. Economy Supple." *Minnesota Star Tribune*, September 4, 2002.

McIntire Peters, Katherine. "Up against the Wall." October 1, 1996, GovExec.com. http://www.govexec.com/magazine/1996/10/up-against-the-wall/427/ (accessed July 1, 2016).

Meissner, Doris. "Two Jobs for One INS." *Washington Post*, April 9, 2002.

"Mexico's Gangs Use 'Narco-Tunnels' to Smuggle Migrants." InSight Crime, September 7, 2011. http://www.insightcrime.org/news-analysis/mexicos-gangs-use-narco-tunnels-to-smuggle-migrants (accessed July 1, 2016).

Meyer, Maureen, and Adam Isacson. "On the Front Lines: Border Security, Migration, and Humanitarian Concerns in South Texas," Advocacy for Human Rights in the Americas, February 27, 2015, http://www.wola.org/publications/south_texas_report (accessed July 2, 2016).

Milbank, Dana. "Bush Poised to Back New Border Agency." *Washington Post*, March 19, 2002.

Milbank, Dana, and Cheryl Thompson. "Panel Agrees on Plan to Split INS." *Washington Post*, March 22, 2002.

Mora, Edwin. "Napolitano: Terrorists Enter U.S. from Mexico from Time to Time." CNSNews.com, July 30, 2012.

Mucino, Kristel. "Mexico's Migration Crackdown Creates Spike in Apprehensions, Dangerous Shifts in Migrant Routes." Washington Office for Latin America, November 9, 2015. http://www.wola.org/news/mexicos_migration_crackdown_creates_spike_in_apprehensions_dangerous_shifts_in_migrant_routes (accessed March 15, 2016).

Muzzafar, Chishti and Faye Hipsman. "Unaccompanied Minors Crisis Has Receded from Headlines but Major Issues Remain." Migration Policy Institute,

September 24, 2014. http://www.migrationpolicy.org/article/unaccompanied
-minors-crisis-has-receded-headlines-major-issues-remain (accessed July 1,
2016).

Myrick, Sue. "Hezbollah Car Bombs on Our Border." *Washington Times*, September 1, 2010. http://www.washingtontimes.com/news/2010/sep/1/hezbollah
-car-bombs-on-our-border/ (accessed July 1, 2016).

Negrete Prieto, Rodrigo, and Gerardo Leyva Parra. "Los NiNis en México: Una
Aproximación Crítica a Su Medición." *Revista Internacional de Estadística y
Geografía* 4, no. 1 (January–April 2013).

Nowrastesh, Alex. "Unaccompanied Minors Crossing the Border—the Facts."
Cato Institute, June 17, 2014. http://www.cato.org/blog/unaccompanied
-minors-crossing-border-facts (accessed July 2, 2016).

Orrenius, Pia. "Illegal Immigration and Enforcement along the Southwest Border." Federal Reserve Bank of Dallas (June 2001). *New York Times*, March 13,
2005. http://www.dallasfed.org/research/border/tbe_orrenius.html (accessed
September 15, 2005).

Passel, Jeffrey S., and D'Vera Cohn. "Homeland Security Produces First Estimate
of Foreign Visitors to U.S. Who Overstay Deadline to Leave." Pew Research
Center, February 3, 2016. http://www.pewresearch.org/fact-tank/2016/02/
03/homeland-security-produces-first-estimate-of-foreign-visitors-to-u-s-who
-overstay-deadline-to-leave/ (accessed June 30, 2016).

Payan, Tony. "Border Killing as a Symbol of Failed Policy." CNN, June 11, 2010.
http://www.cnn.com/2010/OPINION/06/10/payan.border.shooting/
(accessed July 1, 2016).

Payan, Tony. "How a Forgotten Border Dispute Tormented U.S.-Mexico Relations
for 100 Years." *Americas Quarterly* (Winter 2016).

Peck, Michael. "DHS's Border Drones Prove Ineffective," *Federal Times*, January 13,
2015. http://www.federaltimes.com/story/government/dhs/programs/
2015/01/07/dhs-border-drone-cbp/21385613/ (accessed March 24, 2016).

Pew Hispanic Center. "Latino Choices in News Media Are Shaping Their Views of
Their Communities, the Nation and the World." Press release. http://www
.pewtrusts.org/en/about/news-room/press-releases/2004/04/19/latinos
-choices-in-news-media-are-shaping-their-views-of-their-communities-the
-nation-and-the-world (accessed December 2, 2005).

Pew Research Center. *Most Mexicans See Better Life in U.S.: One in Three Would
Migrate*, September 23, 2009. http://www.pewglobal.org/2009/09/23/most-
mexicans-see-better-life-in-us-one-in-three-would-migrate/ (accessed June 30,
2016).

Porter, Eduardo. "Illegal Immigrants Are Bolstering Social Security with Billions."
New York Times, April 5, 2005.

"Portrait of a Mexican Drug Lord." CBS News, December 24, 2003. http://www
.cbsnews.com/stories/2003/10/24/world/main579960.shtml (accessed
October 10, 2005).

"Pot-Laden Truck Creates Armed Standoff." *El Paso Times*, November 19, 2005.

Robbins, Ted. "Illegal Immigrant Deaths Burden Border Towns." *The Nation*,
October 6, 2005. http://www.npr.org/templates/story/story.php?storyId
=4948382 (accessed November 19, 2005).

Ruiz, Rubén. "Ejecutan a Tres Ex Policías." *El Imparcial*, June 7, 2005.

Salamanca Pacheco, Elizabeth. "New Migration Patterns: High-Skilled Entrepreneurial Migration from Mexico to the United States." Mexico Center at Rice University's Baker Institute, November 2015. http://bakerinstitute.org/media/files/files/25c21136/MC-pub-EntrepreneurialMigration-111715.pdf (accessed July 1, 2016).

Saldaña, Juan Diego, and Tony Payan. "The Evolution of Cartels in Mexico: 1980–2015." Rice University's Baker Institute Mexico Center. http://baker institute.org/research/evolution-cartels-mexico-1980-2015/ (accessed July 1, 2016).

Schwartz, Elaine. "Transaction Costs: Delays at the San Diego-Tijuana Border." *EconLife*, May 31, 2013. http://econlife.com/2013/05/transaction-costs-delays -at-the-san-diego-tijuana-border/ (accessed July 1, 2016).

Sheehan, Matt. "Born in the USA: Why Chinese 'Birth Tourism' Is Booming in California." *Huffington Post*, May 14, 2015. http://www.huffingtonpost .com/2015/05/01/china-us-birth-tourism_n_7187180.html (accessed July 2, 2016).

Shoichet, Catherine E. "The Last Flight and First Steps: 'Historic' Surge of Cubans Crossing into U.S." CNN, June 1, 2016. http://www.cnn.com/2016/05/31/us/border-cuban-migrants-el-paso/ (accessed July 1, 2016).

Singel, Ryan. "Passport Chip Criticism Grows." *Wired News*, March 31, 2005. http://www.wired.com/news/privacy/0,1848,67066,00.html?tw=wn_story _related (accessed November 1, 2005).

Sohn, Christophe. "Modelling Cross-Border Integration: The Role of Borders as a Resource." *Geopolitics* 19, no. 3 (August 2014).

Spagat, Elliot. "Half-Mile Drug Tunnel and a Massive Bust: Ton of Coke, 7 Tons Pot Seized." Associated Press, April 21, 2016. http://www.thecannabist.co/2016/04/21/half-mile-tunnel-found-on-us-mexico-border-cocaine-seized/52500/ (accessed July 1, 2016).

Stevens, Elijah. "Mexico's Southern Border Plan Fuels Violence," InSight Crime: Investigation and Analysis of Organized Crime, November 10, 2015. http://www.insightcrime.org/news-briefs/mexico-southern-border-plan-fuels-violence (accessed June 30, 2016).

Stock, Margaret D., and Benjamin Johnson. "The Lessons of 9/11: A Failure of Intelligence, Not Immigration Law." *Immigration Policy Focus* 2, no. 3 (December 2003).

Strand, Paul. "Border Invasion: Stemming the Illegal Flood." CBN News, April 14, 2005. http://www.cbn.com/cbnnews/news/050414a.asp (accessed November 23, 2005).

"Stryker Training." *The Monitor*, March 3, 2005, 30–31.

Suro, Roberto. *Attitudes toward Immigrants and Immigration Policy: Surveys among Latinos in the U.S. and Mexico*, 2005. http://pewhispanic.org/files/reports/52 .pdf (accessed November 15, 2005).

"Survey: Illegal Drugs: Stumbling in the Dark." *The Economist*, July 28, 2001.

Terrazas, Aaron. "Mexican Immigrants in the United States." Migration Policy Institute, February 22, 2010. http://www.migrationpolicy.org/article/mexican-immigrants-united-states-0 (accessed June 30, 2016).

Thompson, Cheryl. "INS Role for the Police Considered." *Washington Post*, April 4, 2002.

Thompson, Cheryl. "INS Tightens Rules for Visitors." *Washington Post*, April 9, 2002.

Trump, Donald J. "Immigration Reform That Will Make America Great Again." https://www.donaldjtrump.com/positions/immigration-reform (accessed July 1, 2016).

"US Border a 'Safety Valve' for Latin Poor." *Providence Journal*, May 11, 2005. http://www.commondreams.org/views05/0511-26.htm (accessed November 27, 2005).

Villalobos, Joaquín. "Doce Mitos de la Guerra Contra el Narco." *Nexos*, January 1, 2010. http://www.nexos.com.mx/?p=13461 (accessed July 2, 2016).

"War on Undocumented Immigrants Threatens to Swell U.S. Prison Population." *Huffington Post*, August 23, 2013. http://www.huffingtonpost.com/2013/08/23/undocumented-immigrants-prison_n_3792187.html (accessed June 30, 2016).

Washington Office for Latin America. *Increased Enforcement at Mexico's Southern Border*, November 2015. http://www.wola.org/files/WOLA_Increased_Enforcement_at_Mexico's_Southern_Border_Nov2015.pdf (accessed June 30, 2016).

Weber, Paul J. "Texas Approves $800 Million for Border Security." *PBS NewsHour*, June 16, 2015. http://www.pbs.org/newshour/rundown/texas-approves-800-million-border-security/ (accessed July 1, 2016).

Windle, James, and Graham Farrell. "Popping the Balloon Effect: Assessing Drug Law Enforcement in Terms of Displacement, Diffusion, and the Containment Hypothesis." *Substance Use and Misuse* 47, nos. 8–9 (June 7, 2012): 868–76.

World Bank. "International Migration at an All-Time High," December 2015. http://www.worldbank.org/en/news/press-release/2015/12/18/international-migrants-and-remittances-continue-to-grow-as-people-search-for-better-opportunities-new-report-finds (accessed July 1, 2016).

Zong, Jie, and Jeanne Batalova. "Asian Immigrants in the United States." Migration Policy Institute, January 6, 2016. http://www.migrationpolicy.org/article/asian-immigrants-united-states (accessed June 29, 2016).

BOOKS

Andreas, Peter. *Border Games: Policing the U.S.-Mexico Divide*. Ithaca: Cornell University Press, first edition 2001 and second edition 2009.

Ankarlo, Darrell. *Illegals: The Unacceptable Cost of America's Failure to Control Its Borders*. Nashville: HarperCollins Christian, 2010.

Bagley, Bruce M., and William O. Walker III. *Drug Trafficking in the Americas*. Boulder, CO: Lynne Rienner, 1994.

Bailey, John, and Jorge Chabat. *Transnational Crime and Public Security: Challenges to Mexico and the United States*. San Diego: Center for U.S.-Mexican Studies, 2004.

Balderrama, Francisco E., and Raymond Rodríguez. *Decade of Betrayal: Mexican Repatriation in the 1930s*. Albuquerque: University of New Mexico Press, 2006.

Bentham, Jeremy. *The Panopticon Writings*. Edited by Miran Bozovic, pp. 29–95. London: Verso, 1995.

Blancornelas, Jesús. *El Cártel: Los Arellano Félix: La mafia más poderosa en la historia de América Latina*. México City: Plaza y Janés, 2002.

Bossard, André. *Transnational Crime and Criminal Law*. Chicago: Office of International Criminal Justice, 1990.

Braunstein, Peter, and Michael William Doyle. *Nation: The American Counterculture of the 1960s and '70s*. New York: Routledge, 2003.

Briody, Dan. *The Iron Triangle: Inside the Secret World of the Carlyle Group*. Hoboken: Wiley and Sons, 2003.

Díaz, George T. *Border Contraband: A History of Smuggling across the Rio Grande*. Austin: University of Texas Press, 2015.

Doty, Roxanne. *The Law into Their Own Hands: Immigration and the Politics of Exceptionalism*. Tucson: University of Arizona Press, 2009.

Dougherty, Jon E. *Illegals: The Imminent Threat Posed by Our Unsecured U.S.-Mexican Border*. Nashville: WND Books, 2004.

Dunn, Timothy J. *The Militarization of the U.S.-Mexico Border 1978–1992: Low-Intensity Conflict Comes Home*. Austin: University of Texas at Austin Press, 1996.

Esparza, Adrian X., and Angela J. Donelson. *Colonias in Arizona and New Mexico: Border Poverty and Community Development Solutions*. Tucson: University of Arizona Press, 2008.

Foucault, Michel. *Discipline and Punish: The Birth of the Prison*. New York: Vintage Books, 1977.

Fuss, Charles M. *Sea of Grass: The Maritime Drug War, 1970–1990*. Annapolis: Naval Institute Press, 1996.

Graebner Anderson, Annelise. *The Business of Organized Crime: A Cosa Nostra Family*. Stanford: Hoover Institution Press, 1980.

Hobbes, Thomas. *The Leviathan*. Project Gutenberg. http://www.gutenberg.org/files/3207/3207-h/3207-h.htm, n.d.

Kaplan, Lawrence J., and Dennis Kessler. *An Economic Analysis of Crime*. Springfield: Thomas, 1976.

Kerry, John. *The New War: The Web of Crime That Threatens America's Security*. New York: Simon & Schuster, 1997.

Kurian, George T., ed. *A Historical Guide to the U.S. Government*. New York: Oxford University Press, 1998.

Laufer, Peter. *Wetback Nation: The Case for Opening the Mexican-American Border*. Chicago: Ivan R. Dee, 2004.

Lipschutz, Ronnie D., ed. *On Security*. New York: Columbia University Press, 1995.

Longmire, Sylvia. *Cartel: The Coming Invasion of Mexico's Drug Wars*. New York: St. Martin's Press, 2011.

Maril, Robert Lee. *Patrolling Chaos: The U.S. Border Patrol in Deep South Texas*. Lubbock: Texas Tech University Press, 2004.

Mason Hart, Jason, ed. *Border Crossings: Mexican and Mexican American Workers*. Wilmington, DE: SR Books, 1998.

Mize, Ronald L., and Alicia C. S. Swords. *Consuming Mexican Labor: From the Bracero Program to NAFTA*. Toronto: University of Toronto Press, 2010.

Mora-Torres, Juan. *The Making of the Mexican Border*. Austin: University of Texas Press, 2001.

Moran, Robert T. *Uniting North American Business: NAFTA Best Practices*, 2nd ed. Boston: Butterworth Heineman, 2002.

Naylor, R. T. *Wages of Crime: Black Markets, Illegal Finance, and the Underworld Economy*. Ithaca: Cornell University, 2002.

Orwell, George. *Nineteen Eighty-Four*. New York: Penguin Group, 2005. Entire text of the book can be found at http://orwell.ru/library/novels/1984/english/en _p_1 (December 5, 2005).

Paredes, Américo. *A Texas-Mexican Cancionero: Folksongs of the Lower Border*. Austin: University of Texas Press, 1995.

Pastor, Robert A. *The North American Idea: A Vision of a Continental Future*. Oxford: Oxford University Press, 2011.

Payan, Tony. *Cops, Soldiers, and Diplomats: Agency Behavior in the War on Drugs*. Lanham: Lexington Books, 2007.

Payan, Tony, and Amanda Vasquez. "The Costs of Homeland Security." In *Borderlands: Comparing Border Security in North America and Europe*. Edited by Emmanuel Brunet-Jailly. Ottawa: University of Ottawa Press, 2007.

Payan, Tony, and Erika de la Garza, eds. *Undecided Nation: Political Gridlock and the Immigration Crisis*. United Kingdom: Springer, 2014.

Payan, Tony, Kathleen Staudt, and Z. Anthony Kruszewski. *A War That Can't Be Won: Binational Perspectives on the War on Drugs*. Tucson: University of Arizona Press, 2014.

Pozo, Susan, ed. *Exploring the Underground Economy*. Kalamazoo: W. E. Upjohn Institute, 1996.

Pyle, David J. *The Economics of Crime and Law Enforcement*. New York: St. Martin's Press, 1983.

Sassen, Saskia. *Expulsions: Brutality and Complexity in the Global Economy*. Cambridge: Harvard University Press, 2014.

Shannon, Elaine. *Desperados: Latin Drug Lords, U.S. Lawmen, and the War America Can't Win*. New York: Penguin, 1989.

Shaw-Taylor, Yoku. *Immigration, Assimilation, and Border Security*. Lanham: Scarecrow Press, 2012.

Smith, Adam. *The Wealth of Nations*. Great Britain: Capstone, 2010.

Sterling, Claire. *Crime without Frontiers: The Worldwide Expansion of Organised Crime and the Pax Mafiosa*. Sacramento: Time Warner Paperbacks, 1995.

Stoddard, Ellwyn R. *U.S.-Mexico Borderlands Issues: The Binational Boundary, Immigration, and Economic Policies: Borderlands Trilogy*, Vol. I. El Paso: The Promontory, 2001.

Thornton, Mark. *The Economics of Prohibition*. Salt Lake City: University of Utah Press, 1991.

Ward, Peter M. *Colonias and Public Policy in Texas and Mexico: Urbanization by Stealth*. Austin: University of Texas Press, 1999.

Wooldridge, Frosty. *Immigration's Unarmed Invasion: Deadly Consequences*. United States: AuthorHouse, 2004.

INTERNET

"American Immigration: An Overview." U.S. English Foundation. http://www.us-english.org/foundation/research/amimmigr/Chapter3.PDF (accessed November 20, 2005).

Birda, Trollinger, Martinez, Eddings and Jewell v. Tyson Foods, Inc. http://www.vdare
.com/misc/tyson_complaint.htm (accessed September 18, 2005).

Borderline data. http://us-mex.irc-online.org/borderlines/PDFs/bl79.pdf
(accessed November 26, 2005).

"Bush Vows to Harden Border Policy." Speech. http://www.chron.com/disp/
story.mpl/metropolitan/3489624.html (accessed November 28, 2005).

"The 1853 Gadsden Purchase Treaty." http://www.yale.edu/lawweb/avalon/
diplomacy/mexico/mx1853.htm (accessed December 10, 2005).

"Governor Schwarzenegger Delivers a Speech on Closing Borders." http://
www.foxnews.com/story/0,2933,153988,00.html (accessed November 28,
2005).

Hear the story of drug smuggling through the Tohona O'odham Reservation on
National Public Radio. http://www.npr.org/templates/story/story.php?
storyId=1125387 (accessed November 20, 2005).

H.R. 3162 RDS, 107th Congress, 1st Session. H.R. 3162 in the Senate of the United
States. Patriot Act. http://www.epic.org/privacy/terrorism/hr3162.html
(accessed December 10, 2005).

"Illegal Immigration and Enforcement Along the U.S.-Mexico Border: An Overview." http://www.dallasfed.org/research/efr/2001/efr0101a.pdf (accessed
December 9, 2005).

"Latino Choices in News Media Are Shaping Their Views of Their Communities,
the Nation and the World." Pew Hispanic Center. http://pewhispanic.org/
newsroom/releases/release.php?ReleaseID=10 (accessed December 2, 2005).

"Militarizing the Border." http://mediafilter.org/CAQ/CAQ56border.html
(accessed December 10, 2005).

"New Requirements for Travelers between the United States and the Western
Hemisphere." http://travel.state.gov/travel/cbpmc/cbpmc_2223.html
(accessed December 5, 2005).

"New Poll Shows Americans Continue to Have Deeply Negative Views of
Mexico, Are Divided Over NAFTA." *PRNewswire*, June 28, 2016. http://www
.prnewswire.com/news-releases/new-poll-shows-americans-continue-to
-have-deeply-negative-views-of-mexico-are-divided-over-nafta-300290940.html
(accessed July 1, 2016).

O'Reilly, Bill. "Interview with Congressman Duncan Hunter." *The O'Reilly Factor*,
November 9, 2005. http://www.foxnews.com/story/0,2933,175030,00.html
(November 20, 2005).

Peters, Katherine McIntire. "Up against the Wall." http://www.govexec.com/
archdoc/1096/1096s1.htm (accessed November 1, 2005).

"Population Statistics." http://www.scerp.org/population.htm (accessed
January 27, 2005).

"President Discusses Border Security and Immigration Reform in Arizona."
Speech. http://www.whitehouse.gov/news/releases/2005/11/20051128-7
.html (accessed November 29, 2005).

Quoteauthors. http://www.quoteauthors.com/charles-caleb-colton-quotes/
(accessed June 28, 2016).

"Rethinking the Role of the U.S. Mexican Border in the Post-9/11 World." http://
www.cfr.org/publication/6906/rethinking_the_role_of_the_us_mexican
_border_in_the_post911_world.html (accessed December 3, 2005).

"A Secure Europe in a Better World." http://ue.eu.int/uedocs/cmsUpload/78367
.pdf (accessed December 5, 2005).

"Sixty Percent Favor Barrier on Mexican Border." http://www.rasmussenreports
.com/2005/Immigration%20November%207.htm (accessed November 15,
2005).

"State Marijuana Laws Map." Governing the States and Localities, May 2016.
http://www.governing.com/gov-data/state-marijuana-laws-map-medical
-recreational.html (accessed June 28, 2016).

"Thirty Years of America's Drug War: A Chronology." *Frontline*. http://www.pbs
.org/wgbh/pages/frontline/shows/drugs/cron/ (accessed December 9,
2005).

"Tightened Border in San Diego Shifts Strain to Areas East." http://www
.signonsandiego.com/news/reports/gatekeeper/20040801-9999-1n1econ.html
(accessed November 29, 2005).

GOVERNMENT DOCUMENTS AND REPORTS

Bureau of Justice Statistics. *National Transportation Statistics 2005*. http://www.bts
.gov/publications/national_transportation_statistics/2005 (accessed October 5,
2005).

Bureau of Transportation Statistics. http://www.bts.gov/programs/international/
border_crossing_entry_data/us_mexico/pdf/entire.pdf (accessed June 21, 2005).

Bureau of Transportation Statistics. *Border Crossing/Entry Data*. http://transborder
.bts.gov/programs/international/transborder/TBDR_BC/TBDR_BC_Index
.html (accessed June 30, 2016).

Bureau of Transportation Statistics. *Major NAFTA Border Crossings: 1996–2000*.
http://www.bts.gov/publications/transportation_statistics_annual_report/
2001/html/chapter_07_table_01_219.html (accessed November 5, 2005).

Census Bureau. "Foreign Trade Division, Data Dissemination Branch."
http://www.census.gov/foreign-trade/balance/c2010.html#2001 (accessed
November 5, 2005).

Census Bureau. "Population Estimates." http://www.census.gov/popest/
estimates.php (accessed November 26, 2005 and June 28, 2016).

Census Bureau. "Top Trading Partners 2016." https://www.census.gov/foreign
-trade/statistics/highlights/toppartners.html (accessed July 1, 2016).

Census Bureau. "Trade in Goods (Exports, Imports and Trade Balance) with
Mexico." http://www.census.gov/foreign-trade/balance/c2010.html#199
(accessed November 5, 2005).

Citizenship and Immigration Services. "Immigration Statistics." http://uscis.gov/
graphics/shared/aboutus/statistics/legishist/456.htm (accessed January 27,
2005).

Congressional Research Service. *Border Security: Inspections, Practices, Policies,
Issues*, May 26, 2004.

Congressional Research Service. *Border Security: The Role of the U.S. Border Patrol*.
http://www.fas.org/sgp/crs/homesec/RL32562.pdf (accessed September 7,
2005).

Congressional Research Service. *Homeland Security: Unmanned Aerial Vehicles and Border Surveillance*, February 7, 2005.

Congressman Tom Tancredo's web page at the U.S. House of Representatives. http://tancredo.house.gov/press/pressers/1212Tancredo51TerroristSuspects -CrossedBorderIllegally.htm (accessed December 13, 2005).

Customs and Border Protection. *CBP Border Security Report FY2015*, December 2015. https://www.dhs.gov/sites/default/files/publications/CBP %20FY15%20Border%20Security%20Report_12-21_0.pdf (accessed June 29, 2016).

Customs and Border Protection. C-TPAT: Customs-Trade Partnership against Terrorism. http://www.cbp.gov/border-security/ports-entry/cargo-security/ c-tpat-customs-trade-partnership-against-terrorism (accessed July 2, 2016).

Customs and Border Protection. *National Border Patrol Strategy.* http://www .customs.gov/linkhandler/cgov/border_security/border_patrol/national _bp_strategy.ctt/national_bp_strategy.pdf (accessed September 7, 2005).

Customs and Border Protection. *Secure Border Initiative.* http://foiarr.cbp.gov/ streamingWord.asp?i=297 (accessed June 29, 2016).

Customs and Border Protection. *Securing the Global Supply Chain.* http://www.cbp .gov/border-security/ports-entry/cargo-security/c-tpat-customs-trade -partnership-against-terrorism (accessed July 1, 2016).

Customs and Border Protection. *2012–2016 Border Patrol Strategy Strategic Plan: The Mission to Protect America.* https://www.cbp.gov/sites/default/files/ documents/bp_strategic_plan.pdf (accessed June 30, 2016).

Customs and Border Protection National Targeting Center. *Identifying Risks Early* (Video). https://www.cbp.gov/newsroom/video-gallery/2014/02/ identifying-risks-early (accessed July 1, 2016).

Department of Homeland Security. http://www.dhs.gov/dhspublic/interapp/ press_release/press_release_0541.xml (accessed October 19, 2005).

Department of Homeland Security. "Testimony by Deputy Secretary of Homeland Security Admiral James Loy Before the Senate Select Committee on Intelligence." http://www.iwar.org.uk/homesec/resources/natsec2005/loy.htm (accessed November 5, 2005).

Department of Homeland Security. "Testimony by Secretary Michael Chertoff before the House Homeland Security Committee," April 13, 2005. http:// www.dhs.gov/dhspublic/display?theme=45&content=4460> (accessed December 1, 2005).

Department of Homeland Security, Office of Immigration Statistics. "Estimates of Unauthorized Immigrant Population Residing in the United States: January 2012," March 2013. http://immigration.procon.org/sourcefiles/illegal -immigration-population-2012.pdf (accessed June 30, 2016).

Department of Homeland Security, Office of the Inspector General. "Detention and Removal of Illegal Aliens," April 2006. https://www.oig.dhs.gov/assets/ Mgmt/OIG_06-33_Apr06.pdf (accessed July 1, 2016).

Department of Homeland Security. Sarah Morgethau. *Interim Report of the CBP Integrity Advisory Panel*, June 29, 2015. https://www.dhs.gov/sites/default/ files/publications/DHS-HSAC-CBP-IAP-Interim-Report.pdf (accessed July 2, 2016).

Department of Justice. "Department of Justice Announces INS Restructuring Plan Splitting Service and Enforcement Functions." Press release, November 14, 2001. http://www.usdoj.gov (accessed November 14, 2004).

Department of Justice. "Justice Department Reaches Settlement in Civil Rights Lawsuit against Maricopa County, Arizona, and Maricopa County Sheriff." Press release, July 17, 2015. https://www.justice.gov/opa/pr/justice -department-reaches-settlement-civil-rights-lawsuit-against-maricopa-county -arizona (accessed July 1, 2016).

Department of State. http://usinfo.state.gov/eap/east_asia_pacific/chinese _human_smuggling/smuggling_in_the_press/crime.htm (accessed November 4, 2005).

Department of State. U.S. Embassy in Mexico City. http://mexico.usembassy.gov/ mexico/ep050610violence.html (accessed October 30, 2005).

Department of State. *U.S.-National Security Strategy: Prevent Our Enemies from Threatening Us, Our Allies, and Our Friends with Weapons of Mass Destruction.* Document found at the Department of State's web page, http://www.state .gov/r/pa/ei/wh/15425.htm (accessed December 1, 2005).

Drug Enforcement Administration. *Illegal Drug Price and Purity Report*, April 2003. http://www.usdoj.gov/dea/pubs/intel/02058/02058.html#2 (accessed September 28, 2005).

Government Accountability Office. *Border Patrol Hiring: Despite Recent Initiatives, Fiscal Year 1999 Hiring Goal Was Not Met.* Washington, DC: Government Accountability Office, December 1999.

Government Accountability Office. *Homeland Security: Overview of Homeland Security Management Challenges*, April 20, 2005.

Government Accountability Office. *Immigration Enforcement: DHS Has Incorporated Immigration Enforcement Objectives and Is Addressing Future Planning Requirements*, October 2004.

Government Accountability Office. *Lack of Progress on Achieving National Goals*, December 2015. http://www.gao.gov/assets/680/673929.pdf.

Government Accountability Office. *Social Security: Better Coordination among Federal Agencies Could Reduce Unidentified Earnings Reports*, February 2005.

Government Accountability Office. *Tax Administration: IRS Needs to Consider Options for Revising Regulations to Increase the Accuracy of Social Security Numbers on Wage Statements*, August 2004.

Government Printing Office. *Remarks from Former Customs and Border Protection Commissioner Robert Bonner.* http://permanent.access.gpo.gov/websites/www .cbp.gov/xp/cgov/newsroom/commissioner/speeches_statements/archives/ 2003/sept092003_2.xml.htm (accessed November 30, 2005).

House of Representatives. "Statement before the U.S. House Committee on the Judiciary, Subcommittee on Immigration and Claims Hearing on Border Security and Deterring Illegal Entry into the United States." 105th Congress, First Session, 1997, House Report 105–32, 16.

House of Representatives. "Testimony of Peter Gadiel before the Committee on the Judiciary." http://judiciary.house.gov/OversightTestimony.aspx?ID=289 (accessed November 5, 2005).

National Archives. "Immigration Statistics." http://www.archives.gov/research
_room/genealogy/immigrant_arrivals/mexican_border_crossings.html#special
(accessed February 1, 2005).
National Commission on Terrorist Attacks upon the United States. *The 9/11
Commission Report.* Washington, DC: Government Printing Office, 2004.
National Institute on Drug Abuse. *Drug Facts: Nationwide Trends,* June 2015.
https://www.drugabuse.gov/publications/drugfacts/nationwide-trends
(accessed June 28, 2016).
Office of Management and Budget. http://www.whitehouse.gov/omb/budget/
fy2006/dhs.html (accessed December 8, 2005).
U.S. Congress. *Homeland Security Act Title IV.* http://www.dhs.gov/dhspublic/
interweb/assetlibrary/hr_5005_enr.pdf (accessed October 20, 2005).
White House. Office of Drug Control Policy. *The Price and Purity of Illicit Drugs:
1981 to 2007,* Institute for Defense Analysis, October 2008. https://www
.whitehouse.gov/sites/default/files/ondcp/policy-and-research/bullet_1.pdf
(accessed June 28, 2016).
White House. "President Discusses War on Terror at National Endowment for
Democracy." http://www.whitehouse.gov/news/releases/2005/10/20051006
-3.html (accessed November 29, 2005).

DATA

"Americans for Immigration Control and Zogby Poll." http://www.immigration
control.com/AIC_Zogby_Mexican_Poll.htm (accessed September 10, 2005).
"Border-Wide Population Projections." http://www.scerp.org/population.htm
(accessed September 7, 2005).
Brookings Institution. Chart: U.S. Trade with Canada and Mexico Equals BRICS +
Japan + Korea Trade. http://www.brookings.edu/blogs/brookings-now/
posts/2013/11/chart-us-trade-canada-mexico-brics-japan-korea (accessed
March 24, 2016).
González Barrera, Ana, and Jens Manuel Krogstad. Pew Research Center. "U.S.
Deportations of Immigrants Reach Record High in 2013," October 2, 2014.
http://www.pewresearch.org/fact-tank/2014/10/02/u-s-deportations-of
-immigrants-reach-record-high-in-2013/ (accessed July 1, 2016).
Governing the States and Localities. *State Marijuana Laws Map,* May 2016. http://
www.governing.com/gov-data/state-marijuana-laws-map-medical-recreational
.html (accessed June 28, 2016).
Instituto Nacional de Estadística, Geografía e Informática (INEGI). See http://
www.inegi.gob.mx (accessed June 27, 2016).
Missing Migrants Project. *Migrant Fatalities Worldwide.* http://missingmigrants
.iom.int/latest-global-figures (accessed June 29, 2016).
Narcodata. "Siete Presidentes, Pocos Resultados: 40 Años de Expansión del
Crimen Organizado," Winter 2015. http://narcodata.animalpolitico.com/
7-presidentes-pocos-resultados-40-anos-de-expansion-del-crimen-organizado/
(accessed June 29, 2016).

Thomas, Brenda, and Tony Payan. "Survey of Recent Immigrants at the U.S.
    Consulate in Ciudad Juárez," 2003–4.
Univisión. Mexico-U.S. Border Survey. Document in the hands of author.

INTERVIEWS

First Interview with "James," a trucking company operator who asked to remain
    anonymous, in San Antonio, TX. Interview conducted on August 5, 2005.
Interview with a federal court employee in El Paso, TX, who wished to remain
    anonymous. Interview conducted on August 18, 2005.
Interview with a former member of the Juárez Cartel, who wished to remain
    anonymous. Interview conducted in Ciudad Juárez, Chihuahua, on August 3,
    2005.
Interview with a member of a drug cartel in Ciudad Juárez, Chihuahua, who
    wished to remain anonymous. Interview conducted on August 4, 2005.
Second Interview with "James," a trucking company operator who asked to
    remain anonymous, in San Antonio, TX. Interview conducted on October 5,
    2005.

Index

Abbott, Greg, 2
African American, 74
Albuquerque, 177
al-Qaeda, 39, 160
American Dream, 105, 188
Anti-immigration, 10, 93, 134, 135, 138
Arizona Daily Star, 156
Arlington, 130
Asia(n), 9, 37, 85, 89, 106, 116, 144–45

B1-B2 visas, 28, 120, 167, 177
Balloon effect, 32, 95–99, 114, 188
Bañarse, 67
Bentham, Jeremy, 180–81
Bocón (big mouth), 67
Bonner, Robert, 18, 169
Border cities, 10, 66, 92, 213;
    Brownsville, 8, 10, 78, 101, 149–50,
    212; Ciudad Juárez, 1, 3, 4, 8, 18, 28,
    30, 37, 40, 42, 44, 47, 53, 57–61,
    72–74, 76, 77, 82, 100–101, 103,
    105–6, 108, 115, 120, 123, 126, 146,
    149, 174, 175, 178; El Paso, 24, 28, 33,
    40, 47, 53, 76, 90, 92, 96, 101, 105,
    108, 113–14, 115–16, 120–21, 122,
    123, 125, 128, 132, 133, 137–38, 146,
    149–50, 151, 174–75, 177–78, 185,

187–90, 200, 205, 212–13; Laredo, 3,
8, 10, 47–48, 57, 60, 78, 122, 149, 169,
212; Matamoros, 37, 59, 100, 126;
McAllen, 3, 78, 101, 149; Nogales, 8,
10, 42, 56, 58, 101, 103, 114, 123, 149;
Nuevo Laredo 1, 3, 8, 37, 57, 59, 60,
61–62, 77, 100, 122, 126, 200;
Reynosa, 100; San Diego, 4–5, 24, 46,
48, 92, 101, 114, 119–20, 128, 149–50,
151, 175, 189, 200; Tijuana, 3, 4, 24,
31, 37, 46, 48, 59, 60, 61–62, 65, 68,
73, 77, 100–101, 108, 114, 119–20,
126, 151, 175
Border czar, 202
Border Patrol 9, 10–11, 13, 15, 18, 19,
24, 43, 53, 87–88, 91–98, 104, 107–8,
110–14, 117–28, 133–34, 138, 146,
152, 156–57, 166, 174, 179, 182,
184–90, 192, 196
Border states, 28, 77, 166–67, 199, 203,
212; Arizona, 2, 8, 13, 24, 43, 50,
86–87, 88, 93, 96, 98–99, 100, 103,
109, 112, 113–14, 119, 123, 125, 127,
135, 137–38, 139, 156–57, 160, 168,
184, 188–89, 192, 197, 199, 210, 212;
Baja California, 48, 50, 73, 81–82,
189, 192, 193; California, 4, 8, 13, 50,

About the Author

TONY PAYAN, PhD, is the Françoise and Edward Djerejian Fellow for Mexico Studies and director of the Mexico Center at the Baker Institute. He is also an adjunct associate professor at Rice University and a full professor at the Universidad Autónoma de Ciudad Juárez. Between 2001 and 2015, Payan was a professor of political science at the University of Texas at El Paso.

Payan's research focuses primarily on border studies, particularly the U.S.-Mexico border. His work includes studies of border governance, border flows, immigration, as well as border security and organized crime. Payan is the author of *Cops, Soldiers, and Diplomats: Explaining Agency Behavior in the War on Drugs* (Lexington Books, 2007). He has also coedited five volumes: *Gobernabilidad e Ingobernabilidad en la Región Paso del Norte*, *Human Rights Along the U.S.-Mexico Border: Gendered Violence and Insecurity*, *De Soldaderas a Activistas: La Mujer Chihuahuense en los Albores del Siglo XXI*, *A War That Can't Be Won: Binational Perspectives on the War on Drugs*, and *Undecided Nation: Political Gridlock and the Immigration Crisis*.

Payan has served on several boards, including the Camino Real Regional Mobility Authority in El Paso, Texas, and the Plan Estratégico de Juárez in Ciudad Juárez, Mexico. He is a member of the Greater Houston Partnership's Immigration Task Force and the Mexico Energy Task Force. He also served as president of the Association of Borderlands Studies between 2009 and 2010.

Payan earned a BA in philosophy and classical languages from the University of Dallas and an MBA from the University of Dallas Graduate School of Management. He received a doctorate degree in international relations from Georgetown University in 2001.